Case Studies
Library and Infor...
Science Ethics

Case Studies in Library and Information Science Ethics

Elizabeth A. Buchanan *and*
Kathrine A. Henderson

with a foreword by Robert Hauptman

McFarland & Company, Inc., Publishers
Jefferson, North Carolina, and London

LIBRARY OF CONGRESS CATALOGUING-IN-PUBLICATION DATA

Buchanan, Elizabeth A., 1968–
Case studies in library and information science ethics /
Elizabeth A. Buchanan and Kathrine A. Henderson ;
with a foreword by Robert Hauptman.
p.   cm.
Includes bibliographical references and index.

ISBN 978-0-7864-3367-4
softcover : 50# alkaline paper ∞

1. Librarians — Professional ethics.   2. Library science — Moral and
ethical aspects.   I. Henderson, Kathrine, 1965–   II. Title.
Z682.35.P75B83   2009   174'.902 — dc22   2008034606

British Library cataloguing data are available

Cover photographs ©2008 Shutterstock

Manufactured in the United States of America

*McFarland & Company, Inc., Publishers
Box 611, Jefferson, North Carolina 28640
www.mcfarlandpub.com*

For bearing with me, yet again,
on a project I swore would be short and sweet,
I thank my dear husband Bill Topritzhofer,
my best friend, love, and research assistant extraordinaire,
without whom nothing would ever get done;
For Jack and Gail Buchanan, parents and grandparents extraordinaire,
who spent countless hours with my children
while I worked on this book; and,
For my truest loves, my children, from whom
I learn more every day about what matters:
Values, morals, rights, and responsibilities,
Zachary, 5, and Annika, 2.
Life is fulfilled by their presence.
— *Elizabeth Buchanan*

To Luc, "The best boy a mama ever had," and
To my husband Scott, thank you for everything.
P.S. Honey, I'll start doing the dishes again after Tuesday.
— *Kathrine Henderson*

Acknowledgments

This book project is the result of many contributions and we thank first and foremost the many librarians and information professionals and students over the years who have told us their stories. We graciously thank Robert Hauptman and Rafael Capurro for their lifelong commitments to library and information ethics and for their visions of a better profession. We extend our most sincere appreciation to each of them for their contributions to this text. We thank Dr. Toni Samek, University of Alberta, Canada, for her scholarship and collegiality and gratefully acknowledge her assistance throughout. We graciously thank the American Library Association; the Canadian Library Association; Fink Verlag; Timothy Ericson, Past President, Society of American Archivists; Teresa Brinati, Director, Society of American Archivists; the American Association of Law Librarians; the American Society for Information Science and Technology; the Reason Foundation; the Ponemon Institute; Thomas Carson; Catherine Hansen; Tomas Lipinski; Johannes Britz and the School of Information Studies, University of Wisconsin–Milwaukee; Charles Ess; Hope Olson; Amy Cooper Cary; James Pekoll; Anthony Hoffman.

Contents

Acknowledgments vii
Foreword by Robert Hauptman 1
Preface 5

1. Ethics in the Library and Information Studies Profession 9
2. Intellectual Freedom 23
3. Privacy 46
4. Intellectual Property 71
5. Professional Ethics 95
6. Intercultural Information Ethics by Rafael Capurro 118

Epilogue 159
Index 161

Foreword
by Robert Hauptman

Nothing is more important than the way we treat each other. Ill treatment results in exploitation, poverty, violence, war and death; respect for and sometimes tolerance of others — their needs, dignity and integrity — offer the possibility of global harmony. In order to achieve economic stability, information must be fairly accessible. This does not imply that all information must be free; rather, the means of accessing crucial economic, business, legal and medical data should be equally available to all peoples regardless of where they reside, under what type of regime they strive for a decent life, and how peers and strangers perceive them socially. Poverty, sexism, racism, classism, and other forms of blatant discrimination harm specifically and generally.

The broad and equitable dissemination of information has a long and glorious history in the western world. Public and subscription libraries have made it possible for all individuals, including society's pariahs — the poor, destitute, homeless, maligned, deranged and even the illiterate — to find both physical and intellectual refuge. Although the specific motivating forces that drove American librarians to furnish material to patrons have changed during the past 150 years, the general desire to provide information (whether factual or fictitious, practical or imaginatively entertaining) has remained a constant impetus. This is true for academic collections as well.

Sometimes well-meaning people cause harm because they do not realize that an action is discriminatory, subversive, self-serving, or unacceptable. Until fairly recently, information specialists, collection curators and librarians were on their own when it came to making ethically acceptable decisions. The frequently non-binding rules laid out by professional organizations offered little more than general (though helpful) platitudes and the unconcerned, uncaring and oblivious acted without regard to the welfare of others. This did not mean that they condoned theft or vandalism, censorship or labeling, but harms nevertheless occurred. Many years ago, I visited the New York Public Library in order to read the holographic letters of Carson McCullers, the subject of a short biographical essay I was writing for the *Dictionary of American Biography*. Although security measures were much more lax than they are today, I was nevertheless shocked when the woman handed me the folder of priceless letters and turned to walk away. I requested that she stay nearby while I quickly glanced at them. I did not want to be accused of theft in the distant future. Those who have such materials entrusted to their care must be vigilant in their protection without, naturally, making the researcher uncomfortable in a room replete with human monitors, cameras and guard dogs.

In 1975, the literature on ethics and librarianship included a handful of articles on decorum and D. J. Foskett's concise 1962 monograph on the obligations of reference librarians, which are nicely summed up in its subtitle: *The Creed of a Librarian: No Politics, No Morals, No Religion*. I believed that relying on a set of dogmatic (and misleading) principles and acting automatically regardless of the situation was not appropriate behavior for a professional information worker. And so, I visited 13 diverse libraries and requested help in building a bomb. I was disconcerted and disappointed that none of these professionals considered my request within an ethical context nor cared at all about the social consequences of blowing up a suburban house, a goal I made patently clear. "Professionalism or Culpability? An Experiment in Ethics" appeared in the April 1976 issue of *Wilson Library Bulletin* and I take it to be the impetus for the subsequent development of interest in ethical matters in information production, storage and dissemination. In 1988, I published *Ethical Challenges in Librarianship* (Oryx), the first such comprehensive study, and other scholars soon followed with a variety of conference papers, articles and monographic works. Not long thereafter, I realized that libraries were but one link in the informational chain and so I founded the *Journal of Information Ethics*, which takes all informational disciplines into its purview. A number of additional seminal works deserve mention: my bibliographical overview of "Information Ethics" (*Choice*, October 1999) and my *Ethics and Librarianship* (McFarland, 2002); Mark Alfino and Linda Pierce's philosophical *Information Ethics for Librarians* (McFarland, 1997); Richard Severson's practical *Principles of Information Ethics* (M. E. Sharpe, 1997); David McMenemy, Alan Poulter and Paul F. Burton's *Handbook of Ethical Practice* (Chandos, 2007); and the helpful online *International Review of Information Ethics*.

These and other materials cover a host of traditional and emerging ethical problems, conundrums and sometimes insoluble dilemmas, including protection of physical and intellectual property; conflicts of interest; censorship; overbearing peers, personnel and administrators who sometimes become what Susan Motin calls academic bullies; anomalous archival rules and agreements that delimit access; research misconduct; judicious collection development;

useful and accurate subject cataloging and classification; computer misapplications (gaming, pornography); and privacy and confidentiality protection.

Despite all the discussions, workshops, conferences, studies, courses, personal controversies, imprecations and sensitization to ethical issues, things are worse in some areas than they were in the past. Consider that the aberrant, homeless, or odoriferous are sometimes harassed or barred from public (governmentally supported) libraries (which is patently unconstitutional), or that the American Library Association (ALA) has stubbornly refused to condemn the Castro regime which has imprisoned some courageous Cubans (who are rotting in foul prisons) because they made books available to their fellow citizens. As I have often noted, sometimes ethical commitment is insufficient and legal sanctions must help to convince people to act correctly. The problem is that correct action is apparently variable depending on one's allegiance. The classic case is now whether a Florida librarian should have protected the confidences of patrons who blew up the World Trade Center (many professionals affirmed this) or whether she should have contacted the FBI (as she did, which in a socially responsible setting is precisely what she should have done). Making the correct choice is often a very difficult task. Elizabeth Buchanan and Kathrine Henderson's volume should sensitize and guide information workers in order to help them reach that goal.

Robert Hauptman, Ph.D., is editor of *Journal of Information Ethics*.

Preface

This book emerged out of a meeting of theory and practice and out of a need for a casebook *specific* to librarians and information studies professionals. Our work is different from computer scientists; thus the many recent casebooks on computer ethics do not always fit in LIS courses and programs. In 1999, when I began teaching in LIS, there was no ethics course offered in my school, so I developed one. I used a small text by Fay Zipkowitz, entitled *Professional Ethics in Librarianship: A Real Life Casebook*. It was comprised of a small but insightful number of cases that librarians in particular faced on a regular basis. Students loved it and they appreciated the application of philosophical theory (which they were not accustomed to in the classroom) to the realistic and challenging scenarios (with which they were well familiar) that were presented. But the text was published in 1996 and, after a few years of using it, it showed signs of datedness. Many of the core principles of intellectual freedom, privacy, rights, and professional responsibilities presented in the cases remain intact and continue to be relevant, but many additional changes — legal, technological, social, political, and cultural — face the field in significant flux. I continued to use case studies, often making up the individual cases myself, so that students could engage on that level of practicality — together we found solutions through discussion; we explored theoretical underpinnings; we identified and applied alternative perspectives; and we learned, most importantly, how to negotiate with and listen to others, who may see things very differently than ourselves. Librarians and information professionals work in an increasingly complex matrix and such negotiation is imperative. Too, case study is widely used across disciplines and I personally embrace its pedagogical power. The beauty of case study: Smooth and simple on the outside, juicy and deeply layered on the inside.

Then, in 2004, I fortuitously met Kathrine Henderson, a practicing librarian, who was very interested in ethics and information policy in LIS. She had herself written some interesting articles on copyright and intellectual property from a very practical perspective, and was able to see clearly through some oftentimes muddied and foggy legal and ethical issues. Our professional interactions progressed and she assisted me in my ethics course a number of times. We mentioned frequently that a new casebook would help us in the classroom, as our students, who were often working professionals, needed a way to operationalize rhetoric into the concrete. Finally, Kat and I decided it was time to collaborate officially and we began discussing the idea of co-authoring a monograph. The work of Robert Hauptman, in particular, assisted us in envisioning this collection of cases and his important visions of and commitment to ethics and librarianship remain unparalleled, as is evidenced in his foreword. This text is the end result of our desire to bring the complexity of contemporary ethical issues in the field to a practical and manageable level. Kathrine and I represent a balance of practical and theoretical experiences and our relationship shows the importance of a healthy, and necessary, dialog between practitioners and academics.

As with any text, the reader will encounter biases and omissions. By the time the text is published, a new technology, a new law, a new library policy, a new disaster, a new conflict, a new opportunity will have emerged and will give us pause. They will cause us to question assumptions, to reevaluate, and to think through a new set of issues. There will always be a new challenge and that should give our field a sense of appeal, while at the same time, we should recognize the responsibilities that come with our work. Our work is underscored by the theme of "thinking critically, acting responsibly." Case study enables both. It made great sense to us to help better instill this hands-on approach in our professional community. It is reflection based on informed reason, individual and collective decision-making, and intellectual development, and it is active engagement. Neither can exist in passivity, in status, or in isolation without diluting itself. Critical thinking must be coupled with responsible action. To think critically without acting means very little, while irresponsible action is arguably very dangerous. We embrace Ghandi's phrase, "Action expresses priority," to enforce our concept. We teach our readers, whether as faculty in an LIS program or our patrons, to be "critical" of their information. We ask them to evaluate and make decisions based on tangible information; we ask them to evaluate their information needs and accept the most appropriate and reliable choices to meet those needs. We provide a *framework* from which their answers can be obtained and then we provide them with a course of action to make appropriate use of that information. We do not always provide answers themselves, but a pathway or exploration of a set of answers.

And, of course, ethics and ethical issues are not always straightforward; ethics is influenced by an amalgamation of personal, institutional, and societal aspects of culture, temporality, technology, law, bias, rights, religion, economic, political, philosophical, ideological and methodological perspectives. When we use case study, we address these influences head-on, as they affect us directly, both personally and professionally. When we are privileged to have the perspectives from, for instance, students or patrons of different cultures, or of different ages, or different sexual orientations, or different socio-economic backgrounds, in our discussions, we learn how blindly, how narrowly, how automatically, how unconsciously we often see things or default to dominant landscapes. Once we have seen and heard differences, our worlds as individuals and as professionals are enhanced. This can only be a positive step for us and our profession and, by extension, our publics.

While the book could be used as a standalone text, we rather encourage readers to refer to the many important works in the growing information ethics field as supplements and complements, as we describe in Chapter One. We provide brief overviews to each chapter, giving readers a sense of the context within which the cases emerge. Each chapter contains twenty-five scenarios. We begin with intellectual freedom — a core value of our field — move into privacy which has emerged as a critical and contentious right in our western society, enter intellectual property which is contradictory and culturally based, review professional ethics and the broad complexities encompassed in that umbrella term, and then end in the exciting, emergent realm of intercultural information ethics (IIE). Readers will most likely be familiar with the concepts presented in the first four chapters, while intercultural information ethics may be novel. We brought in Rafael Capurro's seminal work on IIE to illustrate the global nature of library and information work in the twenty-first century; few have the breadth and depth of this emerging field as Capurro. In advance, we acknowledge we are not entirely comprehensive in our coverage of every culture: We simply could not do this in this U.S.-conceived English language print text (or perhaps, any text, as cultures are elusive, while our inherent limitations as American professionals may prevent us from presenting an issue truly accurately). Our goal in introducing the concept is to spark further interest and awareness of the issues to show interconnections and walls between and among the profession as it exists currently in the U.S. in particular, and the global discourse of information. While Capurro's IIE completes our text, it should be seen as an open door, as opposed to an ending: This realm demands serious attention in our field.

Finally, our introductions are not designed to provide final *answers* to the scenarios, nor do we think it helpful to offer deceptively simple solutions within each case. Perhaps some will wish we did, but that would undermine the commitment to reflection that this work pushes. My experience teaching has shown that there is no "one" answer to many of these cases. And to suggest to the reader that there is would be unethical in itself. Typically, case studies do not have definitive answers. Thus the need for case studies! They are place-specific, time-specific, person-specific. Librarians are citizens as well as workers and the dilemmas they face are grounded in the varied contexts in which they live and labor. While our professional associations, such as the American Library Association (ALA), provide guidance, or guidelines, there is always interpretation and application to a specific event. We provide readers with appropriate references and again, we provide a context. But the librarian in a small rural public library or a Catholic school library may interpret intellectual freedom differently based on their realities — their practicalities, their limitations, their communities. This is not a pejorative comment; it is the result of talking with many librarians and information professionals who believe theoretically in the profession's philosophical foundations but are also faced with the everyday realities of their library or information center homes — homes which are concurrently inhabited by federal law makers, local politicians, parents, library or governing boards, corporate owners, private contractors, sponsors, technology itself, and many others who walk through, wheel through, skip through, peer through, flood through, monitor, and sometimes break through our doors — all with an agenda. Again, we acknowledge the meeting of the theoretical and the practical with our profession and its stakeholders — and regulators.

Herein, we offer questions for discussion, a dialogic text in a human-centered, thriving, active, and participatory context. This could be a classroom or a staff meeting, a library board or town hall meeting, perhaps, before the real case hits the floor. Too, students may find research questions ripe for exploration.

Decisions cannot — indeed should not — be made in isolation, without consultation. The important thing to remember is that the cases throughout are based on reality and thus meant to elicit the necessary critical thinking, devil's advocacy, and then responsible reaction that a reflective, relevant profession displays inward and outward. We hope others find this text useful — as both theory and practice.

Elizabeth A. Buchanan

CHAPTER 1

Ethics in the Library and Information Studies Profession

Ethical dilemmas are certainly not novel to the field of library and information studies. Censorship and freedom-of-expression challenges have faced the field for centuries; monopolies have existed since the earliest days of printing; privacy has been tested as a fundamental philosophical — and legal — value over time. Technologies, laws, policies, and practices have changed dramatically, with sometimes dire, sometimes positive consequences for the field of library and information studies. Whether ethics, or a core set of values for LIS, has changed in light of these is certainly debatable, though many believe that ethics do not change, but only surrounding circumstances do. This casebook explores the often increasingly complex situations information professionals experience in their daily work, encouraging them to consider their actions, their decisions, and the consequences that arise. We present these situations through a series of cases which span library settings, from public to academic to special and archival.

To understand the complexities of LIS professional ethics and in order to move into the major areas of case study throughout the book, it is important to review the foundations of ethics in general. Ethics is related to morals, moral systems, and human conduct. As a branch of philosophy, it systematically examines and studies such concepts as "right" and "wrong." Ethics deals with what we should and should not do, what acts are "good" and "evil." It examines such concepts and constructs as responsibility and rights. As the basis for ethics, morality is a set or system of rules, principles, or values (cultural, professional, religious, *et cetera*) that prescribe behavior and how we evaluate those behaviors. "Whenever we try to defend or criticize a moral belief we enter the realm of ethics. Ethics is not concerned with specific moral rules but with the foundation of morality and with providing general principles that will both help us evaluate the validity of a moral rule and choose between different moralities (different sets of moral rules)" (Solomon, 1993, p. 651). Too, Severson (1997, p. 8) suggests that "ethics is ... structured and deliberative; it is a kind of thinking about the moral life." Finally, ethical decision-making presupposes that people are free, that they want to do what is "right," and that they can make conscious, thoughtful and reflective decisions, in that their capacities are not diminished or compromised. Ethics is notably distinct from law, religion, and policy; it will be important to consider that ethics is distinct from law "in that the law provides a structured context to which we look for 'reasonable' decisions; the law does not necessarily tell us what is inherently good or bad. It prescribes behavior not for the purpose of morality but for the purpose of satisfying a societal requirement or rule; rules are dictated by authority, not necessarily morality" (Buchanan, 2004, p. 618). Likewise, Spinello (1997) asserts that

> law and morality do not always overlap or easily substitute for one another. Legal constraints and judicial decisions, no matter how nuanced, do not necessarily provide sufficient guidelines for addressing the complicated ethics issues in information ... science.... Law is essentially reactive. Laws and regulations are rarely proactive, anticipating problems or possible inequities; rather, they react to problems that have surfaced and usually in a manner that is painstakingly slow [p. 24].

We LIS professionals are bound by many laws and regulations: laws surrounding intellectual property, laws surrounding privacy, laws surrounding unionization and striking. But we face challenges beyond legal specificity when we enter the realm of ethics. Throughout, we will suggest our readers consult with legal council where necessary and where appropriate, while also encouraging our readers to think about the inherent connections *and* disjunctions between law and ethics as they affect our daily work. We will be working in the realm of *applied ethics*.

Ethics is divided systematically into such areas as *descriptive, normative, applied,* and *meta-ethics*. Descriptive ethics involves the study of people's beliefs and feelings about morality—it works to articulate (or describe) a situation or set of conditions, but does not express a value or moral judgment: It stops at the level of description. It contrasts with normative ethics, which is the study of how people *ought* to act, or what *ought* to be the case; normative ethics helps us consider and accept moral standards to regulate right and wrong conduct. Thus, we may assert that corporatization is harmful to public libraries. This is a descriptive statement. We may move beyond that by considering what *should* or what *ought* to be the role of corporate influence or privatization on public goods. Applied ethics is then the application of ethical theory to real-world, practical situations; common examples include bioethics, business ethics, or cyberethics (see Spinello & Tavani, 2004). In our example, then, we may consider the influence of LSSI on the public libraries in Los Angeles, California, in an applied ethics case. Finally, at a more philosophically complex level, meta-ethics is the study of ethics itself, of ethical language itself, what our ethical principles mean, and the fundamental nature of the justification of ethical statements. For example, what do we mean when we say someone is a "good" professional?

Theories of ethical thinking include utility-based (utilitarianism, which is a general philosophy holding that we should act in the way that maximizes happiness for the greatest number of people), duty-based (deontological, which stresses adherence to a set of principles as opposed to a strict consideration of consequences and is typically aligned with Immanuel Kant), justice-based (most recently associated with the theories of justice and rights of John Rawls), and character-based (associated with Aristotelian models). This casebook will not delve deeply into the details of ethical theory, as it instead focuses on practical scenarios and examples that allow us to consider deep ethical issues in practice: It is an applied ethics text for the profession and we encourage its use in conjunction with other texts. There are many important philosophy and information ethics texts available that delve into core philosophical theories in great detail and provide a useful framework for understanding such ethical theories (see, for example, Freeman & Peace, 2005; Hauptman, 2002; Himma, 2007; Himma & Tavani, 2008; Hongladaram & Ess, 2007; Moore, 2005; Quinn, 2005; Schultz, 2005; Spinello & Tavani, 2004; Tavani, 2006).

The formal application of ethical theory to information is termed "information ethics," concurrently coined such by Dr. Robert Hauptman in the United States and Dr. Rafael Capurro in Germany in the mid–1980s, though, as Capurro notes, the concept dates back throughout history (Capurro, 2006). Notably, information ethics was being taught in South Africa as early as 1990, at the University of Pretoria. In 1996, in her doctoral dissertation, Smith identified a taxonomy in which information ethics areas generally fall: ownership, access, and security, categories which still apply over ten years later. More specifically, information ethics "concerns itself with the production, storage, retrieval, security, and application of information within an ethical context" (Hauptman, 2002, p. 121). More broadly, information ethics explores and evaluates the following fundamental information issues:

- the development of moral values in the information field,
- the creation of new power structures in the information field,
- information myths,
- hidden contradictions and intentionalities in information theories and practices, and
- the development of ethical conflicts in the information field [Capurro, 2006].

As such, information ethics has evolved as a critical field of study over the past twenty years. It is a broader arena than computer ethics or cyberethics, which are notable subsets of the field. Scholars across disciplines and across cultures are now engaging in information ethics work and the field is burgeoning. Such international research centers as the International Center for Information Ethics (ICIE), directed by Rafael Capurro, show the vibrant state of information ethics across the globe; it is impossible to speak of information ethics without addressing the intercultural aspects that affect us as information professionals. Thus, we conclude this text with Capurro's important essay on *intercultural information ethics* (IIE) and introduce cases that promote an awareness of these intercultural aspects. Capurro (2007) considers intercultural information ethics through a series of questions:

How far is the Internet changing local cultural values and traditional ways of life? How far do these changes affect the life and culture of future societies in a global and local sense? Put another way, how far do traditional cultures and their moral values communicate and transform themselves under the impact of the digital "infosphere" in general and of the Internet in particular? In other words, intercultural information ethics can be conceived as a field of research where moral questions of the "infosphere" are reflected in a comparative manner on the basis of different cultural traditions.... The key question of intercultural information ethics is thus how far and in which ways are we going to be able to enlarge both freedom and justice within a perspective of sustainable cultural development that protects and encourages cultural diversity as well as the interaction between them.

With this awareness of the intercultural aspects, we acknowledge that our cases are generally grounded in American law and, generally, American perspectives; but, we further acknowledge that librarians and information professionals must be aware of the global nature of our profession; as noted in the preface, our future work will delve considerably deeper into IIE and we acknowledge that our scope is limited. It is, however, a healthy beginning for information professionals who have limited exposure to global librarianship and information studies work. Such issues as transborder data flow, cultural differences with regards to intellectual freedom and property norms, online research ethics, and data integrity and security are never too far afield from our local workplaces. Thus, the complexities abound in the face of local, global, and professional traditions. We believe that case study works well to explore these dimensions and the myriad ethical challenges facing LIS professionals today. Spinello (1997) describes case study as a

popular instrument of provoking students to grapple with complicated moral problems and quandaries. Cases present such problems in a particular context and as a result, they require students to discern the ethical dimension of a situation among a plethora of intricate, perplexing, and sometimes conflicting information.... The most significant benefit of using the case study method is that it engages students and requires them to become active participants rather than passive observers [p. xii].

Case studies have been used to explore the deep dimensions of ethics in such previous works as Herbert White's *Ethical Dilemmas in Libraries: A Collection of Case Studies* (1992), Fay Zipkowitz's *Professional Ethics in Librarianship: A Real Life Casebook* (1996), Gary Edson's *Museum Ethics* (1997) and Richard Spinello's *Case Studies in Information and Computer Ethics* (1997). Most recently, McMenemy, Poulter & Burton (2006) have used case studies to promote ethical reflection in the LIS field. We hope our contribution further promotes ethical consideration of our local and our global responsibilities in and to the profession.

How we learn morals and how we learn to use ethics as a framework for decision-making in general or in a profession is, of course, a philosophically complex discussion. We must first understand the potential differences between personal morals and professional values, as well as differences within our professional values. Typically, on the personal level, we *accept* that we learn and internalize moral values from our parents, schools, churches, society, and customs (though this could be debated). But how do we learn professional values? We *assume* we learn these through formal education and through practice in the field, but what of those professionals who seemingly lack values? Or those who have very different values systems than "the rest of us"?

As a profession, do we consider how ethics *should* be taught? Library and information science programs are increasingly offering courses in ethics, intellectual freedom, law, and policy as standalone courses, as well as integrating these themes across the curriculum. Core classes—such as reference, collection development, management, and foundations—of LIS typically include a component of applied ethics, though standards of coverage and pedagogy vary widely (Buchanan, 2004). At the present time, there is no *required* coursework in ethics in LIS schools or programs, as dictated by the accrediting bodies of LIS education. The major educational association of the LIS field, the Association for Library and Information Science, has a special interest group on ethics that was formed in April 2005, but at the time of this writing, no statement or explicit endorsement of ethics in the curriculum has been issued. As professionals, we then look to the Codes of Ethics of such associations as the ALA, Canadian Library Association (CLA), or appropriate organization, but, notably, such associations as the ALA are consensus building, rather than regulatory. We *accept* that professional ethics, the underlying, and explicit, values of a given profession, are generally embodied in codes of ethics or professional mission statements. Yet conflicts and dilemmas occur in light of, or in response to, technologies, policies, laws, and cultural norms. Changes may threaten one's personal values *or* a profession's values; when one is a member of a profession, he or she must navigate these distinct realms and come to some reconciliation if one's personal values are misaligned with the professional. Codes of ethics do not always provide answers and they of course do not operate on levels of deep specificity; they provide guidelines, not rules, which is probably best; and, certainly, they are not laws.

Typically, in LIS education in North America, we are introduced to ethical practice and professional ethics through two main organizations: the Canadian Library Association (CLA) and the American Library Association (ALA). The CLA's Code of Ethics is as follows:

Canadian Library Association's Code of Ethics, adopted June 1976

Members of the Canadian Library Association have the individual and collective responsibility to:
1. support and implement the principles and practices embodied in the current Canadian Library Association Statement on Intellectual Freedom;
2. make every effort to promote and maintain the highest possible range and standards of library service to all segments of Canadian society;
3. facilitate access to any or all sources of information which may be of assistance to library users;
4. protect the privacy and dignity of library users and staff [Canadian Library Association, reprinted with permission].

The American Library Association's Code of Ethics dates to 1930, with subsequent revisions in 1939, 1975, 1979, 1981, and 1995. The current ALA Code of Ethics is succinct, as many codes of ethics are:

As members of the American Library Association, we recognize the importance of codifying and making known to the profession and to the general public the ethical principles that guide the work of librarians, other professionals providing information services, library trustees and library staffs.

Ethical dilemmas occur when values are in conflict. The American Library Association Code of Ethics states the values to which we are committed, and embodies the ethical responsibilities of the profession in this changing information environment.

We significantly influence or control the selection, organization, preservation, and dissemination of information. In a political system grounded in an informed citizenry, we are members of a profession explicitly committed to intellectual freedom and the freedom of access to information. We have a special obligation to ensure the free flow of information and ideas to present and future generations.

The principles of this Code are expressed in broad statements to guide ethical decision making. These statements provide a framework; they cannot and do not dictate conduct to cover particular situations.

   I. *We provide the highest level of service to all library users through appropriate and usefully organized resources; equitable service policies; equitable access; and accurate, unbiased, and courteous responses to all requests.*

  II. *We uphold the principles of intellectual freedom and resist all efforts to censor library resources.*

 III. *We protect each library user's right to privacy and confidentiality with respect to information sought or received and resources consulted, borrowed, acquired or transmitted.*

 IV. *We recognize and respect intellectual property rights.*

  V. *We treat co-workers and other colleagues with respect, fairness and good faith, and advocate conditions of employment that safeguard the rights and welfare of all employees of our institutions.*

 VI. *We do not advance private interests at the expense of library users, colleagues, or our employing institutions.*

VII. *We distinguish between our personal convictions and professional duties and do not allow our personal beliefs to interfere with fair representation of the aims of our institutions or the provision of access to their information resources.*

VIII. *We strive for excellence in the profession by maintaining and enhancing our own knowledge and skills, by encouraging the professional development of co-workers, and by fostering the aspirations of potential members of the profession* [American Library Association, 1995; reprinted with permission].

Society of American Archivists: Code of Ethics for Archivists

Preamble

The Code of Ethics for Archivists establishes standards for the archival profession. It introduces new members of the profession to those standards, reminds experienced archivists of their professional responsibilities, and serves as a model for institutional policies. It also is intended to inspire public confidence in the profession.

This code provides an ethical framework to guide members of the profession. It does not provide the solution to specific problems.

The term "archivist" as used in this code encompasses all those concerned with the selection, control, care, preservation, and administration of historical and documentary records of enduring value.

I. Purpose
The Society of American Archivists recognizes the importance of educating the profession and general public about archival ethics by codifying ethical principles to guide the work of archivists. This code provides a set of principles to which archivists aspire.

II. Professional Relationships
Archivists select, preserve, and make available historical and documentary records of enduring value. Archivists cooperate, collaborate, and respect each institution and its mission and collecting policy. Respect and cooperation form the basis of all professional relationships with colleagues and users.

III. Judgment
Archivists should exercise professional judgment in acquiring, appraising, and processing historical materials. They should not allow personal beliefs or perspectives to affect their decisions.

IV. Trust
Archivists should not profit or otherwise benefit from their privileged access to and control of historical records and documentary materials.

V. Authenticity and Integrity
Archivists strive to preserve and protect the authenticity of records in their holdings by documenting their creation and use in hard copy and electronic formats. They have a fundamental obligation to preserve the intellectual and physical integrity of those records.

Archivists may not alter, manipulate, or destroy data or records to conceal facts or distort evidence.

VI. Access
Archivists strive to promote open and equitable access to their services and the records in their care without discrimination or preferential treatment, and in accordance with legal requirements, cultural sensitivities, and institutional policies. Archivists recognize their responsibility to promote the use of records as a fundamental purpose of the keeping of archives. Archivists may place restrictions on access for the protection of privacy or confidentiality of information in the records.

VII. Privacy
Archivists protect the privacy rights of donors and individuals or groups who are the subject of records. They respect all users' right to privacy by maintaining the confidentiality of their research and protecting any personal information collected about them in accordance with the institution's security procedures.

VIII. Security/Protection
Archivists protect all documentary materials for which they are responsible and guard them against defacement, physical damage, deterioration, and theft. Archivists should cooperate with colleagues and law enforcement agencies to apprehend and prosecute thieves and vandals.

IX. Law
Archivists must uphold all federal, state, and local laws.

Reprinted with permission from the Society of American Archivists.

These codes are intended for all library and information science professionals, but they are purely advisory, with no enforcement or regulatory significance. As with many codes of ethics, as we discuss in Chapter Five, the value comes in great part through symbolism. The codes dictate the underlying moral system of the profession. Yet, a librarian will not lose her "library license" should she violate the ALA code. In fact, she may not even know the code exists. Others have decided this code and the American Library Association in general do not speak for them. For instance, the Family Friendly Libraries Association was founded in 1996 with the goal of providing an alternative model of library advocacy; this organization, for instance, has questioned the "political" work and/or "liberal tendencies" of the ALA. Of course, library and information studies faculty may not belong to the ALA and instead to the Association for Library and Information Science Education. There is no *requirement* to belong to any professional association, in fact. Subsets of librarianship and information studies may find more suitable homes in associations such as the American Association of School Librarians (a direct unit of the ALA), the American Society for Information Science and Technology (see below), the American Association of Law Libraries (see below), the Special Libraries Association, the Medical Libraries Association, the Society of American Archivists (see below), or the Association of Computing Machinery. It is important to understand that even if one *individually* elects not to adhere to a particular code, professional associations' values may be used to determine policies and as frameworks for *institutional* codes of conduct and professional expectations.

American Society for Information Science and Technology Professional Guidelines *(reprinted with permission)*

Dedicated to the Memory of Diana Woodward

ASIS&T recognizes the plurality of uses and users of information technologies, services, systems and products as well as the diversity of goals or objectives, sometimes conflicting, among producers, vendors, mediators, and users of information systems.

ASIS&T urges its members to be ever aware of the social, economic, cultural, and political impacts of their actions or inaction.

ASIS&T members have obligations to employers, clients, and system users, to the profession, and to society, to use judgment and discretion in making choices, providing equitable service, and in defending the rights of open inquiry.

Responsibilities to Employers/Clients/System Users
• To act faithfully for their employers or clients in professional matters
• To uphold each user's, provider's, or employer's right to privacy and confidentiality and to respect whatever proprietary rights belong to them, by limiting access to, providing proper security for and ensuring proper disposal of data about clients, patrons or users
• To treat all persons fairly.

Responsibility to the Profession
To truthfully represent themselves and the information systems which they utilize or which they represent, by

- not knowingly making false statements or providing erroneous or misleading information
- informing their employers, clients or sponsors of any circumstances that create a conflict of interest
- not using their position beyond their authorized limits or by not using their credentials to misrepresent themselves
- following and promoting standards of conduct in accord with the best current practices
- undertaking their research conscientiously, in gathering, tabulating or interpreting data; in following proper approval procedures for subjects; and in producing or disseminating their research results
- pursuing ongoing professional development and encouraging and assisting colleagues and others to do the same
- adhering to principles of due process and equality of opportunity.

Responsibility to Society

To improve the information systems with which they work or which they represent, to the best of their means and abilities by

- providing the most reliable and accurate information and acknowledging the credibility of the sources as known or unknown
- resisting all forms of censorship, inappropriate selection and acquisitions policies, and biases in information selection, provision and dissemination
- making known any biases, errors and inaccuracies found to exist and striving to correct those which can be remedied.

To promote open and equal access to information, within the scope permitted by their organizations or work, and to resist procedures that promote unlawful discriminatory practices in access to and provision of information, by

- seeking to extend public awareness and appreciation of information availability and provision as well as the role of information professionals in providing such information
- freely reporting, publishing or disseminating information subject to legal and proprietary restraints of producers, vendors and employers, and the best interests of their employers or clients.

Information professionals shall engage in principled conduct whether on their own behalf or at the request of employers, colleagues, clients, agencies or the profession [ASIST].

American Association of Law Libraries Ethical Principles
(reprinted with permission)

Approved by the AALL membership, April 5, 1999

Preamble

When individuals have ready access to legal information, they can participate fully in the affairs of their government. By collecting, organizing, preserving, and retrieving legal information, the members of the American Association of Law Libraries enable people to make this ideal of democracy a reality.

Legal information professionals have an obligation to satisfy the needs, to promote the interests and to respect the values of their clientele. Law firms, corporations, academic and governmental institutions and the general public have legal information needs that are best addressed by professionals committed to the belief that serving these information needs is a noble calling and that fostering the equal participation of diverse people in library services underscores one of our basic tenets, open access to information for all individuals.

Service

We promote open and effective access to legal and related information. Further we recognize the need to establish methods of preserving, maintaining and retrieving legal information in many different forms.

We uphold a duty to our clientele to develop service policies that respect confidentiality and privacy.

We provide zealous service using the most appropriate resources and implementing programs consistent with our institution's mission and goals.

We acknowledge the limits on service imposed by our institutions and by the duty to avoid the unauthorized practice of law.

Business Relationships

We promote fair and ethical trade practices.

We have a duty to avoid situations in which personal interests might be served or significant benefits gained at the expense of library users, colleagues, or our employing institutions.

We strive to obtain the maximum value for our institution's fiscal resources, while at the same time making judicious, analytical and rational use of our institution's information resources.

Professional Responsibilities

We relate to our colleagues with respect and in a spirit of cooperation.

We distinguish between our personal convictions and professional duties and do not allow our personal beliefs to interfere with the service we provide.

We recognize and respect the rights of the owner and the user of intellectual property.

We strive for excellence in the profession by maintaining and enhancing our own knowledge and skills, by encouraging the professional development of co-workers, and by fostering the aspirations of potential members of the profession [American Association of Law Libraries].

While some appreciate the symbolic value of such codes of ethics, others appreciate their pragmatism. Some codes will be used more informally to consider day-to-day moral conflicts. But decisions must ultimately be made and a code of ethics does not necessarily provide an answer, but it does provide a context. When we enter the realm of ethical decision-making, we will undoubtedly look to a framework from which to make responsible and sound decisions. As we explore the ethical implications surrounding library and information studies through case study, we enable readers to adapt various perspectives, see multiple issues in a scenario, and see how various stakeholders are affected. We promote an ethical decision-making model that includes critical reflection and consideration and responsible action.

We begin by defining the situation, recognizing our biases and prejudices. We look to our professional codes and/or our organizational or institutional policies to assess the situation within our professional context. We identify the stakeholders and the implications for those involved. We look at how the situation occurred and examine both significant and seemingly insignificant variables. We explore various perspectives of the issue, looking to understand views that are very different than our own, seeking out alternative perspectives where possible and where necessary. Finally, we guarantee our competence in evaluating the situation and educate ourselves, whether this entails speaking to a technology specialist to understand the implications of some new technological innovation or speaking to a lawyer to understand the details of a pending law or policy change. Critical thinking requires information; it requires analysis and interpretation and it is a process that requires we examine our thought processes to unearth our own biases and tenacity. Critical thinking is being informed. Being informed is being responsible; one can consider the Aristotelian concept of excusable and inexcusable ignorance in this regard (see *Nichomachean Ethics*). Responsibility underscores decision-making and hopefully eliminates irresponsible decisions and unethical behaviors that damage individuals, professions, or society in general. Responsibility also implies accountability to our users and various stakeholders. Spinello (1997) discusses the concept of legal liability, in connection with responsibility and accountability in computer scientists in particular. Typically, librarians are not held legally liable within their workplaces.

We then consider the boundaries of our actions and inactions and we consider the intentions behind these. We evaluate alternatives to a given situation and we explore their repercussions. We determine a reasonable, logical, safe, responsible course of action, noting the stakeholders and how they will be affected. Ethical issues reach far and wide and a decision ultimately affects many individuals personally and society generally. How confident, and how comfortable, will we be with our decision? It is critical to engage in self-evaluation as part of the decision-making process. Will we be confident disclosing our decisions or would we prefer to hide our decisions behind a "closed door meeting" or in a "non-public contract"? Finally, we consider the cumulative effect of each and every decision. We do not make decisions in isolation. How will this decision potentially affect subsequent decisions and policy? For many years, in the library and information studies world, we have talked of a "slippery slope" when referring to matters of intellectual freedom. If we give in on this challenge, do we set in motion an uncontrollable downslide where the next challenge is "easily" granted, based on the previous decision? One action sets off others, with unintended consequences. Ethical decision-making must occur with careful, critical reason, with consideration of the generalization of such decisions. We must ask if we are confident with our decision in order to generalize it. Applied ethics is making decisions — decisions affect real people's existences and decisions affect professions for years to come: In short, "nothing is more important than the way we treat each other" (Hauptman, foreword), and as we consider the issues presented throughout these cases, we must think and reflect on multiple levels — personal, professional, societal — local to global, global to local.

Thus, our objective through this book is to use case study to allow individuals and organizations the opportunity to explore the personal, the professional, the local and the global realms involved in LIS work and come, hopefully, to a place of understanding of and respect for ethical debate. We believe case studies are valuable and pragmatic: They provide the opportunity for "lessons" prior to the "test" instead of the other way around, which can be costly, literally and figuratively, to society, the organization, and the individuals involved in a complex situation. Case study enables us, in educational settings, the opportunity to think critically about a set of conditions before we are knee-deep in them. Finally, case study is a viable way to raise awareness, to question standing beliefs and perspectives, and to assume alternative roles as part of a larger decision-making process. And, given the innumerable issues facing information professionals in the field through complexities surrounding technologies, law, policy and practice, we as information professionals must consider an understanding of ethics in general and professional ethics in particular as an essential proficiency, part of our skill set. For instance, it is notable that a recent job announcement at the Seattle Public Library included a "commitment to intellectual freedom" as a requisite skill for applicants. We've become more accustomed to technical skills listed as the essentials, but perhaps a new trend will emerge where we see "understanding of ethics and ethical decision-making processes" as a primary qualification, next to "ability to search online databases."

As Ghandi said, action expresses priorities. At its core, ethical decision-making must be action-oriented or it is meaningless. As Hauptman (2002) suggested, we are not always used to making reflective decisions: "if we are faced with a dilemma ... we do not call upon Aristotle, the principal, or the Dean. We make a quick decision and act upon it ... so acculturated we are to providing help unthinkingly" (p. 9). We often act from a place of fear, of reaction, or of convenience. Ethical decision-making removes us from those places and gives us appropriate license to decide and act. Using cases as a means to explore and to ask important questions moves us from the realm of the symbolic into the realm of action. *Action expresses priorities.*

The book is structured around the following themes: Intellectual Freedom, Censorship, and Rights to Expression and Access to Information; Privacy; Intellectual Property, Copyright, Ownership, and Licensing; Professional Ethics; and Intercultural Information Ethics. These are significant areas of concern for a wide range of library and information professionals and our cases span library and information settings and introduce readers to various stakeholders' perspectives. There are "classic" ethical issues, dealing with censorship and copyright issues, and emergent ethical issues, such as the PATRIOT Act, RFID, social networking sites, privatization and corporatization, and contingent worker model cases. Information professionals will face this host of issues in their daily work. We hope the cases spark engagement and discussion; such discussion enables us as professionals to think critically and make sound and responsible decisions, based on the above suggestions for ethical decision-making. The cases are designed to be accessible; they may seem simplistic on the surface, but upon consideration, deep ethical complexities are embedded. Yet the cases are succinct and are thus easy to incorporate into a classroom setting or a staff meeting. To promote reflection, we provide questions for discussion on each case. The majority of the cases are based in actual situations and we graciously thank the many individuals who have shared their cases with us. Fact is stranger than fiction, we have learned yet again — we as librarians and information professionals face some interesting challenges in our work!

And, if we accept the importance of information, the power of information, then we, as information professionals, are dealing with enormous power on a daily basis. We should know the value of what we're dealing with and be able to defend our actions and positions within these positions of power. Education — and therefore information — helps to find the answer to almost any problem or issue we face as individuals or as a society. Since the most accessible source of information has historically been a library, we are, as information professionals, directing, controlling, and altering the future of our societies, local and global.

Ethics is not easy work. It requires commitment and diligence. It is a thoughtful process, but, as Socrates once said, the unexamined life is not worth living (*Apology*, 38A). As information professionals in an increasingly complex field and world around us, such ethical examination is integral to our success.

REFERENCES

American Library Association. (1995). *Code of Ethics*. Retrieved August 29, 2007, from http://www.ala. org/alaorg/oif/ethics.html.

Buchanan, E. (2004). Ethical Considerations for the Information Professions. In R. Spinello & H. Tavani (Eds.), *Readings in Cyberethics* (2nd ed.) (pp. 613–624). Boston, MA: Jones and Bartlett.

Buchanan, E. (2004). Ethics in Library and Information Science: What Are We Teaching. *Journal of Information Ethics*, 13, 51–61.

Capurro, R. (2006). *International Review of Information Ethics*. Retrieved August 15, 2007, from http://icie.zkm.de/research.

Capurro, R. (2006). Towards an Ontological Foundation of Information Ethics. *Ethics and Information Technology*, 8 (4), 157–186.

Capurro, R., Frühbauer, J., & Hausmanninger, T. (Eds.). (2007). Localizing the Internet. *Ethical Aspects in Intercultural Perspective ICIE Series*, 4, 21–38.

Edson, G. (Ed.). (1997). *Museum Ethics*. London: Routledge.

Floridi, L. (forthcoming). Information Ethics, Its Nature and Scope. In J. van den Hoven & J. Weckert (Eds.), *Moral Philosophy and Information Technology*. Cambridge: Cambridge University Press.

Freeman, L., & Peace, A. G. (Eds.). (2005). *Information Ethics: Privacy and Intellectual Property*. Hershey, PA: Information Science Publishing.

Hauptman, R. (2002). *Ethics and Librarianship*. Jefferson, NC: McFarland.

Himma, K. (2007). Foundational Issues in Information Ethics. *Library Hi-Tech*, 25(1), 79–94.

Himma, K., and Tavani, H. (2008). *The Handbook of Information and Computer Ethics*. Hoboken, NJ: John Wiley.

Hongladaram, S., & Ess, C. (Eds.). (2007). *Information Technology Ethics: Cultural Perspectives*. Hershey, PA: IGI Global.

McMenemy, D., Poulter, A., & Burton, P. (2006). *Handbook of Ethical Practice: A Practical Guide to Dealing With Ethical Issues in Information and Library Work*. Oxford: Chandos Publishing.

Moore, A. (Ed.). (2005). *Information Ethics: Privacy, Property, and Power*. Seattle: University of Washington Press.

Quinn, M. (2005). *Ethics for the Information Age*. Boston: Pearson.

Schultz, R. (2005). *Contemporary Issues in Ethics and Information Technology*. Hershey, PA: IRM Press.

Severson, R.J. (1997). *Principles of Information Ethics:* Armonk, NY: M. E. Sharpe.

Smith, M. (1996). *Information Ethics: An Hermeneutical Analysis of An Emerging Area in Applied Ethics.* Chapel Hill, NC: University of North Carolina at Chapel Hill.

Solomon, R. (1993). *Introducing Philosophy: A Text with Integrated Readings* (5th ed.). Orlando, FL: Harcourt Brace.

Spinello, R. (1997). *Case Studies in Information and Computer Ethics.* Upper Saddle River, NJ: Prentice Hall.

Spinello, R., & Tavani, H. (Eds.). (2004). *Intellectual Property Rights in a Networked World: Theory and Practice.* Hershey, PA: Information Science Publishing.

Tavani, H. (2006). *Ethics and Technology: Ethical Issues in an Age of Information and Communication Technology.* Hoboken, NJ: John Wiley.

Vaagan, E. (Ed.). (2002). *The Ethics of Librarianship: An International Survey.* Munchen, Germany: K. G. Saur.

CHAPTER 2

Intellectual Freedom

Restriction of free thought and free speech is the most dangerous of all subversions. It is the one un–American act that could most easily defeat us.
— *Justice William O. Douglas*

Intellectual freedom, the prerequisite to a functioning, effective democracy, is about the free exchange of information: All facets of the information life cycle are encompassed, from thought to creation to articulation to access. It is, as the American Library Association (2006b) describes it, "the right of every individual to both seek and receive information from all points of view without restriction. It provides for free access to all expressions of ideas through which any and all sides of a question, cause or movement may be explored. Intellectual freedom encompasses the freedom to hold, receive and disseminate ideas." It is critical to understand intellectual freedom on the personal *and* societal levels and to accept that it only thrives when certain criteria are indeed satisfied.

> Intellectual freedom can exist only where two essential conditions are met: first, that all individuals have the right to hold any belief on any subject and to convey their ideas in any form they deem appropriate; and second, that society makes an equal commitment to the right of unrestricted access to information and ideas regardless of the communication medium used, the content of the work, and the viewpoints of both the author and receiver of information.... Freedom to express oneself through a chosen mode of communication, including the Internet, becomes virtually meaningless if access to that information is not protected. Intellectual freedom implies a circle, and that circle is broken if either freedom of expression or access to ideas is stifled [Fitzsimmons, 1998].

Thus, we must make personal and societal commitments to the protection of intellectual freedom. And, as Samek (2001) asserted, "In order for intellectual freedom to move beyond rhetoric and function in day-to-day life, a full range of information on any given topic or issue must be available to the voting public. When a full spectrum of opinion is not fairly represented, forms of censorship exist" (p. 29).

As with any right, the "right" to intellectual freedom must not be taken for granted. Rights once lost are not easily regained, we have been told. Intellectual freedom is closely intertwined with privacy and readers will note overlap between this chapter and the chapter on privacy. When we eliminate the freedom to pursue information through fear or suspicion, we simultaneously curtail intellectual freedom. Our "circle" is indeed broken when personal *or* societal rights are diminished. As information professionals, we must consider the basic foundations of intellectual freedom, as it is a philosophical and practical reality for us. Intellectual freedom is complicated by culture and locale, however, and sometimes it is not as easy to wave our professional flag of intellectual freedom in the face of adversity. Technologies, laws, cross-cultural differences, and ethical relativism combine to make intellectual freedom one of the most challenging principles facing the field.

Legally, in the United States, we understand intellectual freedom through the First Amendment. It states, "Congress shall make no law respecting an establishment of religion, or prohibiting the free exercise thereof; or abridging the freedom of speech, or of the press; or the right of the people peaceably to assemble, and to petition the Government for a redress of grievances" (Bill of Rights, 1789). Numerous court decisions over the years have supported the legal right to free expression, with many directly evolving from challenges in and issues around libraries as a public space in which the free exchange of information is a right (see, for instance, *Miller v. California*, 413 U.S. 15, 24 [1973], *Board of Education, Island Trees Union School District No. 26 v. Pico*, 457 U.S. 853, 874 [1982], *Via v. City of Richmond*, 543 F. Supp. 382 [D.C.Va., 1982], *Kreimer v. Bureau of Police for Town of Morristown*, 958 F.2d 1242 [3d Cir. 1992], *Mainstream Loudoun v. Board of Trustees of the Loudoun County Library*, 2 F. Supp. 2d 783 [*Loudoun I*]; 24 F. Supp. 2d 552 [*Loudoun II*] [E.D. Va. 1998], *Sund v. City of Wichita Falls, Texas*, 121 F. Supp. 2d 530 [N.D. Texas 2000], *United States v. American Library Association*, 539 U.S. 194, 123 S. Ct. 2297 [2003]).

Philosophically, intellectual freedom as a core human right is articulated in the United Nations Universal Declaration of Human Rights, Articles 18–20 (1948).

Article 18: Everyone has the right to freedom of thought, conscience and religion; this right includes freedom to change his religion or belief, and freedom, either alone or in community with others and in public or private, to manifest his religion or belief in teaching, practice, worship and observance.

Article 19: Everyone has the right to freedom of opinion and expression; this right includes freedom to hold opinions without interference and to seek, receive and impart information and ideas through any media and regardless of frontiers.

Article 20: (1) Everyone has the right to freedom of peaceful assembly and association. (2) No one may be compelled to belong to an association.

As a profession, we also uphold and value highly intellectual freedom as a core principle, as defined in and through the Library Bill of Rights (American Library Association, 1996, reprinted with permission) or the Canadian Statement on Intellectual Freedom (reprinted with permission), both of which follow:

The American Library Association affirms that all libraries are forums for information and ideas, and that the following basic policies should guide their services.

24

I. Books and other library resources should be provided for the interest, information, and enlightenment of all people of the community the library serves. Materials should not be excluded because of the origin, background, or views of those contributing to their creation.

II. Libraries should provide materials and information presenting all points of view on current and historical issues. Materials should not be proscribed or removed because of partisan or doctrinal disapproval.

III. Libraries should challenge censorship in the fulfillment of their responsibility to provide information and enlightenment.

IV. Libraries should cooperate with all persons and groups concerned with resisting abridgment of free expression and free access to ideas.

V. A person's right to use a library should not be denied or abridged because of origin, age, background, or views.

VI. Libraries which make exhibit spaces and meeting rooms available to the public they serve should make such facilities available on an equitable basis, regardless of the beliefs or affiliations of individuals or groups requesting their use. (Adopted June 18, 1948, by the American Library Association Council; amended February 2, 1961; amended June 28, 1967; amended January 23, 1980; inclusion of "age" reaffirmed January 24, 1996.)

Statement on Intellectual Freedom

All persons in Canada have the fundamental right, as embodied in the nation's Bill of Rights and the Canadian Charter of Rights and Freedoms, to have access to all expressions of knowledge, creativity and intellectual activity, and to express their thoughts publicly. This right to intellectual freedom, under the law, is essential to the health and development of Canadian society.

Libraries have a basic responsibility for the development and maintenance of intellectual freedom.

It is the responsibility of libraries to guarantee and facilitate access to all expressions of knowledge and intellectual activity, including those which some elements of society may consider to be unconventional, unpopular or unacceptable. To this end, libraries shall acquire and make available the widest variety of materials.

It is the responsibility of libraries to guarantee the right of free expression by making available all of the library's public facilities and services to all individuals and groups who need them.

Libraries should resist all efforts to limit the exercise of these responsibilities while recognizing the right of criticism by individuals and groups.

Both employees and employers in libraries have a duty, in addition to their institutional responsibilities, to uphold these principles.

(Approved by Executive Council, June 27, 1974; amended November 17, 1983; and November 18, 1985.)

Despite these legal, philosophical, and professional commitments, there are a number of ways intellectual freedom has been threatened and comprised (Buchanan and Campbell, 2004). From media consolidation and conglomeration, to radio frequency identification (RFID) and mass surveillance, to such laws as the Digital Millennium Copyright Act and the Sony Bono Copyright Extension Act and filtering laws such as Children's Internet Protection Act, to such major political pushes as Academic Bills of Rights and political interference with science and research, we face limits on what we can see, read,

In what specific way?

say, and access without fear or restrictions. We recognize, in Chapter Four, the power and peril of ownership over intellectual property to chill intellectual freedom economically and, in the case of the DMCA, legally to inhibit the receipt of information. We will discuss the PATRIOT Act in greater depth in our next chapter on privacy, though we must acknowledge its grave implications for intellectual freedom. In the aftermath of 9/11, "questionable" television programs were shelved or pulled. Radio stations had "no play" lists. We were told to watch what we said — and even what we thought. Libraries once again became a hot spot of inquiry and investigation, once it was suspected that a terrorist had used a local public library in Florida. One has to wonder how the Hauptman experiment would play out today — if an individual asked for bomb-making materials, would librarians respond the way they did thirty years ago? Would it depend on what the patron looked like? Would we vacillate? Would we report the request? In addition to these newfound challenges, old-fashioned censorship rages on in libraries, with concerns revolving around homosexuality, "anti-family," and "offensive language" leading the challenges. Scholars' views are scrutinized, with a fierce attention on the "liberal" academy and its "leftist" views. Research itself is politicized, says the American Union of Concerned Scientists (2007): "Data is being misrepresented for political reasons."

This is probably true, but I'd like to see proof

Intellectual freedom itself seems dramatically malleable in this vastly different political climate. How we as a profession respond, or fail to respond to the challenges around us, is beyond significant.

We see these differences affecting adults as well as children — and this should concern all of us; how we choose to instill, or not, intellectual freedom as a core principle in society affects our future tremendously. Children and young adults fit oddly into the intellectual freedom equation. As a western society in particular, we equivocate over children's and young adults' rights. The U.S. has the notorious stigma of being one of only two nations (with Somalia) not to ratify the UN's Convention on the Rights of the Child, for instance. And, intellectual freedom *is* a large part of the Convention. I might be ok w/ this

Overall, libraries have long adopted the position that children and young adults have the right to free expression. The American Association of School Librarians has suggested, "School library media professionals assume a leadership role in promoting the principles of intellectual freedom within the school by providing resources and services that create and sustain an atmosphere of free inquiry." Importantly, Toni Samek, Chair of the Canadian Library Association's Intellectual Freedom Committee, has expressed great concern over the widespread devaluation and elimination of school librarians. She sees these as an ultimate threat to intellectual freedom. "Broadly in society, the cutting of teacher librarians is the surest way to curtail intellectual freedom from the ground up in a person's lived experience.... In my firm view, critical inquiry will not be fully realized in a school without a professional librarian and a well stocked library. That saddens me deeply as a parent, not just for my kids but for all our kids. What does their future hold? What will their notions of freedom be? Will they ever really internalize the difference between the right to read and the right to read anonymously?" (Samek, as quoted in Buchanan, 2007).

Providing an environment of safety and intellectual freedom for children extends well beyond the classroom and is especially challenging in the digital environment. Children do enjoy the right to receive information; however, the First Amendment does not hinder parents in any way from restricting their children's access to information (Minow and Lipinski, 2003, p. 129). With the exception of public schools in which teachers act *in loco parentis*, that is, in the place of the parents, parents are responsible for providing access to information that they believe appropriate for their children, protecting their children from harmful materials and keeping them safe on the Internet. The reality is that even with parental diligence, children may be exposed to materials that are emotionally harmful or traumatic. As a society, we determined, long before the Internet, that protecting our children from certain kinds of materials is the "right" thing to do. Information professionals are all too aware of the kinds of shockingly offensive materials, including scenes of extreme violence and depravity, children and any of our patrons may encounter while pursuing their information interests, especially on the Internet. This prevalence of online pornography and material characterized as "harmful to minors" has naturally been the catalyst for new legislation designed to protect children in the online environment. The phrase "harmful to minors" is described as "material that is considered 'obscene' for minors even if the materials are protected [speech] for adults" (Minow and Lipinski, 2003, p. 127). Definitions are extremely important: "Public libraries and public academic libraries may not deny access to 'inappropriate' or 'offensive' sites, since those terms have no legal meaning under state, federal or constitutional law" (Minow and Lipinski, 2003, p. 129). The setting in which the information will be received makes a difference, too. "In a school library setting, the Supreme Court has limited minors' right to receive information if the information is 'educationally unsuitable'—but not based on a school's disapproval of the content of information" (Minow and Lipinski, 2003, p. 127).

Three laws have currently dominated the intellectual freedom landscape. The Child Pornography Prevention Act (CPPA) expanded the definition of child pornography and criminalized virtual child pornography. Images in which children appear to be engaged in sexual activity were prohibited under this law even if the individuals photographed, filmed or otherwise displayed were not actually children and/or created via digital manipulation. This law was found to be unconstitutional because it was overly broad; among other things, it prohibited such things as artistic, non-pornographic depictions of sexual activity among teenagers in film to be transmitted via the web. This law only applied to works which were transmitted over the Internet and did not directly affect libraries (American Library Association, 2006a). But we include this reference to bring us to the Children's Internet Protection Act (CIPA) and, later in this chapter, the Children's Online Protection Act (COPA).

CIPA requires that libraries who receive certain federal funds (E-rate or LSTA monies) install Internet filters on every computer. A lower court ruled that this law was overly broad and that filters blocked large amounts of legal, constitutionally protected content for everyone and was therefore constitutionally unacceptable. In a 6-to-3 decision, the

Supreme Court overruled the lower court's decision and opined that CIPA was constitutional as crafted, primarily because the law applies only to children; if it applied to adults, it would not pass constitutional measure. Moreover, in the Court's Opinion, the majority stated outright: "1. Because public libraries' use of Internet filtering software does not violate their patrons' First Amendment rights, CIPA does not induce libraries to violate the Constitution, and is a valid exercise of Congress' spending power. Congress has wide latitude to attach conditions to the receipt of federal assistance to further its policy objectives" (539 U.S. 194; 123 S. Ct. 2297; 156 L. Ed. 2d 221; 2003 U.S.). Thus, the Court seemingly couched the decision less as an issue of intellectual freedom and more as an issue of congressional oversight.

Nonetheless, this decision was a terrible loss for libraries seeking to protect intellectual freedom for all of their patrons. The dissenting justices specifically cite the vagaries in the CIPA legislation and its clear potential to limit constitutionally protected content. And, the 6–3 vote concerned many: "Although it does not make the loss any easier to bear, the decision in *United States v. American Library Association* was a plurality" (American Library Association, 2006a); Adam Hoschild states, "A plurality opinion, which represents the rationale of less than half of the Justices, is ... problematic. A majority opinion may command more authority than a plurality decision, but precisely what authority does a plurality decision command? In other words, how should courts apply a plurality decision to subsequent controversies involving similar issues?" (quoted in ALA, 2006a).

Thus, it remains unclear what will happen as these issues arise time and time again. The vagaries surrounding "obscenity" remain with us. Do we still "know it when we see it," as Justice Stewart argued in *Miller v. California*, and now that we see it through many different channels, must we protect ourselves differently? Proponents of the CIPA argue that it does not place an undue burden on libraries or adult patrons, practically speaking, if adults need to seek out assistance to access legal content; but would a patron stop and reconsider his or her request for information if he or she needed unfiltered access? If so, we are stepping into the circle of intellectual freedom we earlier described and we are interfering. Intellectual freedom *is* chilled. Privacy, too, is at issue, as anonymity is compromised whenever a patron requests unfiltered access to a particular site or sites. Unfortunately, most public libraries rely on these funds and have no choice but to follow the mandatory rules on filtering. Within that framework of funding and mandate, we must acknowledge issues of equity and fairness that consequently arise. If a school or a library is located in a more affluent area and can afford to reject the filtering laws, while those in poorer districts face such interference, what are we saying about intellectual freedom for all? We are saying those that can afford it are privileged and have greater rights. Indeed, the ACLU asserted, "Libraries have traditionally promoted free speech values by providing free books and information resources to people regardless of their age or income" (2001, p. 159). Intellectual freedom cannot — should not — be for sale.

The last piece of legislation under discussion is COPA, the Child Online Protection Act. This act is similar to CPPA in that it relates to materials transmitted over the Internet. Specifically, COPA prohibits any material deemed "harmful to minors" to be transmitted over the Internet for commercial purposes. COPA was unanimously struck down by the Supreme Court and remanded to the lower court for additional exploration as to its constitutionality (American Library Association, 2006a). Like CPPA, COPA does not directly affect libraries, as it is concerned with web site operators as opposed to end users. The impetus to prevent access to inappropriate materials fell *not* to the library, as in CIPA. Still, COPA warrants attention from information professionals as it has the same potential to chill intellectual freedom and interfere with the right to gather information anonymously. The ALA responded to the COPA ruling by stating that the "ALA believes that libraries and the public need to be able to use new technologies.... The only thing that is really going to protect children is education" (Sheketoff, quoted in Lau Whelan, 2007). *Bull Shit*

Echoing back to earlier statements in this chapter, as information professionals, we advocate intellectual freedom and this naturally leads to providing *resources and services that create and sustain an atmosphere of free inquiry.* This is a difficult task in an environment fraught with conflicting and politically charged mandates of protecting children, and even adults, from "harmful" materials and from laws which erode civil rights in exchange for "safety."

Intellectual Freedom Cases

CASE #2.1

In 1995, then president William Jefferson Clinton, by executive order, declassified records 25 or more years old. The order included provisions that exempted certain kinds of records relating to security and other critical state issues. In other words, some things would remain classified. The deadline for declassification was 1999. Some agencies, such as the State Department, were quick to respond, others less so. Some of the declassified records were published in *Foreign Relations of the United States.* Over a couple of years' time, resistance grew and the conflict came to a head in 1999 when a group of six agencies, including the CIA, took action against the State Department. The group claimed that the State Department had declassified records that should have remained classified. Ultimately, approximately 1400 records were reclassified under this action. However, and to the chagrin of the National Archives and Records Administration, the reclassifications continued, far beyond the original records the group sought to reclassify. In fact, the Bush Administration expanded the original reclassification order in 2001. According to *Declassification in Reverse,* a report published in early 2006 by Matthew Aid, some 9500 documents have been reclassified. Aid's report indicated that the work was expected to continue through March 2007. An audit conducted at the time of this report, by

J. William Leonard, Director of the Information Security Oversight Office, revealed that none of the 16 documents reviewed need to remain secret (Aid, 2006).

Notes: This case provides an extremely brief overview of a complex, politically charged conflict across multiple agencies and two administrations. The 16 documents reviewed by Leonard are included on the webpage referenced below. The NARA is obligated by law to remove the declassified materials.

QUESTIONS TO CONSIDER

1. Leonard had not taken action at the time of Aid's report. Discuss possible options he could take and the moral implications of each.
2. Make a list of talking points that should be included in an ALA resolution on reverse declassification
3. How does such classification affect the practical collection development and information access of libraries?
4. How political should librarians as a profession become?

CASE REFERENCES

Aid, M. (2006). The national security archive, *Declassification in reverse* retrieved on September 5, 2007 from http://www.gwu.edu/~nsarchiv/NSAEBB/NSAEBB179/.

American Libraries (2006). *Historian discovers intelligence-agency scheme to reclassify NARA documents* retrieved on September 5, 2007 from http://www.ala.org/ala/alonline/currentnews/newsarchive/2006abc/february2006a/reclassify.cfm.

CASE #2.2

John was a young information professional who enjoyed music and, in his free time, attended many conferences. He recently attended a Pearl Jam event and was telling another staff member about it on Monday after the show. "It was awesome. They are so politically inclined and critical of censorship. They are a great band and have a lot to say. You should watch this concert on their web site; it is webcasted." On their break, John and Marta sat down to watch some of the show. John was horrified to hear that some of the band's words had been muted out. It was not the profanity, but the political ideas that were gone. Specifically, the anti-war comments that the band's singer had made were muted.

John then learned that the media company who owned the rights to the broadcast was also the digital phone and Internet provider of the library. He spoke with the director and encouraged her to consider changing the provider in light of their "overt censorship." John argued, "How can we as a library, a place of un-stifled ideas, give our money to that censor? It is not right. We need to take a stand." The director agreed with John, in principle. She had to make a case to the city board. This was, in her mind, a very different discussion than any of the previous book challenges she had faced in her career.

QUESTIONS TO CONSIDER

1. Write a brief from the director to the board. Should the city change providers over something like this?
2. How is net neutrality an issue in this case?
3. Discuss the changing arena of intellectual freedom in libraries, as it moves from a print-based to an electronic arena.
4. Is John overstepping his personal convictions into a professional area? Should he, in this sort of case?

CASE #2.3

The statewide library association had an electronic mailing list for its members. Individuals were automatically subscribed when they joined the association, but could opt out of the list if they chose, by emailing the list administrator. The list, historically, had been informational only, with limited or no discussions and messages typically sent about events, association news, or business-related topics. The chair of the intellectual freedom committee began sending more posts out, as the current political climate was increasingly hostile to civil liberties and intellectual freedom issues. Specifically, he sent out messages concerning the state of libraries and librarians in Cuba, as well as on the public library strike in Vancouver, Canada. He saw a need to keep members informed about these political encroachments and workplace rights, given their direct impact on all libraries and information workers. Other members disagreed and asked him to stop posting "political trash" and "cluttering others' email boxes." The chair was very offended and saw such comments as contrary to his role on the intellectual freedom committee. He refused to stop and suggested others remove themselves from the mailing list if they didn't want to be informed.

QUESTIONS TO CONSIDER

1. Is the chair of the committee correct?
2. Should the list administrator screen messages before posting them?
3. What policies should be set to govern the list communications?
4. Discuss the idea of the "personal as the political" and how this affects the profession.
5. What moral obligations do information professionals have to each other — that is, to their colleagues? Is the chair acting with a greater good in mind?

CASE #2.4

The University of Cedarburg is a public, four-year college. It is home to 25,000 undergraduate and 500 graduate students and 3000 full-time faculty in a number of academic disciplines. A talk by a scholar, who argued that the U.S. government knew about the 9/11 attacks before they happened, was scheduled to take place in the library.

There was both support and opposition to hosting the speaker at the university. There were threats made against the library, as well as calls from politicians that funding be withdrawn from the university — and the library in particular — if the talk was not canceled. The library director was asked to make a recommendation to the University Chancellor. The library director argued that while controversial, the library would remain open to the speaker, as hosting all points of view, regardless of political orientation, was important to the library in particular and to the mission of public education in general.

QUESTIONS TO CONSIDER

1. Discuss the decision of the library director.
2. Would your decision be different if the institution were a private academic institution or a public library?
3. Step into the director's position. Write a statement presenting your decision to the University Chancellor.
4. How should libraries handle "controversial" speakers/authors, who wish to use a library's space? (Also see Case 2.5.)

CASE #2.5

The Allendale Public Library had meeting rooms available for rentals. As the building is a publicly funded space, it is open to all. The Director of Facilities received a request from a neo-Nazi group, who wished to hold an annual meeting in the room. The facilities director found the nature of the group to be disturbing, citing that patrons would be offended by the presence of the group and that allowing them to host a meeting there implied that its objective was acceptable. She chose to deny the request for the room. The group maintained that as a public space, as long as it was not doing anything illegal, it was able to conduct business in the space. The group filed a discrimination suit with the ACLU against the library and the town of Allendale.

QUESTIONS TO CONSIDER

1. What policies should govern a situation like this?
2. Should a public library have the right to restrict access to its facilities?
3. What ethical issues does this scenario address?
4. If the group were a pro-life or pro-choice group, how would that affect your decision?

CASE #2.6

Bill was with his 5-year-old son at their small public library, in their town of Graderton. Recently, the town was engaged in a debate over the teaching of evolution and creationism in their public schools. Notably, the children's collection at the public library was one of the best in the area. As Bill and Zach looked in the non-fiction shelving for dinosaur books, they saw one entitled *Jesus Walks with the Dinosaurs*. It was cataloged as non-fiction and placed in the Qs with other science materials. Bill asked the librarian why it was wrongly cataloged: "Why would you have a fictional book shelved with the science materials?" The librarian responded, "There are scientists who believe dinosaurs lived with humans. In fact, there is evidence that dinosaurs were on the Ark. This book is for all children to learn about Jesus while reading about dinosaurs, too." "But," argued Bill, "this is fiction. All I am asking is for you to re-catalog and reclassify the book. I do not want my child reading scientific inaccuracies and religion that I do not support. But I am not asking you to remove the book altogether."

The library council met to review the request. After some discussion, they chose to re-catalog the book into the religion area.

QUESTIONS TO CONSIDER

1. What are the ethical issues in this scenario?
2. Is Bill's request to move the book appropriate?
3. Was the library's response appropriate?

CASE #2.7

The statewide prison library system was, like most state agencies, facing severe budget cuts and the prison librarian was told that he was going to need to cut back on acquisitions. The warden thought he would help by donating many books from his personal collection, which was heavily dominated by Christian-themed books. He remarked, "Not only will it help the collection, but it will help the prisoners by learning some religion." The librarian was concerned. He had worked towards a balanced collection, one which represented many religious perspectives, and he felt that by accepting the warden's collection, such balance and diversity would be sacrificed. He felt that prisoners had rights to a balanced collection and to violate such rights was unethical. Now, he had to explain his decision to the warden.

QUESTIONS TO CONSIDER

1. Did the librarian act correctly? What course of action should he follow?
2. Do prisoners have rights to intellectual freedom?
3. Should prison libraries represent a balanced collection, as other public libraries portend to do?
4. If, as is increasingly the case, the prison were not federally funded, but instead a privatized entity, must the library offer a fair collection?
5. If a private entity operates the prison library and the entity has a religious or social bias that is embedded in the library's collection, are the prisoners' intellectual freedom rights violated?

CASE #2.8

June was a senior academic librarian at the public university. She had been on staff for nearly thirty years and had seen many changes over the years in terms of technologies and policies. While not always happy with the changes, June remained professional. One day, June was helping a patron at the public computer terminals when she saw what she considered very offensive pornographic images on the next computer. The university had an acceptable computing policy, but it did not prohibit access to pornography, except as defined by legal standards in cases of child pornography. June complained at the library staff meeting that her rights to feeling safe and secure in her workplace had been violated and that she and others should not have to see such "degradation and smut." She continued that she "supported others' rights to free speech and expression, but not where they violated her own rights." She demanded that the library restrict access to "adult themed" sites in the main computing area.

QUESTIONS TO CONSIDER

1. Are there legitimate conflicting rights in this case?
2. Should academic libraries use filters?
3. Would it be different if the site in question were a racial hate site or a pro-anorexia site?

CASE #2.9

Significant budget cuts faced the State. The public school district, which enrolled 2000 children from kindergarten to eighth grade, shared two full-time librarians and two part-time assistants across three school buildings and resources were already stretched. Music programs were being cut and sports programs were on the chopping block. Parents were outraged and demanded something else be cut. The superintendent, then, decided the schools could save significantly if they reduced to one professional librarian and three assistants or paraprofessionals. "What do those librarians really do anymore," he said, only half-jokingly, "since we have everything online? Kids use the Internet anyway. They aren't interested in using those old books. The assistants can handle whatever comes their way." The librarians were obviously shocked. They argued that not only are librarians important in curriculum and teaching, but they played a significant role in teaching children about intellectual freedom. "These children need a safe place where a diversity of opinions is represented. That is the school library. What kind of message are we sending about libraries and their role in society if we don't support it within their own school?" the librarians argued.

QUESTIONS TO CONSIDER

1. Do children deserve the same rights to intellectual freedom as adults?
2. How do you, as a member of a civil society, respond to the mentalities around libraries expressed in this case?

3. What is the importance of teaching children about intellectual freedom?
4. How do you describe intellectual freedom to a child?
5. What does the ALA say about age and intellectual freedom?

CASE #2.10

Annette Micco was a prominent children's author and frequent critic of the national laws that were recently passed that required standardized testing in classrooms. She was invited to present the keynote speech at a major conference for publishers. She accepted the offer, signed a contract outlining what sorts of issues she was to present, and began preparing her remarks. About one month prior to the talk, she received a request to review her speech. Annette was not pleased and refused to share her speech. The organization sponsoring her insisted that she must allow them to preview it. This was not in the original contract and, becoming suspicious, Annette further researched the sponsors of the conference. She learned that a major publisher of standardized tests was behind the conference sponsorship and she believed that they were attempting to censor her criticisms of such tests. Announcements soon were issued that Ms. Micco's talk was canceled and both Annette and the sponsor claimed the other broke the contract.

QUESTIONS TO CONSIDER

1. How do corporate sponsorships influence public good?
2. Research the Patricia Polacco case and discuss the ethical issues behind it.
3. Discuss the various ways corporate influence can stifle research and, in doing so, curtail intellectual freedoms.

CASE #2.11

One of the most controversial topics for years has been the scientific theory of evolution. Two major movements in the United States, creationism and, more recently, intelligent design, have sought to emphasize the idea that evolution is only one theory among many and, as with any theory, it has flaws. Both movements have pushed public schools to offer alternative theories of human existence alongside evolution in science classes and have pushed public libraries to present all sides through their collections. Some of the outcomes of these movements included adding labels to textbooks in Texas and Georgia, consisting of "clarifying statements" describing evolution as "just one of several theories" explaining the diversity of life on earth, and changing science curriculums to include biblical explanations.

This controversy is not limited to the classroom. At the Grand Canyon National Park Bookstore, alongside scientific books about the canyon's geology, evolution, diverse flora and fauna, and indigenous peoples, there is another book which reveals the canyon's history according to biblical timelines. There has been a challenge against selling this book at the national park. Adding fuel to the fire, there is no longer an official Park Service statement on its web site or in its literature on the geological age of the canyon. The individual, a scientist, who challenged the bookstore's inclusion of the text argued that the park was a governmental agency and, as such, it should not be including the biblical version of the canyon's history. He maintained, "The bookstore at the Canyon *is* different than other for-profit bookstores because of its very relationship to the U.S. government. This is not about that author's right to free speech — he can write whatever he wants, but this book should not be presented as science in this Park's bookstore."

QUESTIONS TO CONSIDER

1. How should the park bookstore respond to the challenge? Should the text be removed?
2. What are the consequences for public, school, and academic libraries if the challenge is upheld or not upheld?
3. How do you respond to the claim that removing the book is a violation of intellectual freedom?

CASE #2.12

Moorestown High School was just down the street from the public library. The school's library and computer lab closed at the end of the school day, at 3:00, thus students were not able to stay and use the Internet. Many walked down the street to the public library to take advantage of the high-speed Internet access. The library had two computer areas with Internet access, one in the reference room and one in the children's area; the library had not implemented a time limit, but, as the winter set in, the high school students were spending more and more time online. Many were involved in role-playing games and spent hours in World of Warcraft and other Massively Multiplayer Role Playing Games. As the reference room computers were frequently occupied, the teens started using the computers in the children's area. Parents complained that the games were violent and their children could see them. Many voiced concerns that the teens should not be in the children's area at all, that they were on too long, and that such games should be filtered out anyway. The teens responded that they had rights, too, and, because the library did not have a policy about teenagers in the children's room, they should be able to do as they wished.

QUESTIONS TO CONSIDER

1. Discuss a policy for the library to cover such issues as gaming.
2. What intellectual freedom and privacy issues apply in this case?
3. Should the library restrict access to the children's room?
4. Should libraries restrict users' access to gaming sites?
5. Why is violence often overlooked in lieu of pornography in discussions of censorship?

CASE #2.13

As with many public libraries, local teens were frequent visitors to the Treestown library, where they had unlimited access to social networking sites. Mrs. Peren, the mother of a 14-year-old girl, came into the library one afternoon and demanded to speak to the director. "My daughter has been approached by *predators* on MySpace and I want this stopped. She has received pornographic images in her account and I want to be able to monitor her use. If she has this unlimited access in the library, however, I can't watch what is going on. I believe you should either restrict access to these sites, or require users to be 18. Then, she would not be allowed to use it here." The director responded with a long discussion of intellectual freedom principles, while also stating that age verification measures were pending but were not very sound in practice. "If you do not want your daughter accessing MySpace, that is a discussion you need to have with her, not with us, ma'am," the director replied politely.

QUESTIONS TO CONSIDER

1. Should libraries have discrete policies guiding social networking sites?
2. Research such technologies as Tubes, a tool that helps social-network users control whom gets to view what information on users' personal pages. How could this sort of technology be useful?
3. In theory and practice, what rights to intellectual freedom and privacy do minors have?
4. How does a right to intellectual freedom affect a right to privacy?

CASE #2.14

Kenoba Public Library was within two miles of a homeless shelter and many homeless individuals, who had to leave the shelter between the hours of 10:00 A.M. and 3:00 P.M., often went to the library. The new director often found these individuals sleeping or simply sitting in the library and decided it was bad for the library and its "real patrons." "People pay taxes to come and use this library and I won't have them scared off by the smell or sight of those people. This library is not a shelter and, if they aren't paying taxes, they have no right to be here." The director then issued a new policy which prohibited sleeping in the library and occupying the same table or desk for longer than 2 hours. Patrons could request the table longer if they had "legitimate" business.

QUESTIONS TO CONSIDER

1. Discuss the director's new policy.
2. What rights do homeless individuals have in public libraries?
3. What ethical and legal principles are significant here?
4. Review the ALA's policy on services to the poor and homeless.

CASE #2.15

The university library was a government repository library and, as such, remained open to the public for use. An elderly woman, Mrs. Marksman, had used the library for years and enjoyed looking through the reports and materials the government produced. She noticed, however, that more and more of the materials were only available on CD and through the Internet. Her arthritis prevented her from spending too much time in front of a computer and she asked the librarian how she could continue to read the materials in print. "We only make available the materials the government sends, Mrs. Marksman. We cannot print out copies for you, unfortunately." Mrs. Marksman maintained that it was her right to be able to read the materials in an easy and accessible way. "My tax dollars contribute to these materials. It is not fair that they are only available electronically. They are *not* fulfilling their purpose of being publicly available."

QUESTIONS TO CONSIDER

1. Do you agree with the patron?
2. How should libraries maintain a balance of materials and media? That is, how should libraries transition from older media to new, from VHS to DVD, when patrons may not have access to newer technologies?
3. How does this case illustrate the digital divide?
4. Explore age as a specific variable in the digital divide. How should libraries respond to the aging population?

CASE #2.16

An eight-school library consortium consisted of some non-religious- and some religious-based colleges, all of which shared a common automation system and resources. One of the schools was a seminary. During a technical services meeting, the librarian from the seminary requested that the cataloging records for their institution be based on the Catholic Subject Headings, an older system that very few libraries used. The LC Subject Headings had been adopted and fit the needs of the Consortium. The librarian was adamant that in keeping with the school's mission, they should use headings that reflect the "true beliefs" of the school. She explained that this was an intellectual freedom for her school and for her students. In particular was the choice of the subject heading "Eucharist," instead of the LC's use of "Lord's Supper — Catholic Church." The Consortium Director explained that, as a consortium, decisions had to be made for the good of all of the schools and that was the point of a consortium — to share resources. Furthermore, the Consortium had agreed that they would avoid the older subject headings where they conflicted with LC. The Consortium Director suggested putting the Catholic Subject Headings in a separate field on the records, so that they would be searchable, but not the main subject headings.

QUESTIONS TO CONSIDER

1. Defend the decision of the Consortium Director.
2. Were the intellectual freedom rights of the seminary library violated?
3. What other options exist for meeting the needs of all stakeholders in this case?
4. What other ethical issues can arise in the face of cataloging and classification?

CASE #2.17

The budget for periodicals at the public library in Whitewater Bay was shrinking, as the costs were increasing. The library director was of the mindset that many people were now reading their newspapers online, as they were more current and convenient. He thought, to save money, the library would reduce the numbers of daily papers from five down to three. The library had to make a decision to deselect two papers. The discussion around this focused on the community's needs. "Well," said one librarian, "we must keep the local paper and we should keep the *Wall Street Journal*, but between the *Times* and *USA Today*, I'd say more people read *USA Today*. People like it; it is easy to read, in short digestible pieces, whereas the *Times* is more political anyway." "Yes," agreed another librarian, "but don't we want a diversity of perspectives? The *Times* offers a bit of an independent perspective, whereas the other is more conservative. We should make every effort to offer both sides to things, as we do in the rest of our collection." "This is not an intellectual freedom issue — it is a practical issue. More patrons read *USA Today*. That should be our deciding factor," the first librarian concluded.

QUESTIONS TO CONSIDER

1. How has media conglomeration affected intellectual freedom?
2. What should libraries do to combat the shrinking perspectives represented, as more and more news outlets are owned by fewer media groups?
3. How do such collection development issues affect intellectual freedom?

CASE #2.18

Maggie was a provisional teacher/librarian at a local elementary school, in her second year of employment. The Maurice Sendak book *In the Night Kitchen* was a favorite among the children. One afternoon, a parent called the media center complaining about the book, as her child said she saw the boy's penis in one of the pictures. The mother was an active parent on the PTA and a vocal individual who attended all school board meetings. The librarian knew the woman would push until she got her way. The school was not prepared with a solid policy on book or materials challenges and Maggie felt alone, being the only librarian in the school. Since she was provisional, she was fearful for her position. She believed if the school board heard the challenge that they would side with the parent. Maggie regretfully moved the book behind the desk, where students could not get it themselves and stopped using it in reading time.

QUESTIONS TO CONSIDER

1. What resources are available to help librarians facing challenges?
2. What arguments should Maggie use in defending her case to the parent and to the school board?
3. Review and discuss the American Library Association's list of 100 Most Frequently Challenged and Banned Books.
4. Review the legal cases cited in the chapter introduction. How are they relevant to this scenario?

CASE #2.19

Nancy and her husband Greg were reading at their local public library when they noticed an Army recruiter chatting with a teenager from their neighborhood. The recruiter was telling him about the education benefits, travel opportunities and high adventure offered by the Army. The recruiter also mentioned other positive things, such as what an honor it was to serve one's country. Nancy and Greg were both very unhappy that the recruiter was recruiting in the public library, especially since they believed that the recruiter was omitting information about the physical and mental cost of the combat the student would likely face, considering the ongoing Iraqi war. Greg knew this first-hand. He had served two tours in Iraq and had only been home a few weeks. Greg got up and spoke to the librarian and asked if it would be all right to hold up a small sign that the teenager could see. The sign said not to join the Army because he could die in combat. Greg told the librarian that he didn't want to cause any problems, but wanted the teenager to consider the dangers. The librarian thought this was fine and Greg proceeded. The recruiter noticed the sign and registered a complaint with the director. The director told Greg to take down the sign immediately. Greg refused and the director told Greg he was not permitted to use the library for 3 months for creating a disturbance. She also gave him a copy of the library policy on disturbing patrons, which indicated that such a disturbance was grounds to revoke library privileges for a maximum of 3 months on a first offense.

QUESTIONS TO CONSIDER

1. Was this a just application of library policy?
2. Is this policy chilling freedom of expression?
3. Was the teenager's right to receive information violated?
4. Should recruiters be allowed to recruit in the public library?
5. If we allow military recruiters, do we also have to allow all recruiters (i.e., seminaries, police or fire departments, universities)?

CASE #2.20

The political climate has become increasingly conservative over the past eight years, with a strong voice of the religious right dominating public discourse. This voice has affected both public and school libraries, which have long balanced the dual challenge of providing information to children and young adults while also keeping them safe from undue harm. Members of various ideological movements across the United States have begun expecting their libraries to fit their models of appropriateness, ranging from books to videos to Internet sites to gaming resources. In some ways, the courts have responded with filtering laws, to differentiate between children's and adults' access and appropriateness. For many, the courts move too slowly and are simply too liberal. Recently, then, libraries have been asked to collect CDs and videos that have been deemed "family friendly." Scenes from major motion pictures, such as *Titanic*, would be edited, blurred, or dubbed. Profanity in music would be beeped. New businesses engaged in such practices were emerging all over the country, to "fill an obvious need," so the argument went. "If the people want good, clean entertainment and Hollywood won't provide it, we will. Our products are sold by Target and Wal-Mart, so why aren't they available in the libraries?"

QUESTIONS TO CONSIDER

1. In addition to the obvious intellectual freedom issues, what intellectual property issues arise in such editing?
2. Discuss the argument, "Why not in the libraries?" What is inherently different between a commercial business and a public entity?
3. When matters of intellectual freedom are pitted in the "us versus them" mentality, what do we all stand to lose?
4. Review the federal court ruling on CleanFlicks. Is intellectual freedom a significant part of the argument? Should it be?

CASE #2.21

The head librarian at Glenhaven Public Library took a great deal of pride in the new book collection. Martha spent several hours every month picking out what she believed to be the best of the best for the citizens of Glenhaven. She was very precise in her selection process, purchasing books across all genres and subjects, carefully adhering to Ranganathan's second law,* "Every reader his book." She would not purchase anything that had not received high praise in respected library journals. If a patron went to the trouble of looking, he or she would discover that many of Glenhaven's new titles have received

---

*Ranganathan, a librarian from India, published his five laws of librarianship in 1931: *Books are for use; Every reader his book; Every book, its reader; Save the time of the reader; A library is a living organism.* These laws continue to be influential today, although expressed somewhat differently to reflect technological innovations.

critical acclaim and many are from small but highly respected presses. Martha often bought two or more copies of these works to ensure that ample copies were available for patrons to borrow. Martha only bought a few popular books each month, relying on the *New York Times* Best Seller list to determine what was "popular." Martha believed that these titles were simply literary "fads" and would not have lasting value. For this reason, she bought only one copy of books that appeared on the list.

QUESTIONS TO CONSIDER

1. Martha was obviously concerned about providing the best possible collection for her patrons. Was she doing them a disservice by only collecting the "best of the best"?
2. Was Martha guilty of censorship? Defend your response.
3. Discuss the "dirty little secret" (Samek, 2001) of librarianship: self-censorship.

CASE #2.22

The president of a university library system was planning to donate $1 million to promote library developments and enhancements over the next two years. She was engaged in talks with the system and the foundation, which would oversee the gift and its implementation. The library president, then, reviewed her annual evaluations, which were done by other administrators and the regents of the system. One of the reviews was quite negative concerning her performance, noting questionable employment practices, elaborate personal spending, and other excesses. Upon reviewing the evaluations, the president decided to withdraw from all talks with the foundation, if the review were not "corrected." The regents and, in particular, the individual who wrote the comments in question refused to change the evaluation, noting this should have nothing do to with the gift to the system. "If this person were acting with integrity and honesty, she would not even consider withdrawing her gift," the regents asserted. The president retorted, "It is unfortunate that the students and members of the university system will lose out because of this individual's personal feelings towards me."

QUESTIONS TO CONSIDER

1. How is workplace speech complicated in this case?
2. If the regents withdrew the evaluation, what message is this sending?
3. How would you respond to the president's demand to have the evaluation comments "corrected"?
4. Consider the ways these events would affect the library staff.

CASE #2.23

Eric, who is 15, and his mother were waiting in line to check out books and movies at the Glenwood Public Library. When it was their turn, Eric's mom checked out her books and stepped a few feet away from the desk. Eric proceeded and the circulation clerk began to check out his books and then to check out his movies. She got to the last one and refused to check it out to Eric. Eric demanded to know why she wasn't checking it out to him. The clerk said Eric couldn't check it out because it was rated R. Eric informed her that he had the right to view whatever he wanted. The clerk still refused. At this point Eric's mom stepped in and told the clerk to check the movie out to her son, as the library did not have a policy on R-rated materials for minors, and that if he ever refused to check something out to her son, she would take it up with the library director.

QUESTIONS TO CONSIDER

1. Did the clerk do the right thing in refusing to check out the materials to Eric?
2. If Eric had been alone, without his mother, would the clerk's refusal have been more appropriate?
3. Should libraries keep a note in minors' records if their guardians allow them to borrow R-rated materials?
4. What does our professional code of ethics tell us about labels on movies, video games, and other materials that are "labeled"?

CASE #2.24

Alison noticed that Rick was rather quiet during the collection development meeting. The chair of the meeting looked worried too when Rick mentioned he was a little behind schedule on acquisitions. Later in the day, she asked him if everything was okay. Rick was a little hesitant, then he told her he felt he was not doing a very good job with his collection development responsibilities. Deciding to take Alison into his confidence, he told her that he never thought it would be so hard to choose the right books. Taking a deep breath, he continued, "I never select anything I actually want to read. I'm beginning to think this is the wrong position for me." Alison assured him that he was not in the wrong position and that he was selected because of his strong political science background. Alison and Rick talked for the better part of an hour. Rick revealed that during the first six months as the social sciences librarian, he hadn't purchased a single book that reflected his own political preferences because he was concerned that his choice was not neutral and objective. Alison advised Rick to attend some professional meetings and conferences to immerse himself in the professional approaches to collection development. As an afterthought, she added, "If you can put together a list of books that you've rejected, just this one time, I'll make some selections for you." Rick was visibly relieved and thanked Alison profusely. Alison let Rick know that she was happy to help out, but "you are going to have to figure out what to do about your own self-censorship issues; otherwise this is not the library, nor the profession, for you."

QUESTIONS TO CONSIDER

1. Do professional codes of ethics discourage librarians from trusting their own judgment?

2. Is it unethical for librarians to make some selections which they personally would like to read? How many selections would be acceptable?

3. Is it possible to create a collection policy which reduces this kind of self-censorship? What would the policy say?

4. If all of our choices are neutral and objective, will our collections meet the information needs of the communities we serve?

CASE #2.25

Tommy was in kindergarten. He had just watched a television show about some very special penguins that live in New York's Central Park Zoo. He loved the television show, as he was adopted, too. He wondered what it would be like to have two dads instead of a mom and a dad. At the end, the narrator told the audience that they could read all about the penguins in a book called *And Tango Makes Three*. The next day, Tommy and his mom went to the children's room at their public library. Tommy told the librarian there that he wanted to check out *And Tango Makes Three*. The librarian, Mrs. Jones, raised an eyebrow at Tommy's mom. Then Mrs. Jones told Tommy that there was a new bunny and suggested he hurry over to see it. Once Tommy was out of earshot, Mrs. Jones asked Tommy's mom if she knew about this story. Tommy's mom said of course she did and asked Mrs. Jones if there was a problem. "Well," said Mrs. Jones, "we don't keep that kind of book in the children's department because it is about..." Mrs. Jones paused and then she continued in a whisper, "It is about alternative lifestyles." Tommy's mom, somewhat puzzled, asked, "So?" Mrs. Jones replied, "It is the library's policy to shelve alternative lifestyle books in the adult section. We made that decision to make sure that children do not come across books like *Tango* accidentally. We had some instances where parents were concerned when their kids saw *Daddy's Roommate* a few years ago, so we decided on the alternative section approach."

Note: *And Tango Makes Three* is one of the most challenged books in the last decade. The picture book is based on the true story of two male penguins who adopt a fertilized egg.

QUESTIONS TO CONSIDER

1. Weigh the pros and cons of this library's decision to shelve alternative lifestyle books in the adult section regardless of the intended audience.

2. If a library makes the decision to keep one type of controversial book, such as this book which falls into GLBTQ (Gay, Lesbian, Bi-sexual, Transgender, Questioning) literature, out of the children's section, does it have an obligation to keep all controversial books, such as those on suicide, out of the children's section?

3. Would Tommy's mom be justified if she challenged the library's policy?

4. How should libraries embrace GLBTQ for young adults, as they may be one of very few safe havens for such individuals?

REFERENCES

Albitz, B. (2005). Dude, Where Are My Civil Rights? *The Journal of Academic Librarianship* 31, 3, 284–286.

American Civil Liberties Association. (2001). Fahrenheit 451.2: Is Cyberspace Burning? How Rating and Blocking Proposals May Torch Free Speech on the Internet. In R. Spinello & H. Tavani (Eds.), *Readings in Cyberethics* (pp.149–162). Boston: Jones and Bartlett.

American Library Association. (2006a). CPPA, COPA, CIPA: Which One Is Which? Retrieved August 10, 2007, from http://www.ala.org/ala/oif/ifissues/issuesrelatedlinks/cppacopacipa.htm.

American Library Association. (2006b). Intellectual Freedom and Censorship Q&A. Retrieved July 8, 2007, from http://www.ala.org/alaorg/oif/intellectualfreedomandcensorship.html.

American Library Association. (2007). Resolution on the Use and Abuse of National Security Letters. Retrieved May 1, 2008, from http://www.ala.org/Template.cfm?Section=ifresolutions&Template=/ContentManagement/ContentDisplay.cfm&ContentID=161325.

American Union of Concerned Scientists. (2007). *The A to Z Guide to Political Interference in Science*. Retrieved September 20, 2007, from http://www.ucsusa.org/scientific_integrity/interference/a-to-z-alphabetical.html.

Bill of Rights, First United States Cong. 1789.

Buchanan, E. (2007). Talking Intellectual Freedom with Toni Samek. *Wisconsin Library Association, Intellectual Freedom Round Table Newsletter*, XIII (2), 5–6.

Buchanan, E., and Campbell, J. (2004). New Threats to Intellectual Freedom: The Loss of the Information Commons through Law and Technology in the United States. In R. Spinello & H. Tavani (Eds.), *Intellectual Property Rights in a Networked World: Theory and Practice* (pp. 225–242). Hershey, PA: Idea Group.

Fitzsimmons, R. (1998). Intellectual Freedom in a Democratic Society. Paper Presented at the International Conference: Freedom of Expression, Censorship, Libraries. Riga, Latvia, October 14–17.

Lau Whelan, D. (23 March, 2007). Federal Judge Strikes Down COPA. *School Library Journal*. Retrieved August 25, 2007, from http://www.schoollibraryjournal.com/article/CA6427357.html.

Minow, M., and Lipinski, T. A. (2003). *The Library's Legal Answer Book*. Chicago: ALA Editions.

Office for Intellectual Freedom, American Library Association (2005). *Intellectual Freedom Manual*. Washington, DC: ALA Editions.

Samek, T. (2001). *Intellectual Freedom and Social Responsibility in American Librarianship, 1967–1974*. Jefferson: McFarland.

UNITED STATES, et al., Appellants v. AMERICAN LIBRARY ASSOCIATION, INC., et al., 539 U.S. 194; 123 S. Ct. 2297; 156 L. Ed. 2d 221; 2003 U.S.

Volokh, E. (2000). Personalization and Privacy. *Communications of the ACM* 43, No. 8, 84–88.

CHAPTER 3

Privacy

Privacy is not something that I'm merely entitled to, it's an absolute prerequisite.
— Marlon Brando

Few would debate the importance of privacy to personal and societal good. Privacy has been defined as the quality or condition of being secluded from the presence or view of others; the state of being free from unsanctioned intrusion, as in a person's right to privacy; it is the state of being concealed and, importantly, it is the necessary context for relationships which would hardly be human if we had to do without. Notions of privacy most certainly vary across cultures. Western conceptions of privacy center around the individual, whereas traditional Eastern conceptions are often more communal: that is, privacy can be viewed as selfishness or a shameful secret. Individual privacy is viewed as antithetical to social harmony and accord (Ess, 2005). Regardless of cultural specificity, as a basic right, the UN Declaration of Human Rights assures in Article 12, "No one shall be subjected to arbitrary interference with his privacy, family, home or correspondence, nor to attacks upon his honor and reputation. Everyone has the right to the protection of the law against such interference or attacks." In this regard, privacy is a primary value.

The cases in this chapter revolve around Western thought; however, as information ethics becomes increasingly global, we must gain "some basic insights into the important similarities and crucial differences between Eastern and Western concepts and emerging data privacy protection laws ... for the sake of furthering an informed and respectful global dialogue. Given the global scope and influences of information technologies, such a global dialogue is critical" (Ess, 2005, p. 1). When we approach intercultural ethics, we will engage in this discussion more immediately; here, we focus on the importance of privacy and implications of privacy violations for the information professions, as employees and for our patrons.

Scholars from vast disciplines discuss and debate privacy, and for good reasons. Concerns around privacy and the protection of personal privacy have truly taken on new dimensions in light of technologies and politics; new encroachments on privacy that many never anticipated in the United States in particular have unfolded. We have, as Brin (1999) described it, become a "transparent society." In some ways, we have consented to this transparency through our acceptance and use of technologies; in other ways, we have rejected this transparency by questioning the validity of such laws as the PATRIOT Act. Privacy has been an important construct over time, but today, we face mass surveillance and registration; we are monitored through our keystrokes and the web sites we visit. During our electronic travels, we each create data personae, an electronic trail of information about us, which is mined and used without our permission. From our medical records to our reading habits, governmental and/or commercial interests gather, use, and misuse our personal information.

Privacy straddles legal, social, cultural, economic, technological, and philosophical boundaries, making it one of the most important and complex issues of the day. In fact, a 1999 survey found that privacy was the issue with which most Americans were concerned, ahead of overpopulation, racial tensions, and global warming (Lester, 2001). More recently, Tavani and Spinello (2004) cite "surveys conducted by *Business Week*, Harris Associates, Equifax, and others suggest that most Americans either are 'concerned' or 'very concerned' about their privacy" (p. 397). With regard to the United States government in particular, the Ponemon Institute has conducted a number of studies in which they queried citizens about their perceptions on privacy and government agencies—the Central Intelligence Agency, the Department of Homeland Security, the Department of National Security, and several social services agencies, including the Department of Health and Human Resources and the Office of Student Financial Assistance Program. In 2004, Ponemon and the CIO Institute at Carnegie Mellon University found "the issues and concerns that were rated by subjects as having the most significant impact on their privacy trust was: loss of civil liberties (64 percent), surveillance into personal life (63 percent), and the monitoring of email and Web activities (47 percent)." Further, over 83 percent of the sample acknowledged the privacy of their personal information as being "important to them" (Ponemon, 2004, p. 2). Ponemon (2007) conducted a similar survey addressing similar issues and government agencies:

> Results of the survey indicate average privacy trust scores in 2007 declined by over 2% from the 2006 survey and more than 7% from 2005. This finding suggests that our sample respondents hold a net unfavorable view of the government organizations than measured in our previous studies. An average privacy trust score of 45 percent for all government organizations listed in our survey—which is 5% points below the midpoint of our PTS [Privacy Trust Scale]—suggests that U.S. residents do not believe that the federal government is committed to protecting privacy. This negative sentiment is not the case for certain government organizations such as USPS, NIH, Census and others [p. 8].

While we are collectively concerned about the state of privacy protections in the United States, we still look to the seminal 1890 Warren and Brandeis article, "The Right to Privacy," as a foundation to our understandings of privacy:

> Political, social, and economic changes entail the recognition of new rights, and the common law, in its eternal youth, grows to meet the new demands of society. Thus, in very early

times, the law gave a remedy only for physical interference with life and property, for trespasses *vi et armis*. Then the "right to life" served only to protect the subject from battery in its various forms; liberty meant freedom from actual restraint; and the right to property secured to the individual his lands and his cattle. Later, there came a recognition of man's spiritual nature, of his feelings and his intellect. Gradually the scope of these legal rights broadened; and now the right to life has come to mean the right to enjoy life — the right to be let alone; the right to liberty secures the exercise of extensive civil privileges; and the term "property" has grown to comprise every form of possession — intangible, as well as tangible.

This "right to be let alone" is physical and psychological, and this is extremely important to us as intellectual beings. We can appreciate the interconnectedness of the physical and the psychological right to be let alone in legal terms in the United States through the First and Fourth Amendments, as we shall see that both are indeed necessary conditions to a functioning and healthy individual and collective life. Cohen (2001) and Volokh (2000) have explored the interconnectedness of the right to intellectual freedom and the right to privacy and, Cohen rightly suggests, "intellectual freedom depends on the degree of informational privacy that individuals enjoy" (p. 7). While our First Amendment protects our intellectual freedoms, as described in Chapter 2, the Fourth Amendment to the Constitution states, "The right of the people to be secure in their persons, houses, papers, and effects, against unreasonable searches and seizures, shall not be violated, and no Warrants shall issue, but upon probable cause, supported by Oath or affirmation, and particularly describing the place to be searched, and the persons or things to be seized." Constitutional scholars have intensely discussed interpretations of the "right" to privacy; it may be a philosophical right, a legal right, an economic right, or some combination of these. Indeed, it may not be a "right" at all. "Judicial restraint in the protection of privacy is understandable, for the right to be let alone appears specifically at no place in the Constitution" ("Fourth Amendment Right of Privacy," 1967, p. 1314).

Such complexity has only increased over time. The concept of privacy has evolved from an original concern over intrusion into one's personal spaces and effects to control over and access to personal information. For instance, online privacy concerns generally fall into three categories: what personal information can be shared with whom; whether messages can be exchanged without anyone else seeing them; and whether and how one can send messages anonymously (WhatIs.com).

In a world of increasing connectivity and surveillance, such control of one's privacy is indeed difficult to maintain. In a rather shocking statement in 1999, then CEO of Sun Microsystems Scott McNealy stated flatly, "You have zero privacy anyway. Get over it" (Sprenger, 1999). While this may be true, others, either the government or private business, should not be the ones to set the parameters of our personal privacy: Philosopher James Moor, for example (2004), suggests that we must embrace a "Publicity Principle," in which rules and conditions governing private situations should be clear and known to the persons affected by them; moreover, he maintains, "A breach of a private situation is justified if and only if there is a great likelihood that the harm caused by the disclosure will be so much less than the harm prevented that an impartial person would permit breach in this and in morally similar situations" (pp. 416–417). And, finally, Moor recommends "The Adjustment Principle," which holds, "If special circumstances justify a change in the parameters of a private situation, then the alteration should become an explicit and public part of the rules and conditions governing the private situation" (pp. 416–417).

The role of privacy in the library and information center is foundational. Recall the American Library Association *Code of Ethics*: "We protect each library user's right to privacy and confidentiality with respect to information sought or received and resources consulted, borrowed, acquired or transmitted." Privacy is codified as a core value and we hold the right of the individual as a primary value. We do not sell our patrons' circulation or usage records, nor do we readily surrender them to authorities. We typically destroy records with identifiable information and we hope, as the ALA advises, we enact privacy-enhancing technologies, we educate our patrons about privacy, and we adopt strong privacy policies for our institutions. Without such privacy protections, we too face curtailed intellectual freedom. If we accept that such freedoms to privacy and to intellectual freedom are indeed intimately connected and bound together and that neither exists in isolation, then librarians and information professionals will acknowledge that both privacy and intellectual freedom are in jeopardy as illustrated in the following discussion.

Reminiscent of the FBI's Library Awareness Program of the 1970s and 1980s (Foerstel, 1991), libraries and information centers, as well as commercial bookstores, are again targets of governmental interest, with renewed threats and powers stemming from uses of the U.S.A. PATRIOT Act. This Act, Uniting and Strengthening America by Providing Appropriate Tools Required to Intercept and Obstruct Terrorism, was made into law just 45 days after the 9/11 events. Notably, the ALA and the American Civil Liberties Union are and have been vehemently opposed to the Act and its far-reaching, seemingly boundless powers. The ACLU has asserted that the PATRIOT Act "violates the Fourth Amendment, which says the government cannot conduct a search without obtaining a warrant and showing probable cause to believe that the person has committed or will commit a crime" and "violates the Fourth Amendment by failing to provide notice — even after the fact — to persons whose privacy has been compromised. Notice is also a key element of due process, which is guaranteed by the Fifth Amendment" (ACLU, 2003). As the American Library Association (2007) describes it:

> The U.S.A. PATRIOT Act amended over 15 federal statutes, including the laws governing criminal procedure, computer fraud and abuse, foreign intelligence, wiretapping, immigration, and the laws governing the privacy of student records. These amendments expanded the authority of the Federal Bureau of Investigation and law enforcement to gain access to business records, medical records, educational records and library records, including stored electronic data and communications. It also expanded the laws governing wiretaps and "trap and trace" phone devices to Internet and electronic communications. These enhanced surveillance procedures pose the greatest challenge to privacy and confidentiality in the library.

One section of the PATRIOT Act directly affects libraries: Section 215 amends the Foreign Intelligence Act of 1978, which originally allowed the FBI to obtain "business records" from a limited group of public or private businesses including vehicle rental companies and storage facilities. "Post PATRIOT Act, any 'tangible thing' (including medical records, library circulation records, book purchase records, membership lists, subscription lists, and lists of web site visitors) has all become valid information sources" (Albitz, 2005, p. 284). As long as the Foreign Intelligence Surveillance Court grants authorization, any of these kinds of records may be searched with or without prior knowledge or consent of the subject of the search. There is also no requirement to inform the subject after the fact (Albitz, 2005). As of August 2005, both Houses had proposals which ultimately reauthorized the bulk of the Act with just two provisions remaining "temporary." "The reauthorizing legislation makes permanent 14 of the 16 sunsetted U.S.A. PATRIOT Act provisions and places four-year sunsets on the other two — the authority to conduct 'roving' surveillance under the Foreign Intelligence Surveillance Act (FISA) and the authority to request production of business records under FISA (U.S.A. PATRIOT Act sections 206 and 215, respectively)" (USDOJ, 2006). The reauthorization includes a few safeguards, such as the signature of application (for a search) signed by either the Director or Deputy Director of the FBI and recipients of National Security Letters (NSL) "may explicitly seek judicial review and disclose receipt of a 215 order to attorneys to obtain legal advice or assistance and to other people necessary to comply with the request" (USDOJ, 2006). However, the reauthorization did not address in a satisfactory way concerns about the notorious "gag orders," which prohibit individuals from talking about receipt of a NSL, except to legal council. Violating the gag order could result in five years of prison.

With this knowledge of what is considered "business records" that are open to requests and given the importance of privacy to our patrons, librarians and information professionals should be cognizant of Nancy Kranich's advice: "Until the protection of civil liberties reaches a balance with the protection of national security, libraries must affirm their responsibility to safeguard patron privacy by avoiding unnecessary creation and maintenance of personally identifiable information [PII] and developing up-to-date privacy policies that cover the scope of collection and retention of PII in data-related logs, digital records, vendor–collected data, and system backups, as well as more traditional circulation information. In short, if information is not collected, it cannot be released" (2003). Yet, most of us do in fact maintain many records and, when a National Security Letter is issued, these records can be searched. Taking a stand (as an individual or an institution) when confronted with an NSL is a frightening proposition; stakes are extremely high.

Four Connecticut librarians learned this the hard way, as they fought the PATRIOT Act after receiving National Security Letters requesting information about a patron. The difficulties went far beyond attempting to protect the patrons' privacy — all were essentially required to lie, due to the gag order surrounding PATRIOT Act requests, to co-workers, spouses, family and friends about their whereabouts and activities. The four, whose identities are now known after the gag order was lifted, Barbara Bailey, Peter Chase, George Christian, and Janet Nocek, have been speaking out on the dangers of the Act in relation to library services: "The fact that the government can and is eavesdropping on patrons in libraries has a chilling effect, because they really don't know if Big Brother is looking over their shoulder" (Christian, as cited in Cowan, 2006). In Christian's testimony to the Senate Judiciary Committee in 2007, he stated:

> The path we chose in Connecticut is based on a longstanding principle of librarianship — our deep-rooted commitment to patron confidentiality that assures that libraries are places of free inquiry, where citizens go to inform themselves on ideas and issues, without fear that their inquiries would be known to anyone else. The freedom to read is part of our First Amendment rights. To function, the public must trust that libraries are committed to such confidentiality. When the U.S.A. PATRIOT Act was signed into law, our Connecticut library community, like the American Library Association, many other librarians as well as booksellers, authors and others, were concerned about the lack of judicial oversight as well as the secrecy associated with a number of the Act's provisions and the NSLs in particular.
>
> Libraries are, of course, subject to law enforcement. Librarians respect the law and most certainly want to do the right thing when it comes to pursuing terrorists and protecting our country. We recognize and accept that, with appropriate judicial review, law enforcement can obtain certain patron information with subpoenas and appropriate court orders. <u>We are not talking about absolute patron privacy.</u> What has disturbed the library community in recent years has been the idea that the government could use the U.S.A. PATRIOT Act, FISA and other laws to learn what our innocent patrons were researching in our libraries with no prior judicial oversight or any after-the-fact review.

It is with reasoned thinking and informed and reflective action that we must make decisions around the complex issue of privacy. As with intellectual property laws, privacy and its related laws such as the PATRIOT Act are often contradictory from legal and philosophical perspectives; Christian's testimony demonstrates this perfectly. The American Library Association continues to advocate for reform. "The American Library Association urges Congress to pursue legislative reforms in order to provide adequate protection of each library user's Constitutional right to be free from unwarranted and unjustified government surveillance" (Resolution on National Security Letters, 2007). This resolution was adopted unanimously by the Council of the American Library Association just weeks before legislation was signed, which temporarily expanded the government's warrantless surveillance.

> The new law gives the attorney general and the director of national intelligence the power to approve the international surveillance, rather than the special intelligence court. The court's only role will be to review and approve the procedures used by the government in the surveillance after it has been conducted. It will not scrutinize the cases of the individuals being monitored [Risen, 2007].

Our goal throughout the cases presented in this chapter is to illustrate this complexity, while encouraging awareness and debate around these issues. Where legal standards apply, consultation with the library or information center's legal council is advised. Although we have allotted a large portion of this discussion to the PATRIOT Act, we

51

also recognize that attention to privacy is required in our regular, sometimes seemingly mundane daily activities, too.

Note: As of September 6, 2007, after the time of our writing, U.S. District Judge Victor Marrero struck down portions of the U.S.A. PATRIOT Act as unconstitutional, ordering the FBI to stop issuing "national security letters" that secretly demand customer information from Internet service providers and other businesses. An appeal is likely. Readers are encouraged to review the ALA web site for updates on the potential impact for libraries and information centers.

Privacy Cases

CASE #3.1

The Sagamore Community Archives was located in a small city of 10,000 people and had a strong collection documenting the role of community service agencies over the years. The archives consisted of city records and a small regional manuscript collection that included personal papers, records of regional organizations, business records, and records from a number of area churches and rural schools. One of the most useful — and unprocessed — collections was from the now-defunct Sagamore Social Service Agency. The records dated from the organization's inception in 1906 until its closing in 1965. There had been strong community and research interest in this collection because of the impact the agency had on the community, so it was a high priority to process and make the archives available.

While the archivist unpacked the collection, a box called "Surveys" was found. There were forty surveys completed by area women in 1943. At that time, each of the respondents had recently given birth out of wedlock and had given the child up for adoption. The survey intended to assess the mental and physical states of the women during their first year after the adoption process. Each survey included the participant's name, address, social security number, religious affiliation, and names of immediate family members. The forms stated that the Agency would protect the privacy of the respondents. After checking the local telephone listings, the archivist found that some families still lived in the area. As far as the archivist can tell, the results were never published, though the data within the surveys would be of great interest to sociologists, historians, and other researchers.

QUESTIONS TO CONSIDER

1. Should the archivist keep the records?
2. What legal and ethical issues must the archivist address if she keeps the records?
3. Should family members be made aware of the data?

4. Should researchers be allowed to use the data?
5. Explore and discuss human subjects' research ethics models in light of this case.

CASE #3.2

Great turmoil unraveled at the Manitowa Public Library. An unidentified individual had been caught masturbating in the stacks. When confronted by another patron and library staff, he pulled a number of books off the shelf, blocking the staff members, and ran out of the library building. Shocked and stunned, the library staff called the police and reported the incident. Fortunately, no children had witnessed the event and only a few other patrons were in the library at the time. The police asked the library director for the surveillance tape, so they could review the events and, hopefully, post the individual's picture on their web site and broadcast it on the news, so anyone having information on the identity of the person could come forward. After consideration, the director realized that turning over the tape, which was a form of a library record and thus legally protected, was not as easy as she thought. While, yes, indeed the library had called in the incident, the reality was library records were not to be turned over to authorities without a warrant. The privacy of the other patrons on the tape had to be considered, the director thought. She decided not to release the tape to the authorities. Once this decision was released, however, local politicians were irate and belittled the director: "Director King would rather see a sexual deviant go free than sacrifice the library's silly privacy policy," the local news reported. State senators then got involved, looking at the laws and language around "library records."

QUESTIONS TO CONSIDER

1. Defend Director King's responses.
2. Was Director King acting irresponsibly by not giving over the surveillance tapes?
3. Should the state laws around library records have some concessions for such instances?

CASE #3.3

Two men sat speaking a foreign language in the reference room at the local library. This was not uncommon as the city had a large population of foreign nationals and a large international student body. The men signed in to use the Internet terminals, as they were required to do. The librarian on the desk noticed that they were viewing Al Jazeera's web site and watched as they became agitated. The librarian was aware of the uses of public libraries by terrorists in planning the 9/11 attacks, and was very sensitive to this. He went to his director and suggested that they report the men to the authorities — "I just have a bad feeling in my gut about this," he said. The director was torn. She felt strongly that the library must protect its patrons' privacy and their rights to intellectual freedom, but she thought, what if...? The librarian said, "If they have nothing to hide, then what is the harm, right? If they check out all right, then no damage was done. The authorities can check them without them even knowing."

QUESTIONS TO CONSIDER

1. How does the slippery slope idea pertain to this case?
2. Review the ALA's Resolutions on the PATRIOT Act; how do these assist libraries?
3. What should the director do to educate her staff about sensitivity and professionalism?
4. What are the dangers in the "if we've got nothing to hide..." mentality?

CASE #3.4

We've been told many times the Internet has changed everything in information services. The speed and accessibility with which information can be found or harvested is stunning, not to mention the unique patterns that can be unearthed through data mining. While such records as court filings, criminal offenses, and driving violations have been open as public records, they were not readily available at our fingertips — someone had to "really want" to know something to go digging through mounds of records to get at some piece of information.

Kris, a librarian at a local public library, was aware of the state's web site where individuals can look up information in the Consolidated Court Automation Programs (CCAP) case management system, a statewide tool. Kris was concerned with the behavior of two patrons who came into the library frequently and "acted suspiciously." She saw them watching the children's room and she knew they did not come in with children. She told her director, but without anything concrete, the director dismissed Kris's concerns. "If you see them doing something questionable, come back. We can't file a complaint for sitting and watching people in the library." So Kris went online to the CCAP site and entered the patron's names. "Aha," she said. "They have records. They aren't listed as child predators, but they have had run-ins with the law. We should keep a very close eye on these two."

QUESTIONS TO CONSIDER

1. Was the patrons' privacy violated, given that the information is public and open record?
2. With the seemingly vast availability of personal information, is there such a thing as privacy at all?
3. Did Kris violate professional responsibilities?
4. What response would you as a librarian have if someone were "sitting and watching" others in the library?

CASE #3.5

The library at GA Healthcare, an international firm, was a large, special library that served the employees of the company, many of whom were international workers. The librarian had used a policy for a number of years where clients signed in with their names, departments, and type of service they were requesting. She had used this to gather usage data, so she could statistically report her workload and services to her administrators. One day, a company manager from the corporate offices arrived and asked to see the sign-in sheets, as they had become concerned about a worker who was suspected of selling pro priety information to a competitor. The manager wanted to know how much time this individual had been in the library and what exactly he had been doing and researching. Given that the library was governed by the policies and practices of the corporation and that employees were informed about surveillance in the workplace, they had no expectation of privacy. The librarian felt conflicted and consulted the Special Libraries Association. While the association does not have a specific code of ethics, it does maintain that librarians should act, among other assertions, "To protect the confidentiality and privacy of individuals requesting information" and "To abide by the legalities governing the employing corporate structure." These two "choices" seemed at odds this time. She felt uneasy about her decision, but provided the data.

QUESTIONS TO CONSIDER

1. Did the librarian act appropriately?
2. What other possibilities should the librarian consider when collecting usage data?
3. How does a special librarian reconcile these seeming contradictions between the corporate structure and intellectual freedom?
4. What are the implications of conflicting values within our professional ethics and behaviors?

CASE #3.6

Kathleen, a librarian, was an avid newspaper reader. She read an article recently that raised a red flag for her. It seemed that RFID was being used to catch cheating spouses. The way they were caught was pretty straightforward. RFID—Radio Frequency Identification Device—was the technology behind fastpass systems that toll roads use—drivers scanned their fastpasses instead of giving cash to tollbooth operators. Use of fastpasses left an electronic trail, which could be used to pinpoint where the driver (or spouse, in this case) entered or exited the toll road and at what time these activities took place.

The library where Kathleen worked used RFID, a kind of wireless technology in which one device can "read" information on another device, often called a tag. Her library uses RFID to read an item's barcode for checkout; tags include catalog information and shelving location and use statistics in addition to the item's barcode. Although there had not been a need to do so, the technology could also be used to identify the patron to whom the material was checked out and it could be used to "find" the remote location of a book if the tag included GPS-tracking ability. The consultant who convinced the library to embrace RFID and incorporate it into their integrated system spent a lot of time "selling" the benefits of this technology and convinced the library that the benefits clearly outweighed any potential privacy violations. Her case included that the technology was quick and convenient and could help with self-serve checkout or check-in and help librarians locate misplaced books or journals, saving the librarians time and money.

Kathleen brought the newspaper article into her director's office. Kathleen suggested that the library should review the ALA's guidelines concerning the uses of RFID with regard to patron privacy and confidentiality, which was at risk with such devices. Kathleen also did some research — the information she found included yet another downside to these devices. She explained how RFID was susceptible to hacking, which increased the potential that someone could intrude on the catalog and patron records and this hacking could also introduce viruses into the computer systems.

QUESTION TO CONSIDER

1. Research the ALA's RFID in Libraries: Privacy and Confidentiality Guidelines. Did the library make a prudent decision to adopt this technology?
2. Write a brief outlining the pros and cons of RFID technology.
3. In addition to the obvious privacy concerns, what intellectual freedom implications arise from this technology?

CASE #3.7

Tom was working at the circulation desk at the Brownsville Public Library. Due to recent problems with patrons acting inappropriately in the restrooms, the library now locked the doors and patrons asked to use the key. One particular day, a patron approached the desk and checked out a number of books and videos. The name on the card was a man's name, though this patron was dressed in women's clothing, wearing a wig and makeup. It was clear to Tom that the patron was a transvestite. The patron then asked for the key to the women's restroom. Tom was not sure how to respond and there was no policy on such an issue. Tom didn't want to make a big issue of this, so he gave the patron the key. He had a nagging feeling, though, that some of the patrons would complain. He considered asking the director to change the policy so patrons did not have to ask for the key.

QUESTIONS TO CONSIDER

1. How would you respond to such a situation?
2. What role does patron privacy play in this case?

3. In public settings, there are always potential conflicts of rights. Discuss these potential conflicts in this case.

CASE #3.8

Two police vehicles parked in front of the Morrisville Public Library and four police officers entered the building and approached the reference desk. They asked the librarian if she had seen this individual in the library and proceeded to show her a picture. The librarian was not sure how to respond, as the officers were not presenting any kind of NSL (National Security Letter) or any warrant for particular information. They simply wanted to know if this individual had been in the library and, if so, when and what was the person doing while there. The librarian looked at the picture again and glanced up to catch the eye of another staff member. He winked to convey, yes, that person had been there, but not to divulge this to the officers. She replied, "We have many individuals coming in every day. It is hard to remember each face, officer." The police left with the warning, "If you should see this person, please call us immediately." The two staff members then spoke. "What if this person is wanted for a serious crime? What if she is some kind of terrorist?" Jone said. "Look, for all we know, they want to know what books she has checked out and, without appropriate paperwork such as a subpoena, we aren't going to just give up that information," Bob replied. "If the library's safety was at risk, they would tell us."

QUESTIONS TO CONSIDER

1. With whom do you agree, Jone or Bob?
2. Was patron privacy at risk in this case?
3. If the police had informed the staff that the person was wanted for murder and had used the 1983 book *Hitman*, would that change your response to the situation?
4. If the police had presented an NSL (National Security Letter), what course of action would be appropriate?

CASE #3.9

Phil worked at a small academic library that was not automated. Library materials were checked in and out by hand, using a log that sat on the circulation desk. Patrons could check materials in and out themselves, if a library staff member was not available. One morning, Professor Fine came into the library and checked the shelves for a specific book. When she did not find it, she inquired at the desk. She was told it was checked out and would be due in one week. She was upset, as she stated she needed the book for class that evening. The librarian apologized for the delay and reiterated she would need to wait to receive the book. The librarian went about his business. Professor Fine then looked in the log book, turning back pages to find the title she was seeking. She informed the librarian that she would herself call the patron, whom she knew, and ask to borrow the book. The librarian was angry and concerned that the Professor would have misused the log in that way and was concerned for the patron's privacy. "I am sorry, Professor Fine, but that is unacceptable. You may not contact the patron and you should not have looked in the log for that information," Phil asserted. "I know her; it is not a violation in any way," Professor Fine responded.

QUESTIONS TO CONSIDER

1. How would you, as a professional, respond to this scenario?
2. Is Professor Fine's argument valid?
3. How should the library handle the log book, given the constraints it has with no automation and few staff?

CASE #3.10

Dave worked in a prison library, where he hoped he could make a difference in the lives of incarcerated individuals. He had hoped that he could create a library setting similar to those on the "outside" and allow prisoners to feel some sense of liberty and independence from their use and access in the library. However, Dave was also aware of the realities of the prison system and of the chain of command mentality that governed his work. One day, Dave's superior officer came to him with a stack of slashed and vandalized books. They were destroyed. The officer demanded to know who had checked them out, so he could be punished. Dave knew if he revealed this information, the prisoner would lose library privileges. However, if Dave had gotten the books back himself, he would have had to report the incident anyway. Dave gave the officer the name of the inmate, realizing he had to maintain a delicate balancing act to preserve inmate's rights with the necessary goodwill between library and the administration that allowed the prison library to function.

QUESTIONS TO CONSIDER

1. Did Dave violate privacy?
2. It is commonly accepted that prisoners have limited rights. Privacy is a major one. Discuss the pros and cons of privacy policies for incarcerated individuals. What limits would be necessary?
3. What general policies on destruction of materials exist for any individual?

CASE #3.11

Marianne had just accepted a librarian position with a major corporation. The first several years of her career were spent in academia and she was excited about the prospect of a new, challenging environment. Her enthusiasm came to an abrupt halt during her orientation session. Her supervisor explained that extensive patron records were kept and shared with other business units — usually finance and accounting, but other units might also request this information. Sensing her duress, George further explained that patron information that was considered private in public and academic settings was not considered private in the corporate setting. He continued, stating that resources were purchased to benefit the company, so the company required the corporate information center to provide reports on who was accessing a particular information source, how frequently they accessed this source, and for what purpose or project. The information center had to justify its expenditures. Marianne asked why the user information had to be at the individual level: "Why not aggregate the data?" George told her that not all materials in the collection were purchased through the information center and might show up on individual expense reports. "We also allocate a portion of certain databases expenses to individual departments. Sometimes, too, we need to post who has a book or a marketing report in case someone else needs it." Marianne managed a quiet "Oh" just as George apologized because he needs to take a call. Marianne was very concerned; privacy is a cornerstone of our profession.

QUESTIONS TO CONSIDER

1. Do companies like the one in the case have a right to know what kind of information their employees are gathering from a corporate library or information center?
2. Should George advocate for new corporate policies that ensure a greater level of employee privacy?
3. Discuss the general issue of workplace surveillance. What are the arguments for and against it?

CASE #3.12

Josey was the library systems administrator. She had access to all of the library's electronic records, including the patron database of logins and passwords, which patrons use for online resources, web circulation, and so on. Patrons could change their passwords online themselves or they could stop at the systems desk in the library and request the change. Typically, when they came to the desk, the staff asked for a photo identification to ensure their authenticity. The library had a policy that they would not change passwords over the phone; however, they saw potential risks in this.

One day, the systems administrator received a phone call from a woman who wanted to access her account online, but lost her ID card and did not know her patron ID or password. She said she had saved these in her computer but hadn't transferred the information when she got a new computer. She further stated she lived thirty minutes away and wanted to resolve this over the phone. The administrator looked up her account and asked her questions on her address and phone numbers, which the patron could verify. However, Josey was nervous. What if she provided the user login and password and it put someone's personal, private information at risk? Furthermore, she would be in violation of the library's policy. She felt badly, as the woman seemed sincere, but decided it was best not to provide the information.

QUESTIONS TO CONSIDER
1. Did the systems administrator act in the best interest of patron privacy?
2. Should the library change its policy and, if so, what recommendations do you have?
3. What are the legal issues in this case? Would Josey be legally liable if a breech of privacy occurred due to her actions?

CASE #3.13

Joy was cleaning up the reference room when she found a flash drive in one of the computers. It did not have a name on it. She thought if she opened one of the files on the drive, she could find the owner and return it to him or her. But, when she saw the names of the files, she grew worried. There were hundreds of image files, all with feminine names. She opened a few and saw they were child pornography. She immediately called her director, who then called the library's legal council. They would give the drive to a computer forensics expert, who may be able to find the owner through the drive's "fingerprints." But, in the meantime, if the person came in looking for the drive, the staff was informed to stall him or her and alert the police.

QUESTIONS TO CONSIDER
1. Did Joy violate the patron's privacy by opening the drive?
2. Did Joy do the right thing in the first place by looking at the files?
3. If they files had been Neo-Nazi or racist images, rather than child porn, discuss an appropriate course of action.

CASE #3.14

In an effort to promote friendliness and a "customer service" attitude, the director at the public library in Jefferson decided staff should wear name tags with both first and last name. This would give patrons the ability to address the staff, to know who they were, and, in the event they wanted to offer praise or criticize a staff member, they would have the information readily. The staff was conflicted on this. Some agreed to wear the name tags, while others said they only wanted their first names available. Others felt it was inappropriate. "We aren't Best Buy, for goodness sakes. Why do we need to have name tags on? I don't want some crazy patron being able to find out where I live," decried Tom, who felt his privacy rights were being violated with this idea. I will not wear one and it is my right to refuse this," he asserted. "I'll call my lawyer if I have to."

QUESTIONS TO CONSIDER

1. Discuss Tom's reaction. Is it valid? Is he overeating?
2. What rights to privacy do staff hold while in a work situation?
3. Given the amount of information we as information professionals have about our patrons, is Tom responding unreasonably?

CASE #3.15

Several students at the university have complained to the circulation desk. All the complaints were similar. Some students were keeping reserve books, especially textbooks, beyond the two-hour limit. The circulation supervisor consulted with the library director and they agreed to raise the fines for late returns to mediate the problem. This did not help much, especially during mid-terms and finals. Students were willing to pay the fines for the extra time. Frustrations grew and the students brought this problem to the attention of the student government. The student government in turn brought this to the attention of the library director. In the view of the students and the student government, the easiest and most prudent solution was to post the names of students who have checked out reserved books. That way if someone kept one of the reserved books longer than she or he should, the student who was waiting could find the student with the book. The library was not large by academic standards and most of the students had posted pictures online, so it would not be hard to find the offender.

QUESTIONS TO CONSIDER

1. Is raising fines a fair solution to problems like the one in the case?
2. Does the penalty imposed have the same impact on all students?
3. Does the student government make a strong enough case that it would be acceptable to breach the privacy of the students who keep books past the time the materials are due?

CASE #3.16

As a cost-cutting measure, many libraries have transferred from mediated to self-service models for patron-requested materials and there are now "on-hold for" shelves in libraries of all types. Graystown Public Library was no exception. It shelved requested materials on a cart located in the circulation area. To help patrons quickly identify their items, the books and materials were labeled with the first five letters of patrons' last names. In some cases, the full name was visible on the spine of the book for all to see. Mary, a frequent patron of the library, was upset by this new practice and confronted the director. The director responded that it was a convenience and, due to budget cuts, the self-service checkout cart was necessary. Prior to the budget cuts, on-hold materials were shelved behind the circulation desk, labeled as they still were with the first five letters of the patron's last name and then arranged alphabetically. This arrangement made finding the material easy when the patron arrived in person to pick up the materials, but, because it was outside of public view, patrons enjoyed relative privacy. Mary maintained the new way of doing things was a violation of patron privacy and demanded that the library reinstate the old practice. "I don't want my neighbors and everyone else in this town knowing what I am reading!" she argued. "It is embarrassing and the library should be taking its job of protecting patron privacy seriously, not putting our reading habits on the shelves for everyone to see."

QUESTIONS TO CONSIDER

1. Do you agree with Mary that such a practice violates patron privacy?
2. Would such a practice have a chilling effect on patrons requesting materials?
3. What other means of labeling should the library consider? Are these methods equally convenient for patron use?
4. How do we balance cost-cutting issues with patron privacy and intellectual freedom?

CASE #3.17

Rick and his mom stopped at the reference desk one Saturday afternoon. Rick had been tracing his family tree for his high school history class. Rick learned that several of his ancestors were gunsmiths; one was somewhat famous for the beauty of his custom pieces and many collectors sought to add his guns to their collections. Rick was excited to learn this — he thought that some of the guns in his grandfather's collection were worth a lot of money. His mom suggested they go to the library to get some books about guns and their history. Another student from Rick's high school happened to be near the desk and caught part of the reference interview. This student went home and told his parents that one of the kids in his class was at the library getting books about guns. The parents of the student contacted the director of the library and asked what action the library had taken about the teenager who was in on Saturday checking out books on guns. The director had not heard of any suspicious patron requests and said as much to the parents. She assured the parents that she would look into the matter and be in touch with the proper authorities if necessary. The director contacted the librarian, who shared her recollections of the interview, including that Rick's mom was there. The director asked the librarian if there was anything suspicious about the situation. The librarian said there was not and that she was happy Rick was expanding his research in a new direction. The director then phoned the parents of the other student and told them that the student asking for the books on guns was working on a class project. The parents demanded to know what kind of assignment would include research on guns — the high school had a zero-tolerance policy on weapons and a teacher would not allow this as a topic. The director refused to disclose any other details and the phone call ended badly, with the parents stating that they would contact the authorities themselves.

QUESTIONS TO CONSIDER

1. Was it necessary to hide the details about the reference interview from the parents who were worried?
2. Did the parents of the other student overreact or was the response justifiable, in light of school and campus shootings?
3. What degree of privacy should patrons reasonably expect, given the openness of most reference desks?
4. Other professions, notably medicine and law, have a relationship of privilege between the professional and his or her "client." Is it reasonable to promote a formal "patron-librarian privilege" in our field?

CASE #3.18

Kim was a distance-education librarian. Her primary responsibility was to facilitate use of library materials in the online classroom setting. This included creating paths to library information via persistent links or web pages that included hyperlinks to the library's databases. Kim also provided library instruction as needed for online classes. The library is short-staffed, so Kim taught library and research skills to on-campus students, too. Access to course pages was a necessity for Kim in her role as the distance-education librarian. It was beneficial when she taught in the traditional setting, but not essential. Although there was no attempt to hide that Kim had unfettered access, the teaching faculty seemed unaware of Kim's ability to proxy into course pages as both professor and student. Kim was quite confident that some were completely unaware of her ability to proxy into the course because they "enrolled" her in the class so she could see assignments or class discussions. Kim wondered how the students would feel if they knew that she had the ability to move into and out of their class at will. If she wanted to, Kim could have altered course materials. Kim was a person of integrity and she did not "lurk" in anyone's class, but she could have easily breached the privacy of the students or the professor. Even though she was in the class for legitimate reasons, it bothered Kim every time she "popped" into a class and no one knew she had been there. If Kim decided to do something unethical, there was a good chance that the IT department would have caught her. Kim's ethical behavior was intrinsic, so this had little bearing on her choice to behave ethically.

QUESTIONS TO CONSIDER

1. What could happen if a person of questionable ethical standards became the distance-education librarian?
2. Is a course a private environment for the students? Should it be?
3. Does the situation call for a proactive decision to create a policy to guide specific behavior or is the ALA's Code of Ethics sufficient?

4. Should online students be informed of the various individuals who have access to their courses and what their purpose is in entering the course?

CASE # 3.19

Many businesses use employee surveillance to monitor such things as numbers of keystrokes, sites viewed, and amount of time spent on various activities. Employees are typically informed about such surveillance and, thus, have no reasonable expectation of privacy. The situation at the library for an all-online college was not quite so clear and situations could arise that stretched the limits of privacy and worker rights. The virtual library was staffed by four librarians and all interactions, including emails and chats, were logged and saved, so that any of the librarians could see the questions and answers between staff and patrons.

The instructors all followed a common curriculum and assigned the same questions and research activities for multiple semesters, so the staff typically received the same, or least similar, questions from semester to semester. The idea behind logging the interactions was to save staff time, but, more importantly, to provide consistency across the responses for students in the school. The librarians were clear that their reference services were thus open to review, but if a personal email came to their work account, this was also open to surveillance. Staff were generally cautious and avoided this, but every so often, a message slipped through.

Kevin received a forwarded message from a friend, who accidentally used the work email address, and the content of the message, meant to be a joke, was ill received by another staff member, who then reported Kevin to the director. She said the message was hostile to women and misogynistic in nature. Kevin apologized and felt truly sorry; the director believed he did not intend this as harassment, but he had no choice but to issue Kevin a reprimand.

QUESTIONS TO CONSIDER

1. Discuss the use of employee surveillance in library settings.
2. Should the students be made aware that their interactions with library staff are logged and reviewed? Is their privacy being violated by this practice?
3. Some contend that worker surveillance is a violation of basic human rights and maintain that workers are in fact more efficient when they are not monitored. Defend or refute this position.
4. Should Kevin be reprimanded in this case?

CASE #3.20

The university archivist received a call from the spouse of a former university president. The president had died some time ago and, at the time, there was no archivist; the university record keeping was not very organized. The president's administrative assistant had simply boxed up what he thought were "personal" papers and effects and had given them to the family, who did not look too closely at the papers for many years. The spouse learned that an archivist had been hired and thought it best to return the papers, for historical purposes, to the university. When the archivist began reviewing the materials, she realized these were not personal papers at all, but official university business. In fact, the papers revealed that a renowned faculty member, who was still affiliated with the university, had been engaged in questionable activities with a student. The papers documented the student's complaint and the legal response from the faculty member. At the time, he had been given a year sabbatical and the student had graduated while he was away from the university. The complaint had never been made public and the faculty member was never punished for this.

QUESTIONS TO CONSIDER

1. Should the archivist make the papers public now?
2. Consider the conflicting rights to privacy in this case.
3. Discuss the legal and ethical implications of the archivist's decisions to make the papers public or to keep them private.

CASE #3.21

Karen was the director at a library that sat on the campus of a high school. The library served the high school students. It also served as the public library for the surrounding suburban neighborhoods. Late in the day last Friday, an upset mother confronted one of the library assistants. The mother dropped a CD on the circulation desk and in a demanding tone asked, "Do you know what this is?" The assistant, recognizing that the mother was upset, said, "No, I do not." "Well, I will tell you what it is," the mother said. "It is a CD full of smut my son downloaded at your library!"

The assistant, now alarmed, asked the mother to wait a moment while she called Karen and asked her to come to the circulation desk right now. Karen quickly assessed the situation and invited the mother into her private office. "Why do you want me to go into a private office? Are you trying to cover this up?" said the mother. Karen stated that she just wanted to protect the student's privacy and the mother reluctantly went with Karen. Once they settled into the office, Karen asked for the parent's name and if her son was a student at the high school. Mrs. Connors wanted to know what difference that made. Karen, keeping her voice level, began, "Mrs. Connors, the library has installed filters on all the public computers to protect children from harmful materials, but it is possible for students to accidentally come across these materials. It is also possible for students to work around the filters. I cannot be certain, but since he created the CD, it looks like your son knows how to get around them." Karen continued, "The library does everything it can to assure that students are using the computers for educational purposes during the school day. We do have tracking software and we could figure out when your son was downloading the materials. You will have to decide if you want to take this step. The library avoids doing this unless legally compelled. Our goal is to respect each person's right to receive information. It is up to you if you want to make this a legal matter. I recommend instead that you and your husband and possibly the principal meet with your son to discuss his use of library computers to download 'smut.'"

QUESTIONS TO CONSIDER

1. Is this a private matter between the Connors and their son?
2. Is the library negligent in this case or is the Connors' son responsible for his actions? Does it make a difference when the downloading take place?
3. Was it ethical to suggest that Mrs. Connors not take legal action?
4. What are the library's obligations to users who are using the library as a public library? Do they need to disclose the tracking software? Is it an invasion of patron privacy to track their activities even if the library avoids reviewing the records unless they receive a court order?

CASE #3.22

A distraught young woman approached Peg, a librarian in a public library. She, the patron, was looking for a book, *12 Easy Steps*. She said that the catalog indicated the book was available, but she could not find it on the shelf. Peg recognized the title. It was a suicide manual new to the collection. Peg hesitated. The book was on the new book cart near the circulation desk waiting for someone to put it away; she noticed it when she was looking for something else. Many thoughts ran through Peg's mind. She was not sure if she should engage the patron and ask some questions about her interest in the book. She was not certain if the woman was a minor, but considered calling the parents. She could, after all, look up personal information about her from her library card and city information database. Peg considered asking the patron if she was all right or if she needed help from a social service agency, but was afraid that was out of the scope of her position and a violation of the woman's privacy. Peg then considered that once the woman had the book, she could call someone to do a well-person check in case the patron is contemplating suicide, but when she discussed this at a staff meeting later that day, the idea was not well received. Most saw this as an intrusion on the woman's privacy.

QUESTIONS TO CONSIDER

1. Is it ethical for Peg to find out private, personal information about the patron?
2. If the patron is a minor, is it ethical to contact the young woman's parents?
3. What guidance does our professional codes of ethics offer in these situations?
4. What legal and ethical responsibilities would a school librarian have to report the case if this were in a school setting?

CASE #3.23

Many libraries have hold shelves for their patrons and many have policies that stipulate the person picking up the material be the same person who requested it. However, not every library does. The Neerland Public Library was in a smaller town of 10,000 people and many people knew each other; notably, the library had no policy on this issue. It had, apparently, never been an issue. The circulation clerks and librarians knew their patrons and knew families. Many of the staff had never questioned the privacy issues involved in a spouse picking up materials requested by the other spouse.

But a new librarian, Erica, fresh out of library school, started at the library and immediately grew concerned about the practice. She thought the library policy should be that only the person whose name was on the hold slip is eligible to retrieve the material, but the rest of the staff said it was inconvenient for the families they served. Her concerns grew more serious when a female patron requested help with a book on abuse. When Erica told her she would have to request it from another library and it would be available at the hold shelf sometime next week, the woman said, "No, never mind." Erica voiced her concerns to a colleague, who said, "Oh, you know, her husband oftentimes comes in and gets their materials. I wonder if she was afraid to get it because of that." Erica felt horrible. What had seemed to be a minor policy issue had become a much larger concern.

QUESTIONS TO CONSIDER

1. Is it a privacy violation to have a spouse or other be allowed to retrieve materials from a hold shelf?
2. Discuss the larger privacy issue in this case. Should Erica be concerned about the type of material the patron first wanted but later refused?
3. What is your library's policy on such circulation?
4. Should spouses sign a consent form to allow each other to retrieve materials?

CASE #3.24

A parent called the Dodgeville Public Library and asked to speak to the director. The parent asserted that the library was trying to "keep secrets" from parents and blamed the library for being "irresponsible" and "promoting danger to children." The director was unsure what Ms. Haas meant and asked for clarification. Apparently, the Haas family had received a call from a library staff member, who asked to speak to Kevin. Kevin was seven years old and had recently received his own library card. Once a child could read and sign his name, he was eligible for his own card. According to Dodgeville's policies, children's cards were treated the same as adults'. It was assumed, and encouraged, that the parent or guardian would assist his or her child in selecting appropriate materials and would prevent a child from borrowing inappropriate materials. Of course, the children's and young adult librarian, Trina, provided guidance and, notably, she was a firm believer in the ALA stance on non-discrimination in regards to age of the patron.

Trina had called Kevin's home to let him know *The Dangerous Book for Boys* had arrived. She asked for him directly and, when Ms. Haas asked who was calling, Trina politely said, "Dodgeville Public Library." Ms. Haas said she would take the call for Kevin, to which Trina said, "No, this is a private matter regarding his library request." "A PRIVATE matter?" Ms. Haas responded. "He is SEVEN. Either you tell me what this book is or I will take his library card away." Trina was shocked; she certainly did not want this to happen and punish the child, who obviously had great potential as a reader; she was surprised that Kevin's mother would react in this way and hoped to diffuse the situation. She provided the name of the book to Ms. Haas. Without knowing anything about the book, Ms. Haas informed Trina she would be calling the director to discuss the matter. "I don't know how you live with yourself. What if my son really hurt himself from that book? You librarians are crazy — you favor some rhetoric about privacy or intellectual freedom over a child's safety. What are you thinking? A seven-year-old doesn't need privacy. He needs to be protected. I thought the library helped us as parents," Ms. Haas stated, before she hung up the phone.

QUESTIONS TO CONSIDER

1. How do we reconcile children's rights to privacy? Is a seven-year-old's privacy less valuable than a fourteen-year-old's?
2. How do you respond to Ms. Haas' claims about librarians favoring "rhetoric" over safety?
3. Should Trina have lied to Ms. Haas? Is lying any more moral than breaching privacy in this case?
4. Discuss the balance between a parent's right to information in the interest of guiding their child and the child's right to autonomy?
5. Discuss the complex issue of age from a cross-cultural perspective, noting the differences in age of "adulthood" across the world.

CASE #3.25

José was a teaching librarian in a public university. He worked with faculty to develop bibliographic information and information literacy sessions. He worked closely with a philosophy professor, who was teaching a "Current Issues in Bioethics" course, which fulfilled an area elective for students. This course dealt with such issues as abortion, physician-assisted suicide, and end-of-life decisions. José assisted the classes by showing how to find both current and historical literature on the topics from a range of materials.

One afternoon, as José was finishing a class, two adults were waiting at the door. The students filed out and the two approached José. They asked if Kayla Smith had been in his library session. "We are her parents and she will not tell us about her work in this philosophy class. We raised her as a Christian, so we want to be sure she is maintaining her beliefs. All we want to see are her assignments. We're afraid they aren't quite appropriate for her and we could work with the professor and you to come up with some alternatives. We called the professor but he said he could not release any information on his students — even to their parents, for goodness sakes. We are paying for this and we don't have a right to know what she is studying? But since you are just a librarian, you can tell us about her work," Mr. Smith argued.

José thought carefully. Then he replied, "Under the Federal Law Family Education Rights and Privacy Act (FERPA), even librarians cannot discuss their students, not even with their parents. I understand your concern, but it is not appropriate for you to sneak around your daughter's education. This is between you and your child. I cannot discuss any student in this fashion. If you are worried about the curriculum in a public university, perhaps you should reconsider your choice of school."

QUESTIONS TO CONSIDER

1. Discuss the impact of such movements as Academic Bills of Rights on libraries.
2. Librarians have long held privacy as a core value; how does FERPA contribute to this in university/educational settings?
3. How would you, as a librarian, respond to parental confrontation such as this?

REFERENCES

Abramson, L. (2006). Librarians Denounce Gag Order in PATRIOT Act Case. Retrieved June 20, 2007, from http://www.npr.org/templates/story/story.php?storyId=5440211.

American Civil Liberties Union. (2003). Surveillance under the U.S.A. PATRIOT Act. Retrieved June 20, 2007, from http://www.aclu.org/safefree/general/17326res20030403.html.

Brin, D. (1999). *The Transparent Society: Will Technology Force Us To Choose Between Privacy and Freedom?* New York: Perseus.

Christian, G. (2007). Testimony to the U.S. Senate Judiciary Committee on April 11, 2007: Responding to the Inspector General's Findings of Improper Use of National Security Letters by the FBI. Retrieved September 15, 2007, from http://judiciary.senate.gov/testimony.cfm?id=2679&wit_id=6284.

Cohen, J. (2001). Information Rights and Intellectual Freedom. In A. Vedder (Ed.), *Ethics and the Internet* (pp. 11–32). Antwerp: Intersentia.

Cowan, A. (2006). Four Librarians Finally Break Silence in Records Case. *New York Times*. Retrieved June 20, 2007, from http://www.nytimes.com/2006/05/31/nyregion/31library.html?ex=1182657600&en=fba40320a8551e62&ei=5070.

Ess, C. (2005). "Lost in Translation"?: Intercultural Dialogues on Privacy and Information Ethics [Special Issue on Privacy and Data Privacy Protection in Asia]. *Ethics and Information Technology*, 7(1), 1–6.

Foerstel, H. (1991). *Surveillance in the Stacks: The FBI's Library Awareness Program*. Westport: Greenwood Press.

The Fourth Amendment Right of Privacy: Mapping the Future (1967, October). *Virginia Law Review*, 53, 1314–1359.

Kranich, N. (2003, May 5). The Impact of the U.S.A. PATRIOT Act on Free Expression. The Free Expression Policy Project Web site. Retrieved July 2, 2007, from http://www.fepproject.org/commentaries/patriotact.html.

Lester, T. (2001, March). The Reinvention of Privacy. *The Atlantic Monthly*, 287, 27–39.

Moor, J. (2004). Towards a Theory of Privacy for the Information Age. In R. Spinello & H. Tavani (Eds.), *Readings in Cyberethics* (pp. 407–417). Boston: Jones and Bartlett.

Ponemon Institute and the CIO Institute of Carnegie Mellon University (2004). Privacy Trust Study of the United States Government: An Executive Summary. Retrieved August 5, 2007, from http://cioi.web.cmu.edu/research/2004PrivacyTrustSurveyoftheUnitedStatesGovernmentExecutiveSummaryV.6.pdf. [Used with Permission].

Ponemon, L. (2007). 2007 Privacy Trust Study of the United States Government. Retrieved August 5, 2007, from http://www.epic.org/privacy/pdf/2007ponemon.pdf [Used with Permission].

Risen, J. (2007, August 5). Bush Signs Law to Widen Reach for Wiretapping. *New York Times*. Retrieved August 10, 2007, from http://www.nytimes.com/2007/08/06/washington/06nsa.html?ex=1344139200&en=24ad2883092e3afb&ei=5124&partner=permalink&exprod=permalink.

Sprenger, P. (1999). Sun on Privacy: 'Get Over It.' *Wired*. Retrieved June 19, 2007, from http://www.wired.com/politics/law/news/1999/01/17538 .

United States Department of Justice (2006, March 6). Fact Sheet: U.S.A. PATRIOT Act Improvement and Reauthorization Act of 2005. Retrieved July 2, 2007, from http://www.usdoj.gov/opa/pr/2006/March/06_opa_113.html.

Warren, S., & Brandeis, L. (1890). The Right to Privacy. *Harvard Law Review*, 4, 190–220.

WhatIs.com. (2005). Privacy. Retrieved September 4, 2005, from http://searchdatamanagement.techtarget.com/sDefinition/0,,sid91_gci212829,00.html.

CHAPTER 4

Intellectual Property

That ideas should freely spread from one to another over the globe, for the moral and mutual instruction of man, and improvement of his condition, seems to have been peculiarly and benevolently designed by nature, when she made them, like fire, expansible over all space, without lessening their density at any point, and like the air in which we breathe, move, and have our physical being, incapable of confinement or exclusive appropriation.
                                                    —*Thomas Jefferson*

Intellectual property (IP) refers to creations of the mind: inventions, literary and artistic works, symbols, names, images, and designs used in commerce. Particular expressions of ideas are things of value to the marketplace and to society and are therefore "protected" under a system of ownership. There are three distinct systems of intellectual property protections: trademark, patent, and copyright, all of which should be familiar to information professionals. All forms have unique sets of laws.

As with laws on privacy and related laws such as the PATRIOT Act, information professionals often find intellectual property dilemmas contradictory from legal and philosophical perspectives. Legal scholars as well as philosophers have struggled and argued vehemently over theories of intellectual property, with some considering IP as a legal, economic, or an ethical construct, or something of a blend of these constructs.

Competing stakeholders further complicate IP laws. Throughout its history, IP law has been influenced by an amalgam of precedent, powerful commercial interests, and international obligations. Information professionals have watched and reacted, as different hands have sorted through the laws, carving out pieces of the pie to best suit their interests; such high profile legislation as the Digital Millennium Copyright Act and the Sonny Bono Copyright Extension Act in the past decade have seriously affected the information professions, as we will describe below.

With the cases presented in this chapter, our goal is to illustrate the complexities around IP, while encouraging awareness and debate of these issues. It is, however, the rules surrounding copyright that typically present most of the ethical difficulties for information professionals and thus are our primary focus in this chapter. A small portion of this chapter will be devoted to licensing issues, which are quickly emerging as hot-button issues for the field; however, a detailed discussion, which would necessarily include matters of contract law, is not within the scope of this work.

Copyright law, in the United States and as international law, has a long history stemming in particular from England's Statute of Anne, codified in 1710. The law is considered by many as the first true copyright law and the cornerstone of U.S. copyright. In the United States, copyright was codified in 1790, when the Congress asserted its power to "promote the progress of science and useful arts ... by securing for limited times to authors and inventors the exclusive rights to their respective writings and discoveries" (United States Copyright Act, 1790). U.S. copyright law was modified in 1831, 1870, 1909, and 1976. Of significance in the original copyright laws was a dedication to balance, a balance between individual reward and social good. The idea of a thriving public domain was critical to social good and the 1909 revision revolved around this balance.

> The main object to be desired in expanding copyright protection to music has been to give the composer an adequate return for the value of his composition and it has been a serious and difficult task to combine the protection of the composer with the protection of the public, and to frame an act that it would accomplish the double purpose of securing to the composer an adequate return for all use made of his composition and at the same time prevent the formation of oppressive monopolies, which might be founded upon the very rights granted to the composer for the purpose of protecting his interests [H.R. Rep. No. 2222 60th Cong., 2nd Sess. 7, 1909].

Libraries were directly affected by the 1976 revisions through sections 106 and 107, which deal with exclusive rights and fair use provisions. But copyright laws became infinitely more complex and controversial — and quite politicized — in 1998. Many believed that two new laws seriously jeopardized the delicate balance between individual rewards and public goods. The Sonny Bono Copyright Extension Act and the Digital Millennium Copyright Act were enacted in part to satisfy international treaties and to harmonize U.S. laws with other countries, especially members of the European Community (see specifically sections 1201–1203 of the DMCA), and in part as a remedy against potential threats to copyrighted works generated through technological innovations. These threats to the content industry resulted in pressure to which Congress responded by including Section 512 (of the DMCA) which describes the responsibilities of Internet Service Providers in relation to copyrighted works.

Both of these laws were codified in 1998, much to the chagrin of information professionals, especially librarians and archivists serving the public and academia. The Extension Act increased term limits on copyright such that copyright is now effectively perpetual. From its original length of fourteen years, the term of copyright ownership is now life of the author/owner plus 70 years or more, depending on the type of work and whether or not the work is published or unpublished, with renewal possible. The DMCA is different from the other major revisions in 1909 and 1976. Protecting copyrights of digital works had become a critical issue by this time and the legislative response, the DMCA, was to solve the problem through technological measures that controlled access. Section

1201 in particular took copyright liability in a completely new direction. Prior to the DMCA, individuals or individual organizations such as corporations were liable for their acts of infringement. Now, persons or organizations that circumvent access controls or assist someone to circumvent these controls by providing tools or guidance are liable. This holds true even if the use of those copyrighted works would be a fair use.

Another major goal of this legislation was to reduce piracy — the copying and distribution of another's copyrighted content movies, music, software, etc., through the aforementioned section 512 of the DMCA. Napster is perhaps the most noteworthy of these online piracy cases; however, it is not just major file-sharing organizations to whom the DMCA applies. The content industry, through organizations such as the Recording Industry Association of America, has aggressively sued individuals, including minors. More recently, academic institutions have been given little choice but to change Internet policies or risk being embroiled in a secondary infringement suit. "Under the 'safe harbor' provision of the Digital Millennium Copyright Act (DMCA) of 1998, colleges and universities are not held liable for copyright-infringing file sharing conducted on their campus networks, provided that they cooperate with copyright holders to identify and deal with users on their networks who illegally share copyrighted materials" (Hearing Charter, 2007). Pending legislation before the 110th Congress to reauthorize the Higher Education Act of 1965, amending Section 485 (20 U.S.C. 1092) would further extend the responsibilities of colleges and universities to protect copyrighted works. In order to receive funds, "institutional policies and sanctions related to copyright infringement that inform students that unauthorized distribution of copyrighted material on the institution's information technology systems, including engaging in peer-to-peer file sharing, may subject the students to civil and criminal penalties" (Higher Education Amendments of 2007, Sec. 477).

Information professionals should anticipate and be prepared for conflicts between shared cultural values — that is, the culture of open access and sharing embodied in the Internet, for instance, and the requirements of copyright law. Intellectual property laws, like other laws discussed throughout the other chapters, are not limited to just those issues included in this chapter. IP laws, especially the DMCA, have the potential to chill intellectual freedom and breach privacy. These laws may also widen the gap between the information haves and have-nots, aggravating broader social ills, poverty, lack of education, and lack of infrastructure directly, because they reduce or deny access to basic information necessary to full participation in society and a healthy life.

With relatively new and emerging technologies, library patrons and other information users look to librarians and information professionals to help them understand what is expected with regard to ethical information behavior. File-sharing programs, digital rights management systems, electronic journals and electronic reserve materials stretch the limits of — or outright challenge — extant laws. These challenges cross over information environments from public libraries to academic to schools or special information centers. IP is a complex issue. Some would argue that information professionals have a responsibility to society that goes beyond adoption of simple policies, which are uncritically compliant with existing laws. This position calls for information professionals to be advocates for expanding access to information for the public good and to push the boundaries of current library and educational exceptions around copyright law.

Ethics and law are not always in sync: Law provides a structured context to which individuals look for a reasonable solution. Law does not prescribe behavior for the purpose of morality, *per se*, but for the purpose of fulfilling a societal requirement. Recall that ethics and ethical decision-making is grounded in morality and that law and ethics must find a comfortable and balanced place. Therefore, the cases presented here include opportunities for the reader to consider both the legal and ethical implications illustrated in the scenarios. We strongly recommend that readers consult with their legal council where necessary to ensure sound and appropriate decisions regarding uses of intellectual property.

This chapter assumes that the reader possesses a working knowledge of IP, but a brief overview on section 107 or Fair Use, section 108 (copies in Libraries and Archives), section 109 or the First Sale Doctrine, and section 110(b) or the TEACH Act begins with the next paragraph. Such highly informative works as *Copyright Law for Librarians and Educators: Creative Strategies and Practical Solutions* (2nd Edition) (Crews, 2006); Minow and Lipinski's (2003) *The Library's Legal Answer Book* (2nd edition forthcoming); Russell's (2004) *Complete Copyright: An Everyday Guide for Librarians*; and Lipinski's (2004) *Copyright Law and the Distance Education Classroom* are recommended reading. These resources are useful for those wishing to gain a deeper understanding of the legal issues librarians face and for those in need of pragmatic advice and solutions. Crews' book in particular has a wonderful appendix, which contains the text of the law for these key sections of Title 17. The authors found this an invaluable reference over the course of writing this chapter. The Copyright Office of the United States Government provides a digital copy of Title 17 as well as a number of brochures designed to guide individuals in the legal uses of copyrighted information. Those who want to learn more about copyright and other intellectual property laws from the global perspective, a perspective which is growing in importance, may wish to explore The World Intellectual Property Organization's *Collection of Electronic Access Laws* (a searchable database) or their brief brochure on the *Collective Management of Copyright and Related Rights*. At the end of this overview, there are some final comments on licensing digital works.

Fair use (Title 17, Section 107) is a set of four criteria or factors that is used to determine if part of a copyrighted work can be used without the owner's permission and/or making royalty payment. In other words, it is a tool used to determine non-infringing uses of copyrighted works. The first factor is the purpose or character of the use itself. Non-profit or educational uses weigh in favor of fair use, whereas commercial use does not. The second factor is the nature of the work itself. A good way to look at this is on a continuum. The more factual the original work is, the more likely its use will be "fair"; conversely, the more creative the original work, the less likely its use will be "fair." Factor three relates to the amount or substantiality of the work that is used in relation to the whole. Using a small portion of a work or using only as much as needed, unless it is the "heart" of the work, is indicative of fair use. The final factor relates to the market for the particular work. Here we consider the effect of the use on the market. Will the fair use affect sales of the original work or will the use dilute either the economic or the artistic value of the work? If the answer is yes to these and similarly framed questions, then obtaining permission is advised. The four factors are of equal weight; however, some may have the impression that the fourth factor, in which we consider market harm, has greater weight.

The four factors are very useful in establishing reasonable expectations of fair use. Only the Court can make that legal determination; however, there is a desire to avoid costly litigation even if a party believes its use is "fair." Individuals and organizations who are formally asked to "cease and desist" in their use of copyrighted works often do. Primary and secondary schools, for instance, are often found in this precarious situation. Information professionals may be too cautious in their use of copyrighted materials in spite of fair use and other legal exceptions because they are afraid of breaking the law and incurring substantial fines. Being cautious is understandable given the uncertainty and potential for statutory damages that permeates fair use and copyright in general. However, these worries should not keep us from our obligation to help our patrons employ fair use in their scholarly or creative endeavors. Crews suggests,

> The law calls on each of us to act in an informed, good faith manner. Reasonable people can and will disagree about the meaning of fair use. Congress recognized that it was enacting a law open to significant differences of interpretation, so Congress provided an important safety valve for educators and librarians.... The law of statutory damages, however, proceeds to give an important break for educators and librarians. In fact, the court may be required to cut the statutory damages to zero. This protection applies if you are an employee or agent of a nonprofit educational institution or library, if you were acting within the scope of your employment, and you believed and had reasonable grounds for believing that the copies you made were fair use [2006, p. 80].

This being said, it is also important for information professionals to know when not to answer or act and immediately consult with their institutional legal counsel, independent counsel, and/or the American Library Association.

Information professionals, especially librarians, should also be familiar with other sections of Title 17. These sections, while less likely to produce the difficulties we see in fair use, are important as they establish other permissible uses of copyrighted works. First, section 108 addresses reproduction of copyrighted works for libraries and archives. Here we see guidance on circumstances in which copies may be made for preservation or replacement purposes, how many copies might be made, and how those copies may be used. There are also rules governing reproduction of works that are contained in obsolete formats and technologies. This section also addresses copies made for individual use in private study, scholarship or research.

As of this writing, section 108 is under review. A study group has been formed to conduct a reexamination of the exceptions and limitations applicable to libraries and archives under the Copyright Act, specifically in light of the changes wrought by digital media. The group will provide findings and recommendations on how to revise the copyright law in order to ensure an appropriate balance among the interests of creators and other copyright holders, libraries and archives in a manner that best serves the national interest. The findings and recommendations will be submitted by mid–2007 to the Librarian of Congress [Section 108 Study Group, Mission Statement].

Section 109, often referred to as the First Sale Doctrine, addresses issues relating to a specific copy of a work, provided that specific copy was lawfully obtained. Simply put, once the "first sale is made," the owner may sell or otherwise dispose of that specific copy. The lawful owner may also display this work. The exceptions contained in the First Sale Doctrine are critical to the essential functions of lending libraries—browsing, borrowing, friends-of-library sales, etc. The basis of these exceptions for libraries is the possession of a lawful copy. Librarians need to be aware that the First Sale Doctrine may not apply to specific kinds of works, such as sound recordings and computer programs. As noted, review of the applicable sections of 109 and/or consulting with legal council is recommended.

Section 110(2), commonly referred to as the TEACH Act, is another area of the law of which information professionals—especially those involved with distance education—should be aware. This act details the rules surrounding the use of copyrighted works in distance learning—the point of which is to mirror as closely as possible exceptions to copyright which are allowed in face-to-face teaching situations. TEACH has numerous requirements that are fulfilled through technological interventions or institutional policies. These requirements cut across multiple academic units—administration, IT, libraries, and faculty (Crews, 2006).

Finally, *licensing* of digital materials moves us into another legal dimension—*contract law*. Licensing requires that librarians or other information professionals work closely with legal council because these contracts must ensure adequate protection for the library and/or parent institution while establishing optimal rules of use.

Moral decision-making takes place at distinct points. The first is during negotiations. Ideally, what we agree to contractually should fall in line with established professional codes of ethics and should align with principles of fair use and other legal exceptions. This is critical because contractual agreements—unless the contracts are deceptive, fraudulent, or unconscionable (a legal concept)—will generally be upheld by the Court even if the contract overrides some aspect of another set of rights like copyright (Lipinski, forthcoming). Once those contracts are signed, the responsibility to fulfill those obligations comes into how we manage day-to-day use of the content. Policies and practice with regard to use of licensed or subscription-based content must take into account the impact of contractual rules on fair use, preservation copies, classroom copies, links for distance education students, and so on.

We conclude this discussion by noting the importance of education in and around copyright and the legal landscape in LIS programs. Our future professionals should be learning these intricacies before they are faced with the challenges of litigation. Thus, we highly recommend students take coursework in legal issues to prepare themselves better as responsible information professionals.

Intellectual Property Cases

CASE #4.1

The circulation supervisor at University of Wildwood Library, a large, public academic institution, was concerned. Their music library did not have its own policy for the number of CDs a patron could check out at once. The music library followed the same circulation policies as the rest of the library where number of items was concerned. For undergraduate students, this was 30 items total. The loan period for CDs, DVDs, and other audio recordings was 7 days.

After one of the university's undergraduate students came to the music library, iPod in tow, and checked out 30 CDs, the circulation supervisor went to the director of the library, requesting that a policy be set limiting CD circulation to 5. "There is no way a person can listen to 30 CDs in one week," she exclaimed. "I know they are simply copying the CDs to their iPods and this is illegal. It is STEALING," she argued. The director firmly disagreed. "We are following the laws. We have our copyright notices posted, we follow fair use guidelines, and it is not our job to ask what a patron is doing with the material she borrows from us. Would you be concerned if the patron checked out 30 books?" "No," responded the circulation supervisor, "because I know a person wouldn't photocopy 30 books, but CDs and iPods have changed everything. The law is the law, stealing is stealing." The director reinforced to the staff that circulation policies were to remain the same regardless of material and would not be changed in light of CDs.

QUESTIONS TO CONSIDER

1. Does the circulation supervisor present a good case? Is her argument sound?
2. If you were a circulation supervisor and faced this issue, how would you handle this situation?
3. If a patron came in and told you that she copied the CDs, how would you respond?
4. Does fair use apply in this situation?

CASE #4.2

Williamstown Public Library now makes wi-fi available for its patrons. It was a good decision, as the public Internet terminals were frequently full. Waiting times for these often exceeded 30 minutes. Patrons became frustrated, leaving for other libraries and Internet cafés. After official library hours, however, people began parking in the library lot and using the wi-fi with their laptops. One night, Joe was reading his favorite blogs when a police officer tapped on his window and asked what he was doing. Joe responded that he was using the free, open-access wi-fi. Joe maintained it was no different than if he had checked out a book, then sat and read it in his car in the parking lot. The police officer was unconvinced, though he could not cite a specific law. After much consultation, the police officer found a law that had to do with unauthorized access, as hackers are often charged, and threatened Joe with arrest.

QUESTIONS TO CONSIDER

1. Was Joe doing anything wrong or immoral?
2. What does such a case suggest about the inabilities of current laws and emerging technologies?
3. What should the library do?

CASE #4.3

Every Tuesday night, the same student came into the campus library. She checked out the algebra textbook that was held in reserve and headed over to the copy machine. She usually copied a chapter or two. The first night this happened, Sara did not think too much of it — maybe the bookstore ran out of the textbook or she forgot to bring her book. After this happened a couple more times, Sara realized that the student was copying the whole book chapter by chapter. She knew that this was unacceptable — there was no way this qualified as a fair use. Sara did not want to confront the student. She knew that this student was poor and trying to support her family on minimum wage. Sara thought that it was likely the family budget did not include buying several required books at a time, but that there was a couple of dollars each week for the photocopies. Sara decided to talk to her colleague, Bob, who had worked at the campus a long time. Bob told Sara that this happened every semester and that the student was just one of many. Bob also mentioned, "just between you and me," that even though the copyright policy for the campus cautioned students against this practice, no one enforced the policy because so many students could not afford to buy textbooks.

QUESTIONS TO CONSIDER

1. Is there a morally sound argument for the librarians to turn a blind eye?
2. Does the responsibility to act within the law rest squarely on the students who are making illegal copies or does the library have some responsibility because it ignores this behavior?
3. Would it be better for the library stop collecting textbooks altogether since it is aware that there is a systemic problem of illegal copies being made?

CASE #4.4

The astronomical cost of college textbooks has many concerned. Professor Smith decided she would not require her students to purchase texts for her class and, instead, sent her students to the academic library, where she had donated five copies of the text, and encouraged students to check out and photocopy the parts they needed. Additional course materials would be available online freely. Professor Smith argued that this was fair use, despite what her colleague argued: Not buying the texts contributed to a negative impact on the market, one of the fair use criteria. Professor Smith maintained that the textbook industry was itself immoral and corrupt and she would no longer contribute to it. The library's director was uncomfortable with Professor Smith's strategies and, while she agreed that textbooks were overpriced, she was concerned that such a practice was obviously not right for the library. She had a long talk with Professor Smith about fair use and the copyright laws, making the argument, "What if every professor decided to do this? What would happen?" Professor Smith replied, "Maybe then the textbook industry *and* copyright laws would get the changes they need. The laws have moved away from their original purpose, to promote the public good."

QUESTIONS TO CONSIDER

1. Do you accept Professor Smith's argument on moral grounds?
2. How would you handle the situation as the library director?
3. If you were an author of a textbook, how would you respond to this situation?

CASE #4.5

Dr. Jones, a popular professor, asked Jim, one of the academic librarians, to read and edit a paper. This wasn't the first time that Jim had done this for Dr. Jones — the two shared common research interests and Jim had an excellent reputation for editing. Jim was a little bit surprised by the request because it had only been a couple of weeks since he reviewed the last paper. "Wow," Jim said, "that was fast." Dr. Jones replied, "All in a day's work!" Jim, joking around, asked, "Did you buy it off the Internet like the desperate students do?" The two had a good laugh over this last question and agreed on a deadline for the edits.

A couple of days later, Jim settled in at home, cup of coffee in hand, and began to read the paper. After he finished the initial reading, Jim was perplexed. Something seemed off about the paper; he could not quite put his finger on it, so he decided to read it again later in the day. After another read-through, Jim was still dissatisfied, but decided to go ahead with the editing. The day before the deadline, it hit him. He had read at least part of the paper before. Since he had a little time, Jim decided to find a copy of the other paper — figuring he would just add the appropriate citation once he had identified the correct passage. As it turned out, there was quite a bit of this paper included in Dr. Jones' paper — some was even word for word even though there was no direct quote indicated.

Hoping his growing suspicion was incorrect, Jim checked another part of the paper. Again, there were several direct quotes that appeared to be Dr. Jones' words. These quotes were not cited in the text or the bibliography. Jim continued to check the paper and found several more passages that were not written by Dr. Jones. Jim shared what he had found with another librarian without revealing who wrote the paper. She asked Jim if he thought the author plagiarized. Sadly, Jim told her, "Yes, as sure as I can be on this kind of thing." The two considered running the paper through the plagiarism detection software to confirm their suspicions.

QUESTIONS TO CONSIDER

1. Is it morally acceptable to run Dr. Jones' paper through the software program? Professionally acceptable?
2. Consider the situation if there was not a software option.
3. What steps should be taken if a librarian believes another faculty member has committed plagiarism?

CASE #4.6

Joe recently graduated from the university. For some reason, he continued to have remote access to databases from the university library. The access should have ended 30 days after graduation, but six months later, he could still get into the system. At his last visit to the library, Joe mentioned to the librarian that he was still able to gain remote access and the librarian responded that the "situation would work itself out." "Don't worry," he said. "You've paid a lot of tuition and we pay a lot of money to these vendors. If you come into the library, you can still use them. What's the harm if you access remotely?"

A few weeks later, Joe checked back and was still able to search the databases. He occasionally felt guilty about using the remote access, but thought if he drove the 20 minutes to campus, he would be able to use any of the databases without question. The university is a public place and anyone with a community borrower's card has the same privileges as undergraduate students, other than remote access. He had told the librarian, after all, and he was told the situation would be resolved.

QUESTIONS TO CONSIDER

1. Is the librarian correct that there is no harm in what Joe is doing?
2. Even if there is no harm, is the librarian's position professionally ethical?
3. If you were this librarian's supervisor or colleague, what would you have done if you overheard this conversation?
4. Does the fact that Joe has paid a great deal of money have any bearing? Could he be violating the law?

CASE #4.7

Alice was an electronic resources librarian at a major state university. She had been asked to make some additions to the business database collection. She planned on adding what she thought was the perfect database by the end of the month — just in time for the new semester. She was happy that the faculty who participated in the trial really liked the content and they were pleased with the user-interface. The database had been available to corporate clients for several years and had only recently begun to offer substantial academic discounts.

As she was leaving for the day one afternoon, Carol, who was in charge of reviewing all of the databases licenses, called her. After a quick hello, Carol got right to the point. There was a clause in the database contract that did not align with library policy and practice. The vendor asked that the library prevent students who worked for a major national company from accessing the content. Apparently, there was an ongoing legal dispute between the vendor and this company. The nature of the dispute was such that the vendor was unwilling to give access to anyone affiliated with the major company. Alice asked, "Did you explain to the vendor that the library doesn't keep track of where students work? Did you tell them that even if we did keep track, we wouldn't discriminate on that basis?" Carol told Alice that she tried to explain, but the vendor seemed to be operating on the corporate model. Alice asked Carol to try again — this content was important to the curriculum and professors were asking when it would be available.

QUESTIONS TO CONSIDER

1. Would you be willing to accept the discriminatory clause? (This assumes that you could actually block certain patrons.)
2. If you are unwilling to accept it, what would you say to the professors to justify your choice?
3. If you are willing to accept the clause, how would you justify your choice to those who were denied access to the database?

CASE #4.8

The new Harry Potter book and audio CDs had arrived at the East Bend Public Library a few days before the official release date. The library director specifically instructed the staff that no one was to remove the books or materials prior to the release date, citing "fairness" to all readers. One of the librarians, while processing the materials, copied the CD files onto his personal laptop, which he brought in to work. He did not remove the original disk from the library and he didn't do anything wrong by copying it, as it was for personal use only. He thought, "If I checked it out when it was officially released, I'd just be preventing someone else from enjoying it. This way, I get to hear it early and others will have access to it immediately. It is not like I am selling it to anyone! This way, no one even knows I have the files."

QUESTIONS TO CONSIDER

1. Were the librarian's actions ethically and/or professionally questionable?
2. Discuss the fair use guidelines. Was the librarian clearly within those rights?

CASE #4.9

In the small town of Trout, everyone knew each other. The public library had a staff of two: the director and another librarian. The Trout Library, while limited with a fairly small collection, had built a nice video and DVD collection, as borrowing movies was a popular activity, especially during the long winter months. Shelly, the librarian, noticed that the local church began a movie series and was advertising the movie nights around town. The events were free of charge and all were invited. The librarian, however, started to realize that the church's community events committee chairperson was renting the library movies and using them for the church movie events.

QUESTIONS TO CONSIDER

1. Is the use of library movies in this kind of public viewing legal?
2. Should the librarian be concerned with what the patron is doing with the materials once they are circulated?
3. Discuss how ethics and law may not be in sync in this case.

CASE #4.10

John was a corporate librarian. He and three other librarians shared the responsibility of running the company's library. John was not looking forward to the next two weeks. He had just finished the contract renewal process for several databases and he had the unfortunate task of telling three divisions that they needed to remove a number of articles that they had uploaded onto their individual units' intranet pages. Prior to the contract renewals, the reposting of these articles, as long as they were on internal web pages, was expressly permitted. Now, though, the database publisher decided that the reposting of articles was only permitted if the company paid substantial additional fees — even the posting of persistent links required additional monies.

John knew that the unit managers would likely decide to pay the additional fees so they would not have to dismantle their web pages — the engineers and other stakeholders need the information readily available, not tucked behind the library's electronic doors. There was nothing new about this problem; last year, two different units were in the same position.

John wished that the units would not repost articles in the first place to avoid this type of situation. He did not like the units paying the reposting fees, either. The company ended up paying for the same information twice. Sometimes the company paid for the same information 4 or 5 times for the convenience of several units. John was tempted not to do anything — it was unlikely that anyone would ever know that the information was posted. He also knew, when the project was over in six weeks, the intranet page would no longer be available.

QUESTIONS TO CONSIDER

1. In what ways, if any, is the database publisher behaving unethically?
2. Do the short run benefits of paying the fees create a situation in which the library is worse off? Better off? In what way?

CASE #4.11

The library at the Tarrington School of Business had just been notified by the vendor that it no longer had access to a core business database. The vendor made this decision because a professor and three of her graduate students, over the course of two semesters, illegally downloaded several thousand documents from the database into another database that they created and shared with individuals outside of the school.

The librarian was extremely upset about the vendor's decision and sent a letter requesting that access be reinstated because it was unfair to all of the other users who used the database appropriately. The letter also described how information about copyright was shared with students, staff and faculty and indicated that the school was addressing the violations according to due process.

The letter softened the vendor's position and the vendor offered to allow in-library, one-user-at-a-time access. This restriction meant that students in the distance-education program would not have access to the materials. Hoping for a better option, the librarian asked the school's legal department if the vendor was within its rights to refuse service. Unfortunately it was. In fact, the legal department said that the single-user offer was very generous and that the school was very lucky it was not facing a lawsuit.

QUESTIONS TO CONSIDER

1. Is the vendor's offer generous? Should the library accept it?
2. What would strengthen the librarian's argument for reinstating access?

CASE #4.12

After the library at Tarrington School of Business was denied access to an important database (see Case #4.11), the library formed a committee to review several practices surrounding database use. The committee successfully revised several policies, but the members had not found a resolution to managing the behavior of students who were hired as interns. The thinking had always been that internships were part of the student's educational experience; the use of library materials to complete projects assigned by the intern's company was similar to the student using materials for any other course. Students paid tuition for internships just as they did for classes. Most of the librarians recognized that at least some of the students were doing more than using the materials to complete projects and reports and were likely sharing full-text articles and reports, copies of book chapters, and other documents with the companies. The library, as an organization, avoided the problem by not asking any pointed questions. Now, they did not have any choice but to sort out the legal and ethical implications.

QUESTIONS TO CONSIDER

1. Is the basic premise that internships are an extension of the classroom reasonable?
2. If so, and as long as the library instructs students about legal and illegal uses of information, is it ethical for the library to let the students make their own choices about sharing materials with the companies for whom they are interning?
3. Is it too risky and therefore unethical to allow students to make their own decisions?

CASE #4.13

Each of Professor Anderson's students was assigned a company as a part of a class research project. The students were required to make predictions about the company's future. Dr. Anderson recommended a particular database from which the students could draw financial data and analysts' reports. She had been using the same company list for the last couple of semesters, so she decided to select some new companies. As she reviewed one of the companies, she noticed some discrepancies in some of the numbers. She reworked the math and she spotted a couple of common mistakes — mistakes which led the database's analyst to make some incorrect assertions about the company. She continued to work through several other companies and came across errors on another company. The mistakes were minor and had a negligible impact on the analysis.

Dr. Anderson took her findings to the business librarian, Allen, who agreed that this was a matter of concern and contacted the database representative. The database representative apologized and said he would check into the problem. After several weeks, the representative called Allen and assured him that these were isolated cases but that they would review practices anyway to make sure that this kind of error didn't happen again.

This answer was less than satisfactory. Allen had doubts, as did Dr. Anderson. Allen decided to review the contract with the vendor. Much to his chagrin, the contract specifically stated that the database publisher was not responsible for the accuracy of the content. After learning this, Allen consulted with the database librarian, Angie, who assured him that some vendors included these kinds of clauses. Allen pressed the matter. "I don't know why vendors do this," said Angie. "Maybe it is to protect themselves from lawsuits in the case of a company or individual who made bad decisions based on the content."

QUESTIONS TO CONSIDER

1. Who should verify the quality of the content: the database publisher, libraries that provide the database to users, the individual user, or the market?
2. Typically, we expect vendors of all sorts of products to stand behind them; should we make an exception when the product is information?
3. If we believe that the database vendor should be responsible for the content, then does it follow that we as librarians and other kinds of information professionals are responsible for decisions that users make?
4. Do IP laws cover data integrity? Should they?

CASE #4.14

ERQ Publishing Company provided digital access to its print content through an aggregated database. One of ERQ's journals was an important information source for public policy. Many professors of public policy published their work in this journal and ERQ required them to assign their copyrights to ERQ as a condition of publication. Naturally, many of these same public policy professors included readings from this journal as part of their course materials and they were delighted when this content became available electronically.

ERQ did not see this journal as a classroom resource but rather as an information source for professionals or as supplemental, self-selected reading for doctoral students and other researchers. Consequently, ERQ required the database publisher to restrict use of this particular journal to reduce or eliminate classroom use. For example, the database stated that posting of persistent links to articles from this journal on course pages was not allowed nor was the making of multiple print copies for classroom use. ERQ allowed users to do these things if the library or department paid additional, substantial fees that ran several thousand dollars annually.

QUESTIONS TO CONSIDER

1. Is ERQ's behavior unethical?
2. If so, is the publisher complicit?
3. What will happen to fair use if other publishers follow ERQ's lead?

CASE #4.15

The institutional price for a number of specialized journals increased to the point that the Ambrose Library considered dropping the journals that received the least amount of use. The circulation staff gathered several months' worth of use statistics and the librarians were to meet later in the week to decide the fate of several subscriptions. Word got out about the meeting and people from several departments asked to speak at the meeting. The library director was anxiously looking for an alternative to cutting the journals.

She held an informal "meeting before the meeting" with the senior librarians. All of the librarians agreed that it did not matter what they cut, someone would be disappointed and perhaps even angry about their decision. Tom, who was famous among his fellow librarians for pushing boundaries, suggested that individuals in each department take out subscriptions to the journals and then systematically "donate" the journals. The library could catalog the "gifts" and everyone would then be able to use the content. It would be up to the individual departments to reimburse individuals for their out-of-pocket expenses.

QUESTIONS TO CONSIDER

1. Is there anything illegal about what Tom is suggesting?
2. Is this an ethical way to combat the year-over-year cost increase of subscriptions?
3. Is there a more ethical way to manage the rising prices of journals?
4. How should researchers themselves work to promote a more equitable system of publication?
5. Consider such movements as Copyleft. What is the moral impetus behind it?

CASE #4.16

Lorna was an academic librarian. One of her responsibilities, one in which she was very uncomfortable, was assisting professors in researching student plagiarism. In about five minutes, she would meet with a professor to discuss yet another case of suspected plagiarism, the fourth one that year. Professor Robin James arrived and proceeded to explain why she thought the student had plagiarized. She told Lorna that she really needed her help to prove that her suspicions were correct. Lorna decided on the spot to make up an excuse about not having enough time to help and said as much to Robin. Robin, sensing that this was not true, asked Lorna why she did not want to help. Lorna tells Robin that she thought that the school's plagiarism policy was Draconian and she did not want to help prove someone was guilty of plagiarism because the consequences were so harsh. Under the school's rules, if a student made even one bad decision, he or she was required to leave the school and the mistake would haunt the student for his or her entire future; even one incident resulted in a permanent "X" grade on transcripts. The "X" designation indicated the student cheated, without explanation as to the seriousness of the offense.

Robin told Lorna that she could not agree more. In fact, Robin told Lorna that several professors had chosen not to pursue cases of suspected plagiarism because of the zero-tolerance policy even on a first or minor offense. Lorna and Robin decided to investigate because, while they believe the consequences were particularly unfair, they also believed that the student must be held accountable for this kind of ethical breach. They agreed that if they find clear evidence of intentional plagiarism, they would confront the student and leave it up to the student to choose between accepting a failing grade or risk the consequences of having the situation formally reviewed.

QUESTIONS TO CONSIDER

1. Is it ethical for Lorna and Robin to bypass the rules instituted by the school given their mutual belief that the consequences are too harsh?

2. Is their approach to the problem any more morally sound than that of the professors who chose to do nothing about plagiarism for the same reasons that Robin and Lorna are following their own path?

3. How would the school administration or students react to Robin and Lorna's decision?

4. Is choosing to receive a failing grade or taking a risk by going through the formal process really a choice for the student?

5. What educational measures should schools and universities take to inform students about plagiarism?

CASE #4.17

Hope Medford was a librarian in a large, multi-national corporation. Most of the library's users were engineers. Only a few worked at the corporate office as Hope did and most worked in various locations around the world. Hope had only met a handful of her users in person. Not knowing the bulk of her users could be a challenge. Hope did not know much about the corporate culture outside of the library and the corporate offices.

At the suggestion of another corporate librarian (who worked in a different company), she decided to do some analysis of circulation figures to help her get to know the users' likes and dislikes. Hope noticed an unusual pattern of use. Every single copy of several critical titles seemed to be in constant circulation. Hope decided to look into this more deeply before she purchased more copies of the same titles. To help allocate expenses fairly, circulation records at the company library were maintained for several years by employee and department.

It did not take Hope long to figure out that all of the copies had been checked out to the same department and that each member of the department had taken his or her turn at checking out the book and then renewing it for the maximum number of times. This made it nearly impossible for anyone in other departments or locations to check out the book. The processing of the books — check-in, check-out, and renewal — obscured the activity.

Hope decided to contact the unit's manager, Rick. Rick chuckled when Hope explained the situation. Rick told Hope that units did this all the time: "Hope, what you need to understand is that good information is a hot commodity around here. Every engineer is competing with every other engineer. Every unit competes with every other unit. Keeping these books in our department gives us an edge." Hope asked Rick if he thought the engineers had done anything wrong. Instead of answering her question, Rick asked if the engineers had broken any library rules. Hope admitted that they had not.

QUESTIONS TO CONSIDER

1. Have the engineers behaved unethically?
2. Is this attitude about information as commodity restricted to private enterprise or does this attitude prevail throughout society?
3. Would changing the library rules make a difference? Would attitudes shift or would this only change behavior?
4. What are some of the consequences of locking up information by subverting the sharing process, whether it is preventing another person from using a resource as in this case or keeping materials that would be fair use under digital lock and key?

CASE #4.18

The Grove Street Library was very cooperative with other libraries when it came to lending books through interlibrary loan. Grove's collection development librarian, Joyce, recently learned that one of their books had become quite valuable. When the book was first published, it received little attention, but recently the demand had grown exponentially. Electronic copies, which may or may not be legal, were available for sale on the web and the purchase price for a used copy hovered around $2000. Many libraries were recalling the book and were no longer willing to lend it to other libraries. One academic library would not allow even its own students to use the book at the library, let alone allow it to circulate.

Joyce debated what she ought to do with the Grove copy. It was a well-used volume and had been repaired several times and rebound twice. She asked herself what good this book was if no one read it. She did not want to risk buying an electronic copy and the publisher had stated that they could not reprint the book because they no longer retained the rights. The author had no interest in republishing his book.

QUESTIONS TO CONSIDER

1. Is it ethical to take this book out of circulation?
2. Does Joyce have any legal options based on exceptions to copyright for libraries?
3. Although the author has no legal obligation to republish, does he have a moral obligation?

CASE #4.19

An academic librarian/researcher, Anna, was mapping a specialized, interdisciplinary thesaurus to an existing, widely used classification scheme; such mapped thesauri are useful for domain-specific vocabulary and they offer insight through exploration of relationships within the language. The researcher had completed a portion of the thesaurus and had created a web page that allowed others to use the resource, as well as offer comments on the project, as it was still a work in progress. After the site had been online for a few days, Anna received a message from the corporate owner of the classification scheme. The owner insisted that this use of the system in the mapping was a violation of copyright, that it did not fall under fair use, nor did the researcher have permission to use the work in this way. "Take it down or we will issue a formal cease-and-desist order," said the message. "Our legal team is prepared to litigate if necessary," it concluded. A lawyer retained by Anna's university advised that Anna was not violating copyright, but that the company did indeed intend to go to court and litigation could take several years. Ultimately, Anna did not think it was worth the battle that would certainly ensue in court and she removed the web page.

QUESTIONS TO CONSIDER

1. Does the use of the classification structure in this research project fall under fair use?
2. Discuss the impact of intellectual property laws on intellectual freedom. How does one ultimately implicate the other?
3. Compare this situation with the now infamous cases of Richard Felton and Dmitry Sklyarov, both of whom faced criminal action for research-based activities.
4. How does corporate ownership and involvement in research affect intellectual freedom?

CASE #4.20

Like many other universities, Polytech had to find ways to cut expenses and to bring in external dollars. A decision was taken about five years ago to offer consulting services to the broader community. The library, anticipating problems with licensed content being shared with external clients, developed a policy which specifically prohibited this activity. The consulting center was quite successful and the director hired several graduate and doctoral students to work with the firms who contracted with the consulting center. The center also hired a few alumni to work there.

Over the past 2 years, the library uncovered a number of incidents in which materials from the databases were printed, compiled, and nicely bound by the consulting center. These compilations were prepared for and distributed to outside clients. These activities were strictly against policy. The director of the center was called on the carpet twice in front of the dean and the university president and both times she repeatedly promised that she would make sure it would not happen again. The problem persisted.

The library learned more about the ways in which the materials were gathered. Some of the student workers were assigned to "help" with research for clients. Students had access to all the materials and asking the librarian for help on a research project was not unusual. It was not unusual to be asked to print out all the research — professors asked students to do this all the time — so the students made the copies and gave them to the staffer in charge of the project.

Sometimes staffers came to the library for help, too. They had clearly been coached in what to say at the library. If the librarians inquired about the project, the response was some variation of "Oh, just a personal interest of mine, not work-related." It was difficult for the library to do anything but help with the research because anyone who worked at the Polytech had library privileges. Only students and faculty had remote-access privileges. This week, a librarian discovered that staffers were sharing an ID which gave them remote access. The dean was at a loss — the director was either asleep on the job or complicit.

QUESTIONS TO CONSIDER

1. What options does the dean have to stop this unethical behavior?
2. Would it be ethical to revoke library privileges of everyone who works at the center? Do not forget that students work there, too.
3. What are the potential consequences of making public accusations of copyright infringement?

CASE #4.21

The Recording Industry Association of America (RIAA) had aggressively pursued pirates for the past several years: teenagers, college students, and anyone else who downloaded music without purchasing it first. There was much debate about the degree to which piracy had affected the bottom line for the content industries — music, television, film, etc. Many universities and colleges were proactive and changed the Internet policies in order to avoid lawsuits for secondary infringement. Carol Davis, an academic librarian, was aware of the piracy issue. She helped craft the Internet policy for her university. Recently, her university was approached by the RIAA and the MPAA to conduct research on students' behavior relating to downloading music and movies; by understanding behavior, they claimed, they could be more proactive in preventing it and therefore avoid litigation. The administration thought this would be an excellent project, but Carol had her doubts. The RIAA had sued several thousand people for copyright infringement and Carol suspected this "research" was another way of identifying downloaders.

QUESTIONS TO CONSIDER

1. Is it reasonable to have doubts about this project?
2. How would the students feel about this research?
3. Research the Safe Harbor clause for universities.
4. What research ethics issues are raised by this case?

CASE #4.22

The relationship between authors and peer-reviewed journals is both cooperative and adversarial. Without the journal, the author has no place to publish his or her work. Without the author's work, the journal has nothing to publish. Ultimately, these two parties must determine which rights the author retains and which rights the publisher holds. The nature of peer-reviewed journals is such that the information contained in each issue affects decisions about courses of action and the finding of solutions to problems. The role of the peer-reviewed journal is fundamental in clinical research trials, especially trials relating to the practice of medicine — efficacy of treatment, standards of care and so forth.

Historically, this kind of research was conducted in academic settings or teaching hospitals and is an increasingly ultra-expensive, time-consuming endeavor complicated by rules governing the treatment of human subjects and more. As costs continue to rise, the response in the market is the emergence of private, nonacademic research centers that are more economical and provide faster results. Neutral, academic researchers do not design the trials conducted by these research centers; rather, the firms seeking approval of their product — i.e., a new drug therapy — are the designers. These firms, as a condition of funding, contractually establish the parameters of the investigation and they make decisions on whether to publish the findings. In these situations, independent researchers are generally unable to review the study's design. The contracts also prohibit access to the raw data; thus, independent review of analysis or checks of validity and reliability checks are impossible.

The publishers of peer-reviewed journals have serious concerns because the contractual obligations and limitations impede the usual process by which research is vetted. They are also concerned about how the research findings are used to advertise the product to the general public. The publishers of these journals have added their own contractual requirements about the autonomy of the researcher and having access to the raw data, methodologies, and so forth. These additional requirements are necessary to facilitate rigorous pre-publication review to which academic researchers must adhere.

QUESTIONS TO CONSIDER

1. Is there an underlying weakness in our intellectual property laws, which has necessitated access to data as a condition of publication?
2. Is the exchange of "rights" for publication sustainable? Ethical?
3. Identify and discuss each party's agenda. In what ways are these agendas self-serving and in what ways are these agendas benefiting all?
4. Is it ethical to use research findings as marketing tools?
5. How are libraries and information centers implicated in this scenario?

CASE #4.23

Compensation for intellectual property has often been a contentious issue between authors and publishers; new mediums only add more tension. A leading case in the digital arena is *New York Times v. Tasini*, decided in 2001. This dispute was between freelance authors and newspaper publishers over whether or not freelancers should receive additional compensation for articles reprinted in electronic databases without the freelancers' knowledge or permission. These electronic versions were not included in the original agreements between the parties because digital formats did not exist or were simply too new to be a viable alternative. The *Tasini* court found in favor of the reporters. An unfortunate unintended consequence of this ruling was the removal of thousands and thousands of unauthorized articles by the publishers, leaving libraries with gaping holes in electronic newspaper collections or CDs containing illegal copies of freelancers' work.

In June 2007, the court settled another major case dating back to 1997. In this situation, freelance authors whose work appeared in *National Geographic* sued the magazine when it made back issues of the magazine available on CDs. This court found in favor of *National Geographic*, comparing digital versions of back issues to microfiche versions of back issues commonly found in libraries. Publishers do not compensate freelancers for works reprinted in the microfiche format and similarly should not compensate freelancers for back issues in the CD-ROM format. This decision opened the door for previously hesitant publishers to release back issues of magazines and journals in the popular DVD format. Notably, the circumstances of the *Tasini* case and the *Greenberg v. National Geographic* case are considerably different according to briefs filed by a number of library associations. These differences warrant careful analysis.

QUESTIONS TO CONSIDER

1. Review the ALA's amicus (friend of the court) briefs for both cases. Is the ALA consistent?
2. Clearly, the tensions between publishers and authors have a negative impact on libraries and their patrons. Is it wise for the ALA and other associations to choose sides in these compensation disputes?
3. If you were an author, how would you respond to these cases? Is it different from a librarian's perspective?

CASE #4.24

Carrie and Jamie had been friends since their college days. Both were librarians: Carrie worked for a law firm and Jamie for an academic library. Jamie was telling Carrie all about their three new databases. Jamie was very excited and had been talking for the last 10 minutes. She realized that Carrie seemed distracted. She asked what was on Carrie's mind. "Since you asked, I will tell you. It is really great that you are able to have so many nice resources for your students and faculty, but you never seem to think about who is paying for those steep discounts. I can promise you, it isn't the publisher. It is law firms, small and big companies, anyone who needs access to high-quality information. You know as well as I do that the Internet doesn't have everything. There are plenty of electronic sources that I would like to have, not to mention all those uses like posting persistent links or emailing links to other people. Just last week, you were teasing me about my library being in the dark ages because we still subscribe to so much print. It is because uses that are fair uses for you add up for us — we either pay more in licensing or permission." "Wow! I never think about that — I'm always just glad to get a good deal." "I'm sorry," says Carrie, "I shouldn't have been so defensive. At least my firm can afford several nice databases. I feel really sorry for some of the smaller firms and libraries — I don't know how they manage."

QUESTIONS TO CONSIDER

1. As a profession, are we advocating laws which help some kinds of libraries to the detriment of other kinds of libraries? If we are, can we argue that the benefits outweigh the harm?
2. As a profession, should we be doing more to address the consequences of the commoditization of information?
3. A major form of the commoditization of information revolves around conglomeration. Discuss the impact of conglomeration on intellectual property and intellectual freedom.

CASE #4.25

One of the librarians at your university was talking about a recent class she had taught. She was very excited because the students had really liked the video clip she had included in the presentation. You joined in the conversation — you had your first instruction session in a week, so you wanted to find out the details.

After some discussion about the assignment and which databases she had recommended, the conversation came back around to the video clip. You thought that you should include some multimedia elements in your class session. You asked where the librarian found the clip. She answered in an off-hand, matter-of-fact way, "Oh, I found it on the Internet, on one of those huge video sites — you know, the ones with 9 million clips." You were very surprised to hear this and you said, "I thought those sites have trouble with copyright infringement. Aren't you worried that we are giving the students the wrong message if we use those clips?" The other librarian said, "I hadn't really thought about it that way. I'm not too worried about it. I was using it in an educational setting and I only used a minute or two, so I think it will be okay under fair use." She noticed that you looked very concerned. She followed this up with, "I'm pretty sure that the site has permission to distribute the clips. The site is free, but there was a lot of advertising. I'm sure the advertising helps pay for all those royalties." You started to disagree, but you weren't sure what to say. You didn't remember anything like this covered in the library's copyright policy. With a quiet sigh, you said, "I guess it is another one of those 'it depends' kind of situations."

QUESTIONS TO CONSIDER

1. What legal and ethical issues are raised by this exchange?
2. Are the librarians sending the wrong message to the students or are they trying to use the media with which their students most identify?
3. Review the educational fair use guidelines for assistance in this case. Is it an "It depends on the situation" situation?

REFERENCES

Crews, K. D. (2006). *Copyright Law for Librarians and Educators: Creative Strategies and Practical Solutions* (2nd ed.). Chicago: American Library Association.

Higher Education Amendments of 2007. S 1642 ES, 110th Cong. 2007.

Library of Congress, Section 108 Study Group. Retrieved August 2, 2007, from http://www.loc.gov/section108/.

Lipinski, T. A. (2004). *Copyright Law and the Distance Education Classroom (Working Within the Information Infrastructure)*. Lanham, MD: Scarecrow Press.

Lipinski, T. A. (2008). *The Librarian's Legal Companion for Buying and Licensing Information Resources*. New York: Neal Schuman Publishers, Inc. [Forthcoming].

Minow, M., & Lipinski, T. A. (2003). *The Library's Legal Answer Book*. Chicago: ALA Editions.

Russell, C. (Ed.). (2004). *Complete Copyright: An Everyday Guide for Librarians*. Chicago: American Library Association.

United States Copyright Office. *Copyright Law*. Retrieved August 13, 2007, from http://www.copyright.gov/title17/.

U.S. House of Representatives Committee on Science and Technology (2007). *Hearing Charter: The Role of Technology in Reducing Illegal Filesharing: A University Perspective*. Retrieved August 3, 2007, from http://democrats.science.house.gov/Media/File/Commdocs/hearings/2007/full/05june/hearing_charter.pdf.

World Intellectual Property Organization. *Collection of Electronic Access Laws*. Retrieved August 26, 2007, from http://www.wipo.int/clea/en/index.jsp.

World Intellectual Property Organization. *Collective Management of Copyright and Related Rights*. Retrieved August 26, 2007, from http://www.wipo.int/freepublications/en/copyright/450/wipo_pub_l450cm.pdf.

CHAPTER 5

Professional Ethics

Professional obligations are necessarily moral obligations.
— *Michael Davis*

This chapter deals with the large domain of professional ethics. Professional ethics, as Spinello and Tavani describe, is a broad area of "applied ethics issues involving the conduct of professionals working in a particular field, such as law, medicine, or computing" (2004, p. 602). Professional ethics in the LIS field is a vast realm and an increasingly complicated realm. Such issues as contingent or part-time worker models, anti–union mentalities, privatization of services, workplace speech, workplace harassment, support of librarian colleagues in war-torn countries, and conflicts of interest — in addition to our daily battles over censorship, privacy, and copyright concerns — feed into an often fragmented notion of the LIS professional.

As the profession itself grows in complexity, our professional ethics do as well. We can, of course, make the argument that all of the discussions presented throughout have to do with professional ethics. It is, certainly, a professional ethics issue to protect our clients' privacy. It is our professional responsibility to understand and work within the environment of intellectual property laws and ethics. We strive daily to protect intellectual freedom for all. We've explored these discretely, insofar as possible, and now the cases presented in this chapter will allow us to explore the implications and issues surrounding the role of librarians and information professionals as *professionals*.

Generally, a professional is considered an expert and capable of making informed decisions. Professionals are autonomous agents who "exercise their autonomous judgment in their work because of their expertise" (Spinello, 1997, p. 47). As Latham (2002) describes, "professionals are persons who employ their authority as experts in an unending mediation between individual private interests and collective public interests." Moreover, the decisions a professional makes and the work of a professional affects large numbers of people — our patrons, our stakeholders, our societies. This clearly differentiates professionals from lay persons. In other terms, as Davis (1988, p. 343) described, "professionalism includes a commitment to benefiting others beyond what ordinary morality requires." A professional librarian, for instance, makes collection development decisions for specific reasons. We enter the collection development process with an educated eye, a trained eye. We understand the difference between selection and censorship. We understand our community and we should know that if our collection offends no one, we have probably done something wrong in our professional judgment. We think differently than a parent does, for instance, where banning books or selecting a "controversial" resource is concerned — and, sometimes, this is highly problematic. As professionals, we must consider our community's values and we must understand our profession's values, while realizing the two may be at odds. A professional negotiates these odds.

It is critical for LIS professionals to have the foundations from which to make reasoned decisions. Professional ethics supports such decision-making and forces us to understand our roles as members of a profession and as members of a larger society. We encourage readers to review the decision-making processes presented in our introduction, as they enable this critical, reflective approach to making decisions in and for our profession. Other professional disciplines — such as medicine, law, social work, nursing, computer science, and education, among others — have large bodies of literature on professional ethics, while discussions of professional ethics in LIS are fairly limited. Notably, Koehler (2003), Shachaf (2005), and Winston (2005) have made recent contributions to this realm of the LIS literature.

LIS programs should look to push the discourse of professional ethics beyond the current boundaries and into these deeper discussions. For instance, Iacovina (2002) has suggested that "academics should be role models for their students.... The teacher-scholar should be the conscience of the profession. Responsibility to conserve the traditions and history of the profession and contribute to its development are core duties of the academic." Moreover, while we can consider codes of ethics and library bills of rights as *part* of our formal ethics training, they should not be the sum of our professional ethics education. Fallis (2007), too, has recently argued for required and meaningful information ethics courses as part of an LIS education, noting "there is frequently too little emphasis on theory in information ethics courses in library science programs" (2007, p. 27).

Of course, codes of ethics, as we presented in Chapter One, have received both praise and criticisms over time. Some have contended that codes of professional conduct are "undesirable" because they are useful only to persons who, lacking decent character, wish to pretend they had one (Baker, 1999). The Center for the Study of Ethics in the Professions states, "Codes of ethics are controversial documents. Some writers have suggested that codes of professional ethics are pointless and unnecessary. Many others believe that codes are useful and important, but disagree about why" (IIT, 2007). Overall, codes of ethics across disciplines share a core commonality, as Mason (1992) described:

> Key ethical principles vary little across different professions. Codes of ethics usually provide guidance on: responsible professional behavior, competence in execution of duties, adherence to moral and legal standards, standards for making public statements, preservation of confidentiality, interest in welfare of the customer, and the development and maintenance of professional knowledge.

And, as Edson (1997) found, there are fundamental problems within codes that span disciplinary boundaries:

1. lack of understanding of the code by the general membership of the profession, therefore minimal endorsement,
2. no method for enforcement of the code,
3. code too general to provide sufficient direction, and
4. code out of date and the mechanism for revision is too cumbersome [p. 120].

Nevertheless, codes of ethics are a foundation, a framework from which we consider professional decisions that are reasonable and equitable, but, again, they are not the whole of professional ethics. Examining local, global, and social issues, adapting a critical stance, and acting responsibility are steps in the right direction for any profession. As members of a profession, we work towards a greater good and sometimes this forces us to reconsider our own personal value system and personal beliefs. How we choose to reconcile conflicting beliefs is a large discussion in professional ethics within LIS and in other professional discourses. Clashes around values arise in any and every profession. The information field has faced great challenges in recent years in particular, through, most readily, technologies, law, and politics, as we have explored in previous chapters.

While information professionals understand the philosophical underpinnings of their professional ethics, the people who are affected by our choices may not. Users, patrons, administrators, and many other stakeholders are often unaware of the professional ethics that guide our policy decisions and day-to-day operations. We may be accused of helping terrorists because we endeavor to protect user privacy or that we approve of pornography or fail to protect children from harmful materials because, as professionals, we choose not to censor or label works. As difficult as it may be to reconcile conflicting personal beliefs and professional responsibilities, defending our policies when confronted with concerned parents or an aggressive town council may prove even more difficult. Working toward the "greater good" may be lost on a society reeling from an incident like 9/11 or a small town shocked by the arrest of a "respected figure" caught with child pornography downloaded at the library.

Externalities complicate things further. In LIS, we have multiple stakeholders, including paraprofessionals, professional librarians and information workers, administrators, LIS faculty and educators, professional associations, and vendors, while other influences include our patrons, taxpayers, boards, and politicians. These stakeholders cross boundaries, too, making clear delineations often difficult. Library policies and practices — from collection development to diversity of staff to how we treat the disenfranchised in our local community, the homeless, the mentally ill, or the functionally illiterate parent seeking books for his or her children — should align with our profession code of ethics. However, what our professional or personal code of ethics tells us about how we should manage the homeless who come into our libraries may not align with the local statutes. Opening our doors to illegal immigrants may not be popular in a small border town. What we see as censorship, others see as guidance for parents or protection of small children. These differences in perspective do exist even among those who ascribe to the ALA, or other professional, codes of ethics. Libraries and information centers do not exist in a vacuum and we must consider other viewpoints or local standards of behavior and respond to the expectations of our funding sources, whether those sources are taxpayers or private corporations. Again, the unending mediation.

Our professional organizations may alienate the very users whose rights they aim to protect. Or their actions may have unintended consequences. Institutional obligations may supersede the ethical practices to which we subscribe; further, we may not have the authority to change laws, rules, policies, or abilities to override another's course of action. But we must mediate those externalities. As professionals, our actions are significant. How we respond to the concerned parents or aggressive town council means everything — locally and globally. As professionals, what we say and do has impact. Our actions must be carefully considered as part of a professional discourse, which contributes to the larger social discourse. One challenge begets another, which begets another. Standing strong in the face of adversity requires commitment.

It is notable that the ALA has shown commitment through its involvement in recent high-profile legal cases in the United States, including the Supreme Court's consideration of the Children's Internet Protection Act (CIPA), the DMCA, and the PATRIOT Act. Such prominent individuals as Judith Krug, of the ALA's Office for Intellectual Freedom, and Nancy Kranich, past president of ALA, have been vocal legislative advocates for the profession and its values. But, in fairness, there are professionals in our field who have found the ALA lacking in its advocacy; some claim the Office for Intellectual Freedom has bowed, has capitulated (see safelibraries.org, for instance). Such debate is indeed healthy for the profession, as it forces us to evaluate our professional values and to reconsider our visions or our codes of ethics. Reflection by and within a profession shows maturity and allows for growth.

Pemberton (1998, p. 76) explains that "professional communities ... have many responsibilities for ethical behavior that transcend the lower order technical concerns of their work. Ethics ... lies in the domain of morality rather than in the ordinary sphere of technical competence." While both information professionals *and* the general public have shown increasingly more sophisticated technical competence in information work and computing, the same cannot be said of a deep understanding around the ethics of information and computing use. Many have experienced our patrons entering our facilities with solid competence in searching and retrieval, for instance, but their moral compasses around such issues as peer-to-peer file sharing and copyright laws may be remiss. We as professionals may be remiss as well. Recall that currently, ethics courses are not required in LIS programs; we may well know the workings of file sharing on a technical level, but may be unprepared to address the ethical implications of such technologies. Thus, fundamental questions need to be considered in a systematic way, through LIS education in particular: What kinds of responsibilities do library and information professionals have?

How must such professionals think critically and act responsibly, with the roles they hold? We agree with Livio Iacovino (2002) who asserts,

> Professionals can marry a number of the principles enunciated in ethical theories to professional ethics. This includes cultivating virtues of integrity and honesty, balancing the rights of and the duties to the client, to society and to fellow professionals, as well as consideration of the "other person" as a fellow human being. Through role models, education and professional discussion, ethics should become an essential part of professional best practice of all information professionals.

As stewards of information, library and information professionals are indeed instrumental in the facilitation of knowledge and thus power. We must accept this theoretically and practically — as professionals, we must embrace our responsibility and act from it, proactively, not reactively. From supporting intellectual freedom to arguing for balance in our intellectual property laws to fighting for basic human rights, librarians have historically been — and continue to be, well into this twenty-first century — a powerful and significant force in and for all societies. Indeed, as Samek asserts, "library and information workers play an important role in preserving and supporting the ideals of tolerance, democracy, human rights, and collective memory" (2007, p. 4). Samek's work in particular shows this connection between theory and practice, as it documents the trials and tribulations of information workers across the world, demonstrating how their actions and ideals promote human rights; librarians and information workers, as Samek reminds us, *are* powerful and must use this power responsibly.

Professional Ethics: Cases

CASE #5.1

In 1997, Riverside County, California, became the first county in the nation the privatize its library operations. Maryland-based Library Systems and Services, Inc. (LSSI) is paid $5.3 million annually for a 1-year renewable contract to run the county's 25-branch, 85-year-old library system. LSSI is a subsidiary of the publisher Follett Corporation and offers cataloging, purchasing, automation, and other services for libraries nationwide, including the Library of Congress, the Boston Public Library, and several federal agencies.

Riverside County's library system was previously run by the city of Riverside, but, due to budget cutbacks, the city voted to drop the contract. The county decided to offer a new contract in a competition open to both public and private bidders. LSSI was the only private-sector bidder, competing against the Riverside County Office of Education and the San Bernardino County Library District.

Under the new contract, LSSI increased library hours by 25 percent and increased the annual book purchasing budget from $144,000 to $180,000. The company planned on investing $200,000 of its own money to improve library services once a countywide assessment of library needs was completed. Other specific improvements would include more Internet terminals at county libraries and a better phone-up library reference service. To maintain oversight of the library operations, Riverside County appointed its own county librarian, Gary Christmas, to work with LSSI. All current library employees were offered employment at their current salaries and some branches even hired more employees. County officials said that LSSI could do more with less money because it was more efficient and had lower overhead. The city of Riverside took a 10 percent administration fee off the top of all library funding, whereas LSSI generated its profits by keeping its costs lower than the $5.3 million contract payment.

(Note: This case reprinted with permission of the Reason Foundation, www.reason. org; http://www.privatization.org/database/policyissues/libraries_local.html)

QUESTIONS TO CONSIDER

1. What are the ethical implications of privatized public library services?
2. Is there a conflict of interest, given Follette's role in library business?
3. Of what potential future ethical issues should the appointed county librarian be cautious?

CASE #5.2

Allenville was a mining town. Its population was approximately 20,000 people, who depended on coal for their livelihood. The day before, there was a major collapse inside of the mine and 50 to 60 miners were trapped. Many people were at the mine, waiting for news. Others were at home, listening to the radio or watching the tragedy unfold on television. The public library was nearly empty. With so few patrons, the librarians and staff talked about the trapped miners. One of the librarians believed that the library should quickly create a web page with current news and information about the situation. Some of others disagreed, but for different reasons. Most thought this would be a waste of time and effort because everyone was at the mine or at home watching or listening to the news.

One of the librarians raised a different concern. She believed that they should not post anything about the situation until the miners were rescued and the investigation into the cause of the collapse completed. The other librarians simultaneously asked her why. She responded, "This town depends on mining for everything and so do we. I think it would be a big mistake to start posting the media's opinion about what is happening here, especially the stories about the mine being unsafe and that the owners knew this and did nothing. Imagine what the mining company might have to say about us posting things that were false. The politics could get ugly." The librarian who suggested the web page spoke up again. "I don't know if our patrons will look to us to provide information about this or not. We should be prepared anyway. This is our community, too." One of the staffers added, "I don't think it is our job to provide news as it happens."

QUESTIONS TO CONSIDER

1. Do libraries have an obligation to provide news and information on catastrophic or tragic events as they are occurring or immediately afterward?
2. What should our response, as information professionals, be to sensationalism in the media?
3. Consider the comment about the politics getting ugly. Do libraries in small towns and cities need to be careful about not offending major employers in their locales? At what risk?
4. Should there be a more formalized professional response to assisting our peer libraries in the face of disaster? Think of Hurricane Katrina and its impact on libraries, for instance.

(Note: The American Library Association provides resources for disaster preparedness. Please see *Disaster Preparedness* (2006). Retrieved on September 17, 2007, from http://www.ala.org/ala/washoff/woissues/disasterpreparedness/distrprep.cfm.)

CASE #5.3

The public library in Trenton, an affluent suburb, had a new director. She was not a librarian, but came from a business background. She saw an opportunity to change the existing structure of the library and, in doing so, maximize efficiency while cutting her budget considerably; like many businesses do to save money, the director saw great potential in eliminating benefits from the personnel budget to save thousands of dollars. She would do this by reducing the number of full-time, professional librarians and realigning the departmental structures. Such realignment would affect the number of unionized librarians. Instead of having a professional librarian as head of each department, she would have one assistant director who would oversee each of the departments and that person would oversee the part-time staff who would work in each area. Only the assistant librarian would then report to the director. In sum, three full-time librarians were eliminated from the staff, while four others were reduced to 19-hour-per-week positions — positions without benefits. There were other changes: the director would not be included in the weekend reference rotation, the library would close by 2:00 P.M. on Saturdays and would be closed on Sundays, and all new release/popular entertainment videos would no longer circulate for free but would cost $1.00. The library board, comprised of high-profile community members, including, among others, a CEO of a local corporation, saw these as positive steps to a "profitable library." The board and the director announced the changes to the public, asserting that such restructuring would contribute to a better collection overall.

QUESTIONS TO CONSIDER

1. What are the professional ethics issues involved in such corporate business models in libraries?

2. What roles should library boards have in the day-to-day operations of libraries?
3. Research the composition of your local public library board. Are any members professional librarians or educators? Should they be?
4. What roles can and should unions play in library work?
5. Discuss the changes made by the director in this case and their ethical implications.

CASE #5.4

The Edwardton Archives, a public resource, received a large collection of personal papers from a prominent local family, the Smiths. Their policy was to accept donations after a careful review process, if they were in fitting with the Archives' mission and if they added substantial merit to the collection. In this case, the papers were important and would prove valuable for researchers interested in the family and their contributions to the city over the years. The family also offered to make a substantial financial donation over time. There was one condition, however. Ms. Smith wanted to have a permanent seat on the Board of Trustees of the Archives, a governing body that made budgetary and personnel decisions. She felt this was only fair and did not see any problems with her request. The archivist was concerned, as they had never made such an agreement before, and was concerned that conflicts of interest could easily arise.

QUESTIONS TO CONSIDER
1. Discuss the potential conflict of interest in this case. Is it an ethical issue?
2. How should the archivist respond to this request?
3. Review the SAA Code of Ethics. Does it help resolve this case? How?

CASE #5.5

The staff at the art museum library, a non-profit entity, dealt with patrons and donors quite frequently. With a restricted budget and given the high costs of acquiring art books, donations were common. The staff, however, had to be quite careful when dealing with two significant questions: How much they thought a particular book or piece of artwork was worth and if they had auction catalogs or price databases that could tell a patron how much theirs was worth. The latter was usually followed by "I don't know what to look for; can you help or do this for me?" The staff assembled a list of appraisers, though appraisers charge a fee for their work, something the library staff did not, and legally could not, do. The staff had a common response to these sorts of inquiries: The staff was not experienced nor qualified in assessing fiscal value and members of the organization were prohibited from suggesting value because they were in the business of acquiring material for the collection.

One patron, who was an important donor, however, became problematic. He wanted to know the value of some materials before his donation would be made. He approached different staff members, played one person's words against the others, implying it was acceptable to tell him since he would not hold any one of them individually responsible for prices that were quoted. Finally, once all of the staff had refused to quote the value for the patron, he called and requested the value for insurance purposes. The librarian was now nervous. They frequently reviewed insurance values, but they were quite sure this patron was insincere in this request, given his past behavior. Providing such information, as an appraisal, the librarian knew, could indeed threaten their non–profit and legal status.

QUESTIONS TO CONSIDER

1. How should the librarian respond to such a patron's requests?
2. How are professional ethics at risk in this case?
3. What conflicts of interest can arise specifically in art museum libraries?
4. Discuss the various ethical obligations in this case: obligations to the organization, to the patron, to the profession.
5. How can the information professions encourage individuals to share memorabilia or valuable books for the greater good, instead of being concerned with the profit aspect of such resources?

CASE #5.6

Johnsonville Library School, like many other academic programs, was facing severe budget cuts from the state and a hiring freeze on full-time, tenure–track faculty had been imposed. The school began hiring many adjunct instructors and assistants, who worked on a semester-to-semester basis, with no contract, minimal pay, and no benefits. This is known as a "contingent worker" model and many universities rely heavily on it, as it saves money and allows more classes to be offered, as full-time faculty become more involved in research grants and outside consulting.

Students in the program were conflicted. On the one hand, they got to take coursework from practicing professionals or other instructors whose only responsibility was to teach. On the other hand, they were paying high tuition dollars to work with esteemed faculty, who were considered experts in the field. But these adjuncts were often working multiple jobs at various institutions, making their availability outside of class difficult. It also raised questions around the coherence of the program, as different instructors were teaching courses all the time. The students decided to write a letter opposing the long-term use of contingent instructors and had a talk with the program director about their concerns.

QUESTIONS TO CONSIDER

1. What are the ethical issues involved in the contingent-worker model?
2. What role should the accrediting bodies play in this debate?

3. Debate the pros and cons of this situation. How would you as a student, as an adjunct, or as a full-time faculty member respond to the debate?
4. Discuss the implications of the contingent-worker model on the "signature pedagogy" of the profession.

CASE #5.7

The Legislative Research Bureau Library was part of the Common Council-City Clerk's Office. The library and its services were available to all city employees for work-related purposes, as it was a special government library. A number of years ago, one of the city officials, who was also an amateur playwright, made information requests of the library staff that were obviously related to this activity. The requests were time consuming and completely unrelated to the true mission of the library. The librarians made an effort to deflect these requests and suggested that he contact the public library. The library manager, however, felt that the staff should handle them, much to the dismay of the staff, who resisted, but typically ended up researching the requests. Notably, the Common Council had oversight of the city budget and this particular official sat on the Finance and Personnel Committee. Therefore, the manager felt it would be safer for the library, fiscally speaking, to comply with the requests. The staff argued that not only was this official using his time at the city to work on his hobby, but he was also taking their time and using resources and services inappropriately.

QUESTIONS TO CONSIDER

1. What are the unique conflicts of interest involved in this case?
2. What would an appropriate course of action be for the library manager?
3. What special ethical issues face special libraries and information centers?

CASE #5.8

Karen, the youth services librarian at the public library, had been in her position for fifteen years and felt that she knew her young patrons well. She watched many of them grow, from their infancy and lapsit programs into young adults, when they got MySpace accounts and read Judy Blume. One young patron had been a vibrant girl and spent many hours in the library. Karen noticed that recently this girl had changed, becoming more and more introverted. She spent more time alone, reading in the library, and less time socializing with her friends. Her appearance worried Karen, as she was losing weight and looked pale. Karen noticed that the young girl was reading web sites that offered "advice" on how to lose weight, sites that promoted strategies how to hide food from one's parents and how to force oneself to vomit. Karen knew these sites as "pro-anas," pro-anorexia sites. They were often missed by the library's filtering software. Karen felt professionally obligated to talk to the girl's parents, but also wanted to keep the trust she had with the girl and wanted to protect her rights.

QUESTIONS TO CONSIDER

1. What is a professional librarian's role in protecting minors from harmful materials?
2. Discuss the conflict the librarian is experiencing.
3. Should the librarian speak to the parents?
4. How should the profession respond to "harmful" sites such as pro-anas or self–mutilation sites?

CASE #5.9

Information professionals, especially librarians, have a lot to cope with as far as what the "library of the future" will be like. Stories circulate declaring that librarians are a dying breed and are being rapidly replaced by Internet search engines like Google. Declaring that librarians are at death's door might be a bit premature. Librarians certainly recognize that the roles of librarians and libraries are no longer the constant they once were or at least what we imagine they once were. Some librarians embrace the changes. They do not worry unduly about keywords, folksonomies, and the eventuality of replacing MARC with the Dublin Core or another metadata scheme. Other librarians hold tightly to the print world despite all of the technological innovations, from the digitization of core works to online reference with patrons half a world away to wiki-driven book discussions. Most librarians fall somewhere along this continuum. Obviously, there is going to be the occasional clash of ideals, especially when new libraries are built or old ones refurbished. How the money is best spent is an important question for librarians and all the other stakeholders to answer. Hopefully, what's best for the community will arise out of the ensuing debates even if the debates are heated.

But what happens when the disagreement becomes extreme — creating factions among librarians or between librarians and administrations, management, governing boards, etc.? What happens if this disagreement becomes ugly in a public way? For instance, the administration in a major public library approved the necessary funds to revamp youth services and resources. The plans included, among other things, a substantial increase the number of DVDs available, a plasma television in the teen room, and an additional 10 computers with every bell and whistle imaginable for enjoying multimedia. The plan did not, however, include any new funds for books. This was a major disappointment for several librarians who were already unhappy about cuts to the book budget over the last several years. This group of librarians thought the overall plan flies in the face of what the library should be and they decided to circulate a petition for a vote of no-confidence in the library's administration. It didn't take long for the newspaper to find out what is going on and headlines such as "Luddite Librarians Standing up for Books" hit the papers.

QUESTIONS TO CONSIDER

1. Are the librarians who are circulating the petition acting in the best interest of their patrons and community?
2. Is there a broader problem within the library profession that fuels these kinds of crises?
3. Consider all of the stakeholders in this case. Role-play these various perspectives.

CASE #5.10

The school media center received a gift of $500,000, with the stipulation that the center be renamed the Time-Harner Media Center. The center would, in addition, receive new computers and high-speed access to the Internet, something the school media center could use desperately. The district offices would also subscribe to Time-Harner's digital phone and business packages for a reduced rate and children would be able to get additional resources if their parents signed up for Time-Harner's services. The principal saw it as a win-win situation: "The school and parents get what they need and Time-Harner gets a little extra business." Some parents, however, were concerned that their kids were exposed to such intense marketing and consumerist practices at such early ages. The librarian was torn, as she wanted the new resources but also saw the concerns of the parents.

QUESTIONS TO CONSIDER

1. Discuss the implications of naming rights used in primary or secondary schools.
2. Should a library have a corporate sponsor?
3. How have libraries faced or embraced commercialism and marketing?
4. What potential impact could a corporate sponsor have on intellectual freedom and other basic informational rights?

CASE #5.11

Like many libraries, the Woodland Public Library, which served a city of about 200,000 people, emulated the look and feel of some of the major bookstores. They added a coffee shop, changed the furniture, and painted the walls for ambiance. One of the changes was the way books were displayed. Instead of the traditional system with spines out, many of the books were placed with covers out. This change required significantly more space for each book. With space at premium, the library made the decision to reduce its print collection, as e-books were readily available. Rather than discard the books, the local friends of the library organized a huge used book sale. The sale was highly successful and generated about $10,000. This money was used to purchase a pair of leather couches, coffee tables, reading lamps, a multimedia entertainment center, and other furnishings for the staff lounge.

QUESTIONS TO CONSIDER

1. Is this an ethical use of the funds?
2. What ethical issues do you see arising from the new display arrangement?

CASE #5.12

Joe was an academic librarian at a private, Catholic university. The university was very good to its employees, thanks to a large donor-supported foundation, and provided all of the faculty and library staff with a professional development stipend. They could use it as they wanted: for books, conferences, memberships, and the like. Joe joined the ALA and, with his membership, had access to his choice of roundtables. He selected the ALA's GLBT Roundtable (GLBTRT), as he was a gay man, though he kept his personal life private while at work. He saw the importance of this roundtable, which highlighted important GLBT literature every year and provided a safe environment for professionals of these orientations. At a staff meeting, Joe mentioned the upcoming roundtable meeting he would be attending and voiced his excitement at the possibility of learning about more "alternative" literature for the library. He expressed hope for networking with professionals who could provide suggestions for creating better environments for GLBT patrons, thinking people would be supportive of his professional endeavors. There were a few comments that this was a "Catholic university" and the presence of such materials was questionable, but no one came outright and said he could not join the roundtable, nor did any disagree with Joe's intentions. But a few weeks later, Joe received a memo from the university president, who expressed her concerns about using the staff development money to explore this "personal life preference." The memo stated, "While the university is supportive of its people, we do not want our donors and our church to think we are actively supporting homosexuality." Joe was astonished at the open level of discrimination and sought legal counsel.

QUESTIONS TO CONSIDER

1. What is the professional value of such roundtables as the GLBT?
2. Consider James Cooke's questions from his "Gay and Lesbian Librarians and the 'Need' for GLBT Library Organizations," *Journal of Information Ethics*, 14 (2), 32–49: "Are groups such as the GLBTRT necessary? What purpose(s) do they serve? Is sexual orientation an issue in the library workplace? Should orientation even be an issue in the workplace? Are GLBT persons feeling threatened at work? What should libraries do with regard to GLBT employees and issues?"

CASE #5.13

Carson was the branch director at one of the three libraries in a system. Recently, he began receiving complaints from his staff about a particular patron because she was very demanding. She wanted answers to her questions right away. She refused to wait and was outright rude to the staff and to other patrons. When the reference staff couldn't find the answers quickly enough, she called them incompetent and threatened to call the director. She then started phoning in reference questions, but got in the habit of hanging up when her calls went into the voice mail system and would continually call until a person answered. Finally, she started demanding that only male staff assist her; in the library, she would stand and wait until Carson or another male staff member arrived and the staff assumed it was her when a caller frequently hung up when female librarians answered the phone.

QUESTIONS TO CONSIDER

1. How should the library handle this situation?
2. Why is this a professional ethics case?
3. Discuss patrons' rights versus staff rights.

CASE #5.14

Betsy confided in one of her colleagues that she was pregnant and would be having the baby later that spring. She was under review for a permanent position at the information center where she was currently under a provisional title and position. She knew that the law prevented discrimination against pregnant women, but was still nervous that she would be overlooked for the permanent position because of it. Betsy assumed her colleague would not tell anyone, as she had expressed her concerns to this colleague and thought she, as another woman, another mother, would understand the potential for discrimination. A few days later, another permanent librarian stopped by Betsy's desk and congratulated her. "Don't worry, you will be fine," she said, and assured her she would not reveal Betsy's pregnancy to the review committee. Betsy was shocked and felt betrayed by her colleague, despite the reassurances.

QUESTIONS TO CONSIDER

1. Did Betsy's colleague violate any laws?
2. What professional values did the colleague violate?
3. Review the ALA's Code of Ethics, principle V: We treat co-workers and other colleagues with respect, fairness and good faith, and advocate conditions of employment that safeguard the rights and welfare of all employees of our institutions. Was this principle violated?
4. If the employee were male and had confided that his wife was pregnant, would your reactions be different and, if so, how?

CASE #5.15

Jane conducted research for a major law firm in a large city. Her role was to locate information for the lawyers in her firm that could be used to help clients resolve their legal problems. Often this required Jane to gather information from companies that were named in disputes. Sometimes Jane needed to obtain information from city, state, or county officials.

One of the most difficult parts of this kind of research was maintaining client confidentiality, which meant Jane had to omit information about who she was when she contacted a particular company or local official. In the past, Jane had never had to outright lie to get the needed information, but this changed the previous week. One of the lawyers had asked Jane to research a local bank and the bank's president. Jane was at a dead end, as the lawyer needed the information right away since the trial was starting in just a few weeks. This information was critical to the firm's case against the bank. Jane was very sympathetic to the client, who has been treated in a deplorable way by the bank in question. The client was one of many bank customers whom the bank has defrauded. Jane wanted to help, but she would have to lie in order to get the information. After wrestling with the problem for a day or two, Jane called the company and led them to believe she was a student working on a project and the bank willingly provided the information to her the same day.

QUESTIONS TO CONSIDER

1. In this circumstance was it okay for Jane to lie? Do the ends justify the means?
2. Discuss this case from various ethical perspectives (utilitarian, deontological, consequentialist, justice-based) to explore different possibilities.
3. The person Jane spoke to at the bank was quite willing to hand over the information to Jane without verifying her story. To what degree is this person legally or ethically responsible if the bank loses its case?

CASE #5.16

Rich was due to graduate from library school, where he was a quiet but solid student. Fellow students were often surprised at his comments before and after class. He said things like "the field is dying" and "librarians will be obsolete soon enough." He was frequently heard saying, "Librarianship is a ridiculous profession." His peers laughed, thinking he was just a cynical type; why would he be completing the degree if he truly felt this way?

Then one of his peers learned of his blog, where he was absolutely vicious and openly hostile in his criticisms of the field, his LIS faculty, and students. Sarah mentioned the blog to her faculty mentor, who read with concern many of the blog postings. Rich was not only disparaging to the field, Professor White thought, he was dangerous. One blog post mentioned how he couldn't wait to get hired into a reference position so he could "suck off the library's resources" and get paid while writing his blog. "These librarians are so clueless, they think I'll be working but little do they know."

Professor White voiced her concerns to the dean and to the school's academic advisor. "How could we as a library school send a person with such a lack of values into the field?" She was told, however, that student privacy was important, that the blog was his personal diary done on his own time and he could say anything he wanted, since it was not an actual threat. Professor White was told not to share this information with fellow faculty, who may still be grading his work or submitting letters of professional reference to potential employers. Professor White was very conflicted. This was her professional responsibility, she thought, to protect others in the field from hiring such a hostile and irresponsible individual.

QUESTIONS TO CONSIDER

1. Should Professor White share Rich's writings with the LIS faculty?
2. Has Rich done anything wrong?
3. What professional responsibility does Professor White have to inform potential employers about Rich's blog and his comments?

CASE #5.17

The special collections of a major university were a well-known repository of "anarchist and radical" papers and materials. In the events following the infamous "Unabomber" capture and arrest, an archivist found herself in an unusual and professionally challenging situation. After communicating with the Unabomber's attorney, some months later, she received a large envelope, full of letters people across the world had written to Kaczynski while he was in prison. The university archives did not, at the time of receipt, have a letter of agreement or any formal deed of gift agreement with Kaczynski, but he had asked the archivist to keep the letters safe, as the prison had a limit on the number of letters he was allowed to keep in his cell. For some time, as the university negotiated the terms of the collection, the archivist kept the materials unopened and protected. Lawyers for both sides were involved in the negotiations, as such issues as media access, privacy, terms of release, and processing the materials took on great complexity. There were fan letters and threats and many were simply letters from people who were "lonely," as Kaczynski described them and as the archivist came to appreciate.

The archivist faced a plethora of ethical and professional challenges: One was third-party privacy. Names of the individuals whom had sent him letters had to be redacted to protect their privacy. Additional information, such as places and personal references, also had to be concealed; thus the processing of the collection was intense. But people's reputations and personal privacy were at stake. There could be no identifying information to connect a letter with an individual. There were concerns that the government could access the materials and consider those people "questionable," given the nature of Kaczynski's crimes.

Moreover, the archivist herself became a target of the media. Since the Unabomber had been overtly critical of the media, they went after her. Her loyalties were questioned; indeed, her professional ethics were questioned. Other donors to the collection were critical; perhaps others decided against a gift.

QUESTIONS TO CONSIDER

1. Discuss the unique ethical challenges facing the archivist in acquiring a collection such as the Unabomber's letters.
2. How is third-party privacy difficult to protect in archival work?
3. When the archivist received the initial package, when the university did not have a deed or contract, did she act responsibly by safeguarding the materials?
4. If a government agent asked for the un–redacted letters, how should the archivist respond?
5. In the face of a media attack on their professional values, what principles should an archivist or librarian discuss to ensure the public understands the roles and responsibilities embodied in the profession?

CASE REFERENCE

Herrada, J. (2003). Letters to the Unabomber. *Archival Issues*, 28(1), 35–46.

CASE #5.18

As in many workplaces, the university's information center staff did not always get along. Two individuals in particular were continually at odds. Toby was a mid–career, tenured academic; Diane was not tenured and would not go through her tenure process for another year. Their disagreements often ran over into staff meetings and into the workplace. Toby often brought their disagreements to a personal level and she was a very vocal and intimidating member of the staff. Many of the newer librarians and library specialists were quite fearful of her. The senior librarians seemed less concerned, often telling the newer staff that Toby's "bark was worse than her bite."

Diane tried as hard as she could to maintain her professionalism; however, it was very difficult. Diane felt her work was solid: She performed very well in her reference capacity, received stellar evaluations, and was a very well-liked colleague, with the exception of Toby. Toby took advantage of Diane's status by using the executive staff meetings as a personal venue to question Diane's performance, while she excused other non–tenured staff's shortcomings. These were "closed-session" meetings. Only tenured individuals could attend and the discussion was private and not to be shared.

When Diane received her annual review, there were some odd comments and Diane approached her mentor about them. "Why would anyone suggest I did not fulfill my outside activities duties? I've done more outside duties than any other non–tenured individ-ual. I do not understand this," Diane lamented. "Well, there was a member of the com-mittee who said you had questionable attendance at meetings," her mentor explained. "And let me guess. It was Toby," replied Diane. "I went to every meeting about which I was informed. The trouble is that Toby conveniently forgot to include me on the elec-tronic distribution list whenever our committee met," Diane vented. "Fortunately, Ann (another librarian) noticed most of the time and forwarded the information to me. Tech-nically, Toby isn't lying, but she sure isn't telling the truth either. Just out of curiosity, does the committee check on everyone's activities attendance?" "Of course, I can't confirm this for you," Diane's mentor responded, "but you might want to consider sending a response to the committee indicating that you disagree with certain comments on your review." Diane asked, "Is this what you would do?"

QUESTIONS TO CONSIDER

1. Toby spoke in private, in a "privileged situation." Could her words still be construed as libel?
2. What are the workplace speech issues in this case?
3. What are the ethical obligations of being a good colleague?
4. How can the power imbalances between tenured and nontenured professionals be resolved in an ethical way?

CASE #5.19

The director in a large, public academic library was a very active member of the library profession. She worked on the state's Library Association, as well as many national and international committees. Such work, while a valuable asset to the profession as a whole, took Director Kline out of the office quite regularly and often at the expense of the library, who paid for her travel out of their operating budget. She felt she was serv-ing her profession and, in doing so, was raising the visibility of her library and its insti-tution. However, Julie, her administrative assistant, started to notice that Director Kline's expense reports were increasing with each trip, trips which were becoming ever more fre-quent. The expense reports had only to be approved by the Director, so there was no one else to notice but Julie. Instead of line-item budgets, Director Kline listed the maximum per diem amounts for each meal. Sometimes, Julie knew, the director had not used these amounts, as when food was provided at the conferences, and was simply taking money out of the budget because she *could*. Julie was concerned about the impropriety of this, but also knew she had no recourse.

QUESTIONS TO CONSIDER

1. How should Julie respond?

2. The thought "Who polices the police?" comes to mind: Must there always be oversight?
3. Do individuals in positions of power have greater ethical responsibilities, by virtue of this power?

CASE #5.20

The librarian at the Pepperton Public Library said hello to a father and two small children, about 7 and 5, when they entered the children's room. This was a nice space for kids, with plenty of couches and pillows and, more importantly, a door, so children could not easily leave. The librarian noticed after a short time that the father had left the children's room; she assumed he was in the restroom or in another area of the library. The policy was to have a parent or guardian with children under 8 in the room at all times, as the children's librarian was quite busy and could not "baby-sit" for patrons.

After about fifteen minutes, the librarian went looking in the library for the father. He was not there. She waited another ten minutes and then made an announcement over the PA system after asking the children for their last name. "Would Mr. Cass please return to the children's area?" There was no response. The older child said, "Daddy told us to wait here and he'd be back soon. He told us to read and relax." After another thirty minutes, the librarian called her director and asked for guidance. "What should we do? Should we call the police?" The director responded, "No, we will wait another hour. Upon his return, we will discuss the matter with him and inform him if he does this again, we will call the police."

QUESTIONS TO CONSIDER

1. Should libraries have explicit policies about leaving children alone?
2. Did the librarian act in the best interests of the children?
3. Were there any privacy violations in asking for Mr. Cass over the PA system?
4. Is this a professional ethics case?

CASE #5.21

The new director of the Westlawn Public Library was a controversial administrator. She frequently sided with the library board over the library staff in matters of personnel, budget, and policies and made no apologies to her staff, many of whom had worked in the library for ten years or more. There were great concerns among the staff about the director's negotiations and the eventual contract she received. Since the library was a public entity, contracts were a matter of public record, so the staff decided to review the contract; but, in this case, the contract was housed at the library, so any requests to see it had to go through the library director's office, as opposed to city hall. When a staff member inquired to see the contract, the director informed him that she would check with the city to see if she was required to release the information and, if so, how much time she had to honor the request. The staff member learned from the city hall that it is up to the library to set a policy, which states how long the library would have to release the contract information. The staff thought they were stuck in a Kafka novel. But, eventually, they gained access to the contract to find some questionable issues: First, the director received a higher salary than what was advertised because she would not be using the city's health care benefits. The contract reflected the argument that that they would either be paying her with the money used to pay the benefits or they could give her a more "appropriate" salary. Second, a clause indicated that if the director could "save" money by a more "judicious collection development policy," she would get a cash bonus at the end of the budget year. Third, the contract contained a clause that she would receive a cash payout if her contract were terminated. The board had considered these options, did not see any legal problems with her requests, and granted her the position with these agreements.

QUESTIONS TO CONSIDER

1. Discuss the ethical issues in this case.
2. Would you be comfortable generalizing the decisions made by the board?
3. What is at stake when core operations of the library are compromised through personal interests?
4. Should the library contracts be a matter of public record? Should the library be the party responsible for holding the contract?

CASE #5.22

When part of a public, state-funded system, libraries (academic, school, or public) face difficult budgetary challenges. When state funding is tight, every dollar is critical. Libraries often show statistics — from numbers of reference questions asked and answered to circulation numbers to hours open — as evidence of their quality and as the basis for justifying their budgetary requests. Beth, the director at the public library, knew this well. And she knew that her requests for additional staff would face criticism if the library's numbers were lower than the previous year. Thus, she informed the head of reference that "transactions" would be counted differently from now on: Questions, responses, and actions, such as going to the stacks or to the computer, would count individually, not as a single transaction. What used to be one transaction would now count as three. Questions such as where the restroom was would now count as a reference transaction, whereas before they did not. The staff were unsure about this new practice, but were assured, "If you want to keep your jobs, and if you want any additional staff, do it this way."

QUESTIONS TO CONSIDER

1. Did the director act unethically by creating this new policy?

2. Do the ends justify the means?
3. Do the staff have any ethical responsibility to report the "accounting" change?

CASE #5.23

Tony and Nancy, two librarians at a public library, talked about work issues with one another frequently. On this occasion, they were discussing the library's web page, which they thought looked dated, with bad color choices and illogical layout. There were so many different fonts that the two of them had renamed the page "the ransom note." But complaining to other staff or administrators was pointless, as the IT department approached usability differently and their priority was on consistency across the pages and branding the library's identity. Unfortunately, the IT staff and the librarians did not always see eye-to-eye on matters of technology.

One afternoon, Tony and Nancy had several humorous and slightly sarcastic exchanges about the web page. Nancy asserted that she was willing to bet that the web pages would flunk if they ran it through one of the ADA test sites. Nancy went back to her desk feeling guilty — she was overtly critical of her colleagues and she was doubting their professional abilities about a very serious matter. But something was nagging at both Tony and Nancy: Was the library's web site truly accessible? They both knew there were legal requirements for accessibility. Tony found it hard to believe that the web page was not ADA compliant; he also knew there were obvious aesthetic issues and he knew the page was hard to navigate. But he also thought about the community the library served — a large population of Spanish–only speakers and many adults with low-literacy skills.

Tony decided that he ought to check into the situation more seriously. The first thing he did was run the website through an ADA online test and discovered that there were a number of problems requiring attention. Tony was concerned — his professional values told him he must address this with the IT staff as well as with the other librarians. But he also wanted to be a friendly colleague and did not want to be seen as a "whistle blower"; too, the IT department did not appreciate hearing negative comments about their pages. Tony was further worried about his own situation. Web page issues were out of his scope of responsibility and his department had plenty of their own difficulties to resolve. He should not have spent time looking into this in the first place. He decided that from this point forward, he would keep his opinion to himself and hoped that the IT staff would take care of the situation themselves.

QUESTIONS TO CONSIDER

1 Does Tony have an obligation, legal and/or ethical, to report his findings to someone who can act on them?
2. If Tony does not report the findings, does he have some culpability or liability if an individual or group brings charges of discrimination toward the disabled?

3. What about the other groups Tony has identified? Is the library discriminating against those groups, too?
4. What moral imperative do librarians and information professionals have to meet the needs of "special" populations?

CASE #5.24

The staffs from the Shoretown Public Library and the Johnsville Library, which were very close in proximity but different counties, met frequently for social events and professional development. Two of the staff librarians began talking about "problem patrons" one evening and they realized they shared someone in common. Mrs. Robbins had been calling the Johnsville reference desk for months, asking very obscure religious questions. The staff suggested that she contact a seminary library or a private university library, as they were not equipped to answer such questions. Mrs. Robbins instead began calling the Shoretown Public Library, which did in fact have a larger religious section, but was not staffed to answer such elaborate reference questions. And the caller ID on the library's reference line revealed the caller was from Johnsville County, so the staff did not feel compelled to respond to such questions.

QUESTIONS TO CONSIDER

1. Should the Shoretown Public Library respond to the reference questions?
2. Is it professional for the library staffs to discuss patrons?
3. Should libraries use caller ID?

CASE #5.25

Maya was a school librarian. On occasion, a child came in with severe bruises and had difficulty explaining how she got them. She knew the mother pretty well and she could not imagine her abusing her child. However, the girl's mother had recently remarried and Maya was quite suspicious of the new stepfather. She thought about calling social services, knowing that even though her call would be anonymous, the parents would easily guess it was her, as they knew the girl spent many hours in the library at school and they knew Maya was a good friend to their daughter. She also knew this would make the mother extremely upset, especially if she was wrong and this wasn't an abusive situation. In the end, Maya decided it would be unprofessional to ignore the situation and made the call to social services. She then contacted the school's principal for additional support. It turned out, sadly, that Maya was right about the abuse and if she had remained silent, she could have been legally responsible.

QUESTIONS TO CONSIDER

1. Discuss the differences in law and ethics between a school library and a public library's responsibilities in such a situation.

2. How does this case illustrate the great responsibilities that come with information work?
3. How should we be trained to deal with this sort of issue?

REFERENCES

Baker, R., Caplan, A., Emmanuel, I. (Eds.). (1999). *The American Medical Ethics Revolution.* Baltimore: Johns Hopkins University Press.

Davis, M. (1988). Professionalism Means Putting Your Profession First. *Georgetown Journal of Legal Ethics*, 2, 341–357.

Edson, G. (1997). *Museum Ethics.* London: Routledge.

Fallis, D. (2007). Information Ethics for Twenty-First Century Library Professionals. *Library Hi-Tech*, 25 (1), 23–36.

Iacovino, L. (2002). Ethical Principles and Information Professionals: Theory, Practice and Education. *Australian Academic and Research Libraries*, 33 (2). Retrieved September 25, 2004, from http://www.alia.org.au/publishing/aarl/33.2/full.text/iacovino.html.

Illinois Institute of Technology. Center for the Study of Ethics in the Professions. (2007). *Introduction*. Retrieved July 25, 2007, from http://ethics.iit.edu/codes/Introduction.html.

Koehler, W. (2003). Professional Values and Ethics as Defined by "The LIS Discipline." *Journal of Education for Library and Information Science*, 44 (2), 99–119.

Latham, S. (2002). Medical Professionalism: A Parsonian View. *The Mount Sinai Journal of Medicine*, 69 (6), 363–369.

Mason, F. (1992). *Ethics and the Electronic Society.* Chicago: American Library Association. Retrieved September 10, 2007, from http://www.cni.org/pub/LITA/Think/Mason.html.

Pemberton, J. M. (1998). "Through a Glass Darkly": Ethics and Information Technology. *ARMA Records Management Quarterly*, 32(1), 76–84.

Samek, T. (2007). *Librarianship and Human Rights: A Twenty-first Century Guide.* Oxford: Chandos.

Shachaf, P. (2005). A Global Perspective on Library Association Codes of Ethics. *Library and Information Science Research*, 27 (4), 513–533.

Spinello, R. (1997). *Case Studies in Information and Computer Ethics.* Upper Saddle River, NJ: Prentice-Hall.

Spinello, R., & Tavani, H. (Eds.). (2004). *Intellectual Property Rights in a Networked World: Theory and Practice.* Hershey, PA: Information Science Publishing.

Winston, M. (2005). Ethical Leadership: Professional Challenges and the Role of LIS Education. *New Library World* (5/6), 234–243.

CHAPTER 6

Intercultural Information Ethics[*]
by Rafael Capurro

Whosoever wishes to know about the world must learn about it in its particular details. Knowledge is not intelligence. In searching for the truth be ready for the unexpected. Change alone is unchanging. The same road goes both up and down. The beginning of a circle is also its end. Not I, but the world says it: all is one. And yet everything comes in season.

— *Heraclitus*

Introduction

The concept of ethics as reflection on morality is widely accepted among philosophers going back to Aristotle as the founder of ethics as an academic discipline. Today's constructivists such as Niklas Luhmann underline the critical function of ethical theory with regard to morality (Luhmann 1990). The Aristotelian *techne ethike* is in fact oriented towards the formation of an individual character. It belongs together with the *techne oikonomike*, that is the science of house administration, and the *techne politike*, that is the science of the *polis*, to what he calls *philosophia praktike* or practical philosophy (Bien 1985). Aristotle's conception of practical philosophy is concerned with the reflection on the ways human beings dwell in the world, with their *ethos*, and their search for good life (*eu zen*). According to Luhmann (1990) the ethical discourse should not provide a given morality with a kind of *fundamentum inconcussum* or even become a meta-perspective beyond all other societal systems but, quite the contrary, it belongs to the self-referential process of morality itself. As a self-referential process ethics is an unending quest on explicit and implicit uses of the moral code, that is to say of respect or disrespect, with regard to individual and social communication. In other words, ethics *observes* the ways we communicate with each other *as* moral persons and the ways this moral identity is understood. There is, indeed, no unbiased ethical observer.

*This chapter is reprinted with permission of Fink Verlag and was originally published in: Capurro, R., Frühbauer, J., & Hausmanninger, T. (Eds.) (2007). *Localizing the Internet. Ethical Aspects in Intercultural Perspective* (pp. 21–38). ICIE Series Vol. 4. Munich: Fink.

The German philosopher Hans Krämer has remarked that Western moral philosophy follows basically two lines, the older one which was predominant until the 18th century and which deals with "striving for the good" ("*Strebensethik*"), and the modern one beginning with the Enlightenment which tries to determine what we ought to do ("*Sollensethik*") (Krämer 1992). If we restrict moral philosophy to the second view most of the questions about the ways we construct the social world, that is to say human culture, do not belong to the realm of ethics. This narrow view also puts aside the ancient meaning of philosophy as a practice of "care of the self" (Hadot 1993, 1995; Foucault 1984; Capurro 1995). Both traditions, the striving for universality and the care for locality, are intertwined in an open-ended process of self-reflection. Our present life-world is shaped by information technology. The Oxford philosopher Luciano Floridi has coined the term "infosphere" to capture this point (Floridi 1999). I use instead the term *digital ontology* in the sense that this world view of the digital embraces today all dimensions of our being-in-the-world (Capurro 2001). This predominant digital world view is not the cyberspace or "the new home of mind" proclaimed by John Perry Barlow in 1996 (Barlow 1996) but the intersection of the digital with the ecological, political, economic, and cultural spheres. *Intercultural information ethics* addresses questions concerning these intersections such as: How far is the Internet changing local cultural values and traditional ways of life? How far do these changes affect the life and culture of future societies in a global and local sense? Put another way, how far do traditional cultures and their moral values communicate and transform themselves under the impact of the digital "infosphere" in general and of the Internet in particular? In other words, intercultural information ethics can be conceived as a field of research where moral questions of the "infosphere" are reflected in a comparative manner on the basis of different cultural traditions. The Internet has become a challenge not only to international but also to intercultural information ethics as I will show in the second part of this paper. But, indeed, intercultural information ethics suggests a paradigm shift not only within traditional (Western) ethics but also within (Western) philosophy itself to which I will first briefly refer.

1. Intercultural Philosophy

Is there a European philosophy? This question sounds strange not just because we speak about, for instance, Indian, Chinese, Latin American or African philosophy, but also because Europe is anything but a homogeneous cultural phenomenon. But even in case we would answer it positively, it sounds chauvinistic and finally irrational because it presupposes that universal rationality could be the specific property of a local culture, or even that other similar cultural formations of human rationality should not be addressed as philosophical. Philosophy would be then a *mono-cultural* property of Europeans or even only of its name givers, namely the ancient Greeks. This Euro-centric or Helleniccentric view of philosophy has been criticized particularly in the last years by what is being called *intercultural philosophy* (Wimmer 2004).

1.1 Is There a European Philosophy?

Is there a European philosophy? One prominent philosopher of the last century, namely Martin Heidegger, has apparently given an affirmative answer in his book "What is Philosophy?" by saying that only the "Western world and Europe" ("das Abendland und Europa") as heirs of the Greeks have developed, on the basis of Greek philosophy, modern sciences that now pervade the whole planet (Heidegger 1976, 7). This Euro-centric thesis has been criticized, for instance, by the Indian philosopher Ram Adhar Mall (1996, 12) who at the same time remarks that although Heidegger does not seem to see the difference between the Greek word *philosophy* and its subject matter, he also remarks in the "Conversation on language" that the different answers given by Western-European and Far-East traditions to the call of language, that is to say to the hermeneutic shaping of our being-in-the-world, might be able to converge on the basis of a dialogue ("*Gespräch*") that would then come out of a common and single source ("*einer einzigen Quelle*") (Heidegger 1975, 94). In other words, Heidegger would be considering what we could call not just an *intercultural* but a *transcultural* philosophy.

According to Heidegger the word "philosophy" points to a specific way of questioning of the kind "what is?" (*ti estin*), and more precisely "what is being?" (*ti to on*) that arose within Greek culture (Heidegger 1976, 9). But already Plato and Aristotle, no less than Kant or Hegel, gave different answers to what is meant by the word *what* in the sense of what is meant when we ask for the essence of something. In other words, the original Greek question opened different paths of thinking in such a way that, according to Heidegger, the answers do not build a kind of dialectical process but a "free sequence" ("*freie Folge*") (Heidegger 1976, 18). This means that philosophy from its very beginning and in its further development in Western culture is not restricted to the Greek origin or that it is not mono-ethnic. Moreover, it opens, on a first step, an *inner-cultural* dialogue in which those who share this questioning, are already embedded without the possibility of an *immediate* liberation. But the fact of asking the question "what is philosophy?" already points to a situation of distance with regard to what we are asking for (Heidegger 1976, 11–12). According to Heidegger the different answers given to the question of what things are, have something in common, namely the conception of language (*logos*) as a gathering of the whole of reality which is what the Greek called science (*episteme*). We, as human beings, are responsible or in charge of this gathering which means no less that the possibility of giving grounds or reasons for what is (Heidegger 1976, 16). Philosophic questioning is of the nature that it binds questions with the essence of the questioner. To answer the question "what is philosophy?" is then by no means possible by referring to one of the possible answers alone, nor is it the result of looking for what is common to all of them as this would provide just a "void formula" ("*leere Formel*") (Heidegger 1976, 19).

It is also not sure that our answer, or Heidegger's own, will be a philosophic one. In fact, this situation of disturbance or insecurity may be a hint and even a "touchstone" ("*Prüfstein*") that we are on a philosophic path (Heidegger 1976, 19). What is basic for grasping the differences among philosophic answers is their corresponding mood, including the sober mood of planning and calculating which is a characteristic of modern science and with it of what we use to call "modernity." In fact, as Heidegger states, it is not possible to be able to ever go back to the original Greek experience of *logos* and it is of course not possible just to incorporate it. We can only get into a historical or *creative* dialogue with it (Heidegger 1976, 30).

1.2 THE PATH OF COMPARATIVE PHILOSOPHY

This dialogue is thus not only an inner one but also an intercultural and finally a transcultural one that goes beyond the local tradition of Western philosophy as well as beyond any mono-cultural foundation of philosophy but remaining attached to it at the same time in the different voices that articulate it. When Heidegger states that we can only get into a historical or creative dialogue with the original Greek experience, "we" is then of course not restricted to Europeans who must overcome their own tradition, starting with an inner-cultural dialogue. This dialogue changes the meaning of the word "we," that is to say, the matter of philosophy. The concept of comparative or intercultural philosophy fosters this paradigmatic change. It makes explicit the difference between traditions of theoretical and practical thinking that arose and were developed more or less independently from each other, on the one hand, and the dialogical appropriation of Western philosophy by non–European traditions and *vice versa*, on the other (Elberfeld 2002, 11). This intercultural appraisal gives rise to a new kind of philosophic thinking, particularly of ethical thinking. An outstanding example of an intercultural philosophic dialogue between Western and Chinese thinking tradition(s) that does not level the differences by looking for some kind of universal human rationality lies the work of François Julien (1998). When this intercultural philosophical dialogue deals with information technology as the pervasive medium of today's being-in-the-world, we speak of *intercultural information ethics* as well as of *intercultural philosophy of information*.

The journal *polylog: Forum for Intercultural Philosophy* (*polylog* 2004) addresses the prospects of the field in this way:

> We understand intercultural philosophy as the endeavor to give expression to the many
> voices of philosophy in their respective cultural contexts and thereby to generate a shared,
> fruitful discussion granting equal rights to all. In intercultural philosophy we see above all a
> new *orientation* and new *practice* of philosophy — of a philosophy that requires an attitude of
> mutual respect, listening, and learning.

It entails a new orientation because, in acknowledgment of the cultural situatedness of philosophy, claims must prove themselves interculturally, and culture and cultures must be consciously kept in view as the context of philosophizing. It entails a new practice because this consciousness demands a departure from an individual, mono-cultural pro-duction of philosophy and seeks instead a dialogical, process-oriented, fundamentally open *polyphony* of cultures and disciplines.

Following Ernst Cassirer's insight about the historical construction of reality on the basis of "symbolic forms" we can say that culture is the shaping or *in-formation* ("*Formung*") of human self-consciousness as well as of the material world. The "philosophy of symbolic forms" and the "philosophy of technology" are two sides of the same coin or different forms of sense production ("*Sinngebung*") (Cassirer 1994, vol. 2, 258–259; 1985). Both processes are based on the processes of selection, conservation, and reconstruction of meaning being accomplished by a *plurality* of actors and leading to what Jan Assmann calls "cultural memory" (Assmann 2003, 2000). Cultural identity is a relative concept as it points to a permanent exchange of messages between social actors (Capurro 2003). Today's digital globalization has accelerated the process of cultural hybridization leading to *global* cultures, to use this neologism suggesting the merging of the global and the local suggested by the sociologist Roland Robertson (1992). Although the outcome is not just homogenization or *MacWorld* new forms of ghettoization, marginalization, and social exclusion might also arise even within democratic societies (Agamben 2002).

The path of comparative philosophy has several important landmarks in the last century. The first East-West Philosopher's conference took place 1939 in Hawaii and was followed by subsequent meetings since 1949. Günter Wohlfart and Helmut Pape have organized similar meetings of the *Académie du Midi* starting in 1989, one of which was particularly concerned with the question of "comparative ethics" (Elberfeld 2002). What does "comparative" mean? It does not mean the mere juxtaposition of different ethical theories, a sort of mere relativism or multiculturalism. It means, in contrast, a dialogue between them following Nietzsche's aphorism that we live in the "age of comparison" ("*Zeitalter der Vergleichung*") in which cultures, customs, and world views that were in former times mostly isolated are being compared and can be "lived through" ("*durch-lebt*"), leading to an epoch beyond the "culture of comparison" ("*Cultur der Vergleichung*") (Nietzsche 1988, 44). We may speak of *multicultural ethics* in which case we just juxta-pose ethical views instead of comparing them. A mono-cultural view of ethics conceives itself as the only valid one. In order to avoid this kind of ethical chauvinism and colo-nialism it is necessary that *transcultural* ethics *arise* from an *intercultural* dialogue instead of thinking of itself as universal without noticing its own cultural bias. In contrast, a mere meta-cultural view is eventually metaphysical or essentialist as it pretends to have a definitive true knowledge on human nature and human reason.

But, indeed, human reason is genuinely *plural*. We constitute a common world on the basis of exchange practices. This is indeed the key question with regard to the dis-cussion on the theoretical foundation of human rights. This foundation cannot be pro-vided by methodological or meta-cultural rules alone, i.e., by formal-logical principles or so-called anthropological constants. Not just because such principles and constants are the object of interpretation and evolution but also, as Gregor Paul himself in his final statement to a comprehensive project sponsored by the *VolkswagenStiftung* remarks, because the foundation of, for instance, such a basic human right as the respect for human dignity, for instance, remains problematic in either of the following foundational possibilities, namely: on authority, on a pure methodological or empirical basis, or on positive law (Paul 2001). In other words, universal principles can only be founded on a *permanent* critical and, I would add, intercultural exchange. This hermeneutic circle between morality, ethics, and law builds also a condition for political legitimacy from the beginning: Modernity in opposition to its foundation in natural law or in metaphysical or religious presuppositions. But it is indeed an open question whether modern nation-state oriented political theories can be *analogically* expanded to include the present digital globalization. Intercultural ethics can provide a ground for an intercultural and not just international dialogue on these matters.

2. Beyond Meta-Cultural Universality: Intercultural Ethics

The UNESCO Universal Declaration on Cultural Diversity defines the concept of culture in line with the conclusions of three world conferences — the World Conference on Cultural Policies (Mexico City, 1982), the world conference of the World Commission on Culture and Development (1995), and the world conference of the Intergovernmental Conference on Cultural Policies for Development (Stockholm, 1998) — as follows:

> *Reaffirming* that culture should be regarded as the set of distinctive spiritual, material, intellectual and emotional features of society or a social group, and that it encompasses, in addition to art and literature, lifestyles, ways of living together, value systems, traditions and beliefs [UNESCO 2003].

The question of culture is, as this Declaration also stresses, at the heart of contemporary social and political debates particularly since the appearance of Samuel P. Huntington's influential book *The Clash of Civilizations and the Remaking of World Order* (1997) and the events of September 11, 2001, and March 11, 2004. The current discussions in the field of intercultural philosophy and sociology (Hoffmann 2003) show that there are no clear borders among cultures and that cultures are not homogeneous and static. A closed and static vision on cultures, as largely presupposed by Huntington, argues with clichés and does not pay attention to the complex diachronic and synchronic hybridizations or "polyphonies" inside as well as between cultures (Jammal 2004). Even the idea of humanity that lies behind universalistic approaches to ethics rests on an essentialist paradigm and can be considered only as a regulative one, as I will show (Merwe 2000). When we speak about cultures we deal, as the UNESCO Declaration stresses, with *fuzzy and contingent sets* of life styles, value systems, and beliefs that are themselves the product of hybridization.

Michael Walzer distinguishes between "thick" and "thin" morality, i.e., between moral arguments as rooted or located in a culture as opposed to disembodied ones (Walzer 1994). It is a misunderstanding to envisage the intercultural "thick" ethical dialogue for instance in relation to the validity of human rights as a kind of moral relativism (Paul 2003). Universality is, in Kantian terms, a regulative idea that can only be perceived and partially achieved within the plural conditions of human reason, i.e., through a patient intercultural dialogue on the maxims that may guide our actions. The fixation of ethical principles in a moral or quasi-legal code such as the *Universal Declaration of Human Rights* (UDHC) has highly *pragmatic* and indeed *political* significance, namely as a global strategy for global survival and well being. But the idea of a universal code of morality remains *problematic* in the Kantian sense of the term. According to Kant *problematic concepts* are those whose object we cannot know about. For the kind of questions arising from them there is no solution ("*Lösung*"), but only a dissolution ("*Auflösung*") of the problem on the basis, for instance, of the difference between the empirical and the transcendental (Kant 1974, A 339). The concept of humanity and consequently the concept of human rights are problematic concepts. In order to deal with them we need a permanent intercultural ethical dialogue, on the one hand, as well as a pragmatic and contingent transcultural consensus, on the other, by retaining universality only as a transcendental or regulative idea. The insight into the theoretical contingency of universal moral codes and their practical utility is not in the same sense valid, I believe, for projects like the one of a "world ethos" (Küng 2001) as far as such a distillation of theological norms retains a religious dimension that is deeply rooted in different "thick" moralities. Thus the real challenge is intercultural theology which is not the same as the question of theological inculturation (IIMO 2004, Wijsen 2001).

Charles Taylor (1993) has pointed to the tension between the modern idea that all human beings are equal with regard to their dignity as stressed by the Enlightenment, and the idea of respect of the uniqueness of human life in its particularity. This tension has less to do with the so-called Euro-centric origin of the human rights as stated in the UDHC (Wimmer 2004, 171) as with the fact that for instance Article 27 of the UDHC explicitly protects "the right freely to participate in the cultural life of the community, to enjoy the arts and to share in scientific advancement and its benefits." This right to individual and social/cultural identity or autonomy has been also stated by the UNESCO Universal Declaration on Cultural Diversity as follows:

> The defence of cultural diversity is an ethical imperative, inseparable form respect for human dignity. It implies a commitment to human rights and fundamental freedoms, in particular the rights of persons belonging to minorities and those of indigenous peoples. No one may invoke cultural diversity to infringe upon human rights guaranteed by international law, nor to limit their scope [UNESCO 2003].

It is a permanent task of intercultural ethics to reflect on these principles as well as on their factual collisions. There are two dangers that may affect this reflection. One is the use of *mono-cultural* or *multi-cultural* arguments in order to undermine the ethical imperative of universality. This is the danger of moral and cultural relativism. The other one is a one-sided plea for *meta-cultural* universality that does not open itself to an inter-cultural dialogue. This is the danger of moral universalism. In both cases ethical think-ing does not meet the challenge of grasping and holding the tension between universality and particularity. The search for good life and the imperative of universality need a per-manent work of translation or exchange that with regard to information society can be called *intercultural* information ethics. This concept of intercultural ethics is *prima facie* related to Jürgen Habermas' "discourse ethics" (Habermas 1991). But intercultural ethics does not address the question of consensus as a transcendent or counter-factual goal of the evolution of human society. It aims, as already stated at the beginning of this paper, at observing or working out the differences in the uses of the moral code within and between societies in order to keep the process of communication between different cul-tural systems going on (Rombach 1996). Luhmann's idea of ethics as a critical reflection on morality means nothing else than the opposition against moral fundamentalism that could even become worse if ethics would provide an apparent solid foundation.

In other words, one main task of intercultural ethics is to foster cultural identities not through their isolation or mere addition or even collision but through a process of communication being held more and more on the basis of the digital "infosphere." This process concerns not only the pragmatic level of everyday life but also the theoretical level of reflection on their implicit and explicit philosophic traditions. When this reflection refers to the communication process itself between cultures we speak of intercultural com-munication ethics in a broad sense or of *intercultural information ethics* in case commu-nication is conveyed via digital information technology.

2.1 INTERCULTURAL INFORMATION ETHICS

Digital information technology has at first sight changed the horizon of human thinking and action in such a way that we have to deal with many problems for which classic ethical theories do not have only any answers but they cannot even provide a sufficient basis to deal with them. This insight into the somehow unique ethical chal-lenges of the technological civilization was clearly seen by Hans Jonas (1979). But, as Rolf Elberfeld remarks, Jonas dealt with this question only within the horizon of European philosophy (Elberfeld 2002, 16). It is indeed necessary to undertake an intercultural dia-logue on information technology which means not only to become aware of the condi-tions under which different lifestyles and life projects can coexist within the new digital environment but also in order to explore how it affects and is being appropriated by dif-ferent cultures particularly as they are conditioned by this new environment. As far as information technology pervades our being-in-the-world itself on a global scale and influ-ences all aspects of life including philosophical thinking itself (Floridi 2004), the ques-tion about the uniqueness of computer ethics can be discussed (Tavani 2002). As far as I can see, the impact of information technology on a global scale and on all aspects of human life gives, on the one hand, a plausible argument in favour of the uniqueness approach not only with regard to the subject matter but also to the theoretical approaches so far. But this does not mean that, on the other hand, the moral code itself and its ethical reflection will be superseded by another one. The basic question concerning the status of moral persons, their respect or disrespect, remains unchanged although we may discuss as to what are the candidates and what this respect means in a specific situation. We may also discuss as to how this code has been interpreted (or not) within different ethical and cultural traditions and how it is being conceived with regard to the challenge of information technology.

Cultural reflection on information technology, with particular emphasis on the Internet, has already a history. Charles Ess (Drury University, U.S.A.) and Fay Sudweeks (Murdoch University, Australia) have been organizing biennial conferences on cultural attitudes towards technology and communication since 1998 (CAtaC 2004, Ess 2001). Other important meetings in the field are: Computer Ethics: Philosophical Enquiry (CEPE 2005), Computing and Philosophy (CAP 2004), Ethics and Computing (ETHICOMP 2005), Ethics of Electronic Information in the 21st Century (EEI21 2004) as well as the ICIE Symposiums (ICIE 2004). The leading journals in the field are *Ethics and Information Technology* (ed. by Jeroen van den Hoven, Lucas D. Introna, Deborah G. Johnson and Helen Nissenbaum), the *Journal of Information, Communication and Ethics in Society* (ed. by Simon Rogerson and N. Ben Fairweather), the *Journal of Information Ethics* (ed. by Robert Hauptman) and the *International Journal of Information Ethics* (ed. by Rafael Capurro, Thomas Hausmanninger and Felix Weil) (ICIE 2004). Particularly since the question of information ethics was addressed by the United Nations it became part of the international political agenda. But, how did we Europeans get to where we are now?

2.2 SPHERICAL PROJECTS IN EUROPEAN HISTORY

There are at least three major global or *spherical* projects in European history (Sloterdijk 1998ff). The *first* one is the globalisation of *reason* in Greek philosophy. Reason conceives itself—from Aristotle until Hegel—as global thinking that goes beyond nature into the realm of the divine as the eternal, infinite or metaphysical sphere. Such a sphere bursts with the rise of modern science. Metaphysical claims are criticised by modern empirical science. In this unequal fight, David, modern empirical science, is the winner over the metaphysics of Goliath. The *second* globalisation is the *earthly* one. It begins in Europe in the 15th century and bursts in the 20th century. The idea of a spherical earth and the attempts to circumnavigate it are indeed older, but the totalitarian ambitions of modern subjectivity are paid off, at least for a while. The *third* globalisation is the *digital* one with predecessors in the late Middle Ages (Raimundus Lullus, Nicholas of Cusa) as well as in modernity (Pascal, Leibniz). Today we are confronted with the digital formatting of mankind. The digital globalisation not only reinforces and expands upon the

126

divide between the digital haves and have-nots but also makes more explicit and even deepens existing inequalities (Warschauer 2002).

Philosophical, earthly, and digital universalisms are intertwined with other kinds of global projects such as modern science with its view of nature as a system of laws that underlie and determine in a partially foreseeable way at least the process of natural evolution, or the project of modern economy with the spread of global capitalism including a universal currency, identical goods for everybody, global marketing, global production and management processes, etc., or the process of universal politics and universal values (United Nations, "Universal Declaration of Human Rights"), or the project(s) of universal cataloguing of and accessibility to scientific literature ("Universal Decimal Classification," bibliographic databases accessible for instance through DIALOG, the Internet as a distribution medium for all kinds of digital material, etc.). The ecological movement has made aware of the global effects of industrialisation on nature and society. Two world wars had deep effects on the physical and moral life of millions of people all over the planet.

What is new in the present situation is the fact that such global perceptions become at least partially transformed by digital media. This new situation is basically characterized by a system of world communication that allows different kinds of social systems to better interact (this is the optimist hope) with each other beyond the top-down vs. bottom-up alternative as well as beyond different kinds of cultural homogenization which is mostly nothing more than cultural colonialism. Although digital communication may not bring a solution either for single societies nor for their global interaction, it can contribute to find new ways of interaction between the local and the global, creating *glocal* cultures (Castells 1996).

3. Intercultural Information Ethics at the WSIS

In the first phase of the World Summit on the Information Society (WSIS 2004) the question of bridging the so-called *digital divide* (Scheule, et al., 2004), a concern that was and is at the core of the Summit, has been addressed from two ethical viewpoints that are closely linked, namely the question of a human right to communicate and the question of cultural diversity to which I will now briefly refer.

3.1 IS THERE A HUMAN RIGHT TO COMMUNICATE?

The issue concerning the human right to communicate has now raised a new dimension based on the discussions of a *New World Information and Communication Order* that led the United States to leave UNESCO some twenty-five years ago (UNESCO 1980). In the meantime, since the rise of the Internet, a paradigm shift in human communication has taken place as the classic structure of still dominant mass media, namely a one-to-many message distribution has been superseded by a structure in which everyone having access to the Internet can receive *and send* digital messages not only on a one-to-one basis, but also in the forms of one-to-many, many-to-one and many-to-many. This is indeed a cultural evolution in communication that occurs for the first time in the history of mankind on a global scale and within a short period of evolution. It is not surprising that many participants of the WSIS considered it necessary to think about the significance of Article 19 of the UDHR:

> Everyone has the right to freedom of opinion and expression; this right includes freedom to hold opinions without interference and to seek, receive and impart information and ideas through any media and regardless of frontiers.

This article was based on an understanding of the communication situation before the advent of the Internet. It is not clear whether the formulation "to seek, receive and impart information" can be applied to the possibilities of communication created by the Internet. Do we need a specific *right to communicate* or *communication rights* in order to underline the new possibilities of writing (right to write = r2w) and reading (right to read =r2r) as building together the right to communicate (r2c) (Kuhlen 2003)? The discussion of these issues is extremely controversial and even polemical. The final text from December 12, 2003, of the *Declaration of Principles* begins with a formulation that mirrors, at least partially, this new perspective without using the formula *right to communicate*:

> We, the representatives of the peoples of the world, assembled in Geneva from 10–12 December 2003 for the first phase of the World Summit on the Information Society, declare our common desire and commitment to build a people-centred, inclusive and development-oriented Information Society, where everyone can create, access, utilize and share information and knowledge, enabling individuals, communities and peoples to achieve their full potential in promoting their sustainable development and improving their quality of life, premised on the purposes and principles of the Charter of the United Nations and respecting fully and upholding the Universal Declaration of Human Rights [WSIS, 2004].

3.2 THE ISSUE OF CULTURAL DIVERSITY

Point 8 of the *Declaration of Principles* deals explicitly with "cultural diversity and identity, linguistic diversity and local content" as follows:

52. Cultural diversity is the common heritage of humankind. The Information Society should be founded on and stimulate respect for cultural identity, cultural and linguistic diversity, traditions and religions, and foster dialogue among cultures and civilizations. The promotion, affirmation and preservation of diverse cultural identities and languages as reflected in relevant agreed United Nations documents including UNESCO's Universal Declaration on Cultural Diversity, will further enrich the Information Society.

53. The creation, dissemination and preservation of content in diverse languages and formats must be accorded high priority in building an inclusive Information Society, paying particular attention to the diversity of supply of creative work and due recognition of the rights of authors and artists. It is essential to promote the production of and

accessibility to all content — educational, scientific, cultural or recreational — in diverse languages and formats. The development of local content suited to domestic or regional needs will encourage social and economic development and will stimulate participation of all stakeholders, including people living in rural, remote and marginal areas.

54. The preservation of cultural heritage is a crucial component of identity and self-understanding of individuals that links a community to its past. The Information Society should harness and preserve cultural heritage for the future by all appropriate methods, including digitisation [WSIS 2004].

The *Plan of Action* of the WSIS foresees corresponding policies. The global and local challenge of WSIS is to develop an *inclusive* digital information society, that is to say to bridge the digital divide by fostering cultural diversity. A *prima facie* similar wording of the cultural article can be found in the *Civil Society Declaration to the World Summit on the Information Society* "Shaping Information Societies for Human Needs" (Civil Society 2004). But, in fact, this *Declaration* stresses under "2.3 Culture, Knowledge and the Public Domain" the role of "oral tradition" as well as a "variety of media" as means through which the diversity of cultures and languages enrich "information and communication societies." It binds the concepts of communication and information by using the plural form "information and communication societies." This *Declaration* is as a whole and in each of its paragraphs a plea for pluralistic, interactive, and *glocal*-oriented *communication rights*. It is not astonishing that the media establishment was not happy with it (Kuhlen 2003, 396). This indeed makes a difference to the official Declaration of the WSIS, explicitly stated in the following footnote to the Preamble:

There is no single information, communication or knowledge society: there are, at the local, national and global levels, possible future societies; moreover, considering communication is a critical aspect of any information society, we use in this document the phrase "information and communication societies." For consistency with previous WSIS language, we retain the use of the phrase "Information Society" when directly referencing WSIS [Civil Society 2004].

The concept of "information and communication societies" underlying this Declaration is not only plural but also historical or dynamic. The Preamble underlines also gender and culture perspectives as follows:

We, women and men from different continents, cultural backgrounds, perspectives, experience and expertise, acting as members of different constituencies of an emerging global civil society, considering civil society participation as fundamental to the first ever held UN Summit on Information and Communication issues, the World Summit on the Information Society, have been working for two years inside the process, devoting our efforts to shaping people-oriented, inclusive and equitable concept of information and communication societies [Civil Society 2004].

Under 2.3.1.3 the Declaration asks for the establishment of an *International Convention on Cultural Diversity* as well as for a review of existing copyright regulation instruments.

During the WSIS meeting a World Forum on Communication Rights took place, which was organized among others by the campaign on Communication Rights in the Information Society (CRIS) and the German *Heinrich-Böll-Foundation*. This last institution published a *Charter of Civil Rights for a Sustainable Knowledge Society* as a contribution to the WSIS (Charter 2003). The *Charter* states the following fundamental right:

1. Knowledge is the heritage and the property of humanity and is thus free. Knowledge represents the reservoir from which new knowledge is created. Knowledge must therefore remain permanently accessible to the public. Limitations on public access such as copyrights and patents must be the exception. Commercial exploitation of knowledge conflicts with the interest of society in knowledge as a public good. Knowledge as a common good must have a higher status in the hierarchy of social values than the protection of private claims.

It also mandates a special right with regard to cultural diversity and it explicitly fosters intercultural dialogue on the basis of common rights and values:

6. Cultural diversity is a prerequisite for individual and social development. Culture is realised in languages, customs, social behavior patterns, norms and ways of life, but also in human artefacts (such as arts, crafts and technology). The emergence of the global knowledge society must not be allowed to lead to cultural homogenisation. Instead, the creative potential of current information and communication technologies must be used to preserve and promote the heterogeneity of cultures and languages as a precondition for the individual and social development of present and future generations. A dialogue of cultures can only be realised in a climate of diversity and equal rights.

4. Case Studies and Best Practices

In his book *Code and Other Laws of Cyberspace* Lawrence Lessig (1999) envisions a situation in which the universality of the cyberspace is endangered by the local codes of the market, the software industry, the laws of nation states, and moral traditions. He writes:

Nature doesn't determine cyberspace. Code does. Code is not constant. It changes. It is changing now in a way that will make cyberspace more regulable. It could change in a way that makes cyberspace less regulable. How it changes depends on the code writers. How code writers change it could depend on us.

If we do nothing, the code of cyberspace will change. The invisible hand will change it in a predictable way. To do nothing is to embrace at least that. It is to accept the changes that this change in code will bring about. It is to accept a cyberspace that is less free, or differently free, than the space it was before [Lessig 1999, 109].

One way of keeping the cyberspace more free and to foster cultural diversity in it is indeed intercultural dialogue as taking place in the context of WSIS as well as in the UNESCO INFOethics congresses on ethical, legal and societal aspects of the information society since 1997 (UNESCO 1998). Intercultural information ethics matters not only in order to overcome the isolation of moral traditions with regard to the Internet but also in order to provide a platform for pragmatic action, for the kind of declarations and (quasi-) legal agreements that can be used as a framework for preservation and fostering of cultural differences in the new digital environment. It is still an open question how far these activities could and should be coordinated by an international agency or by one of the existing UN bodies or by some other kind of institution. Ethics, law and pragmatic actions are needed in order to keep the net as free as possible, avoiding ghettoization of group morals and encouraging intercultural dialogue (Hausmanninger 2004). But, indeed, the good is not necessarily on the side of the universal and the bad on the side of the local, at least when we understand these concepts not only, as Lessig does, within a normative context but within a cultural one. In this last case the question of localizing the Internet does not mean maintaining or even creating normative ghettos or imposing the norms of one ghetto to the rest of them even with the *best intentions* in a kind of *paternalist communitarianism*. Rather it is a matter of giving communities the possibility of appropriating the Internet according to their own cultural traditions. I call this view *bottom-up communitarianism* (Capurro 2004). The Latin American virtual community MISTICA ("*Metodología e Impacto Social de las Tecnologías de Información y Comunicación en América*") has published a document with the title "*Working the Internet with a Social Vision*" that clearly shows how the ethical question of justice and the Internet can and should be reflected within a specific economic, social, and cultural setting such as the Latin American one (MISTICA 2002).

The German sociologist Ulrich Beck opposes a totalitarian view of globalisation, which he calls "globalism," to a view in which the cultural differences are preserved and that he calls, following Robertson (1992), "glocalisation" (Beck 1997). This implies a view of "networked justice" (Scheule 2004) that is not identical with the classical conceptions of commutative or distributive justice but is more related to what Tomas Lipinski and Johannes Britz call "contributive justice":

> That an individual has an obligation to be active in the society (individual responsibility), and that society itself has a duty to facilitate participation and productivity without impairing individual freedom and dignity [Lipinski & Britz 2000, 65].

This obligation implies the society's responsibility to enable cultural appropriation, for instance, through an equal right of access to (digital) information which implies a right to read (r2r) and a right to write (r2w) within the new interactive digital environment, as already said. Modern political philosophy is based on nation-oriented conceptions of justice and mostly does not deal explicitly with the question of *glocal* cultures intertwined with cyberspace. But, as Soraj Hongladarom remarks:

> [...] justice and culture are linked in many ways. Firstly, justice, if it is to be workable in a cultural entity, must be integrated to the tradition or the normal practices of that entity. Secondly, when cultures interact as closely as they are now due to globalization, one finds many cases of cultural intermingling, a result of which is that systems of practices born in one culture become "exported" to other cultures when the latter find such systems appealing and useful to them [Hongladarom 2001].

Justice is, according to Hongladarom, both cultural and intercultural. Following Michael Walzer, Hongladarom argues that moral arguments are "thin" when they are not embodied in culture and history(ies), that is to say, if they are not contextualized or localized (Hongladarom 2001a, 318). But, on the other hand, "thick" moral arguments must overcome their "thick" mono-cultural horizon as they interact with other cultures, a process that does not start with the Internet. Thus, Hongladarom's terminology corresponds only partially to what I call mono-cultural, intercultural, and trans-cultural (information) ethics, the latter being the result of the intercultural interaction as opposed to a purely meta-cultural or "thin" universality. The question of what kind of culture(s) will the Internet bring about is, on the one hand, a question of fact(s), that is to say, of how different cultures integrate it within their local environment(s). But it is also, on the other hand, a question of ethical reflection on these facts that we call intercultural information ethics in which "thick" and "thin" arguments are intertwined. The Kantian imperative of universalizability does not mean that universally proved maxims should be followed by the same kind of actions by everybody. It only states a basic condition for human action, a kind of elementary *touchstone for conviviality*. But Kant is not facing the kind of culture-oriented justice as made explicit by Hongladarom. His imperative is a necessary but not a sufficient condition for a view of justice that takes care *positively* and *empirically* of fostering different lifestyles as something belonging essentially to human communities, the humanness of humans not being reduced to their being rational or even to their membership in a *noumenal* world. Hongladarom's ethical approach meets the older pre- and post-modern Western traditions of self-care and striving for the good. According to Eben Moglen (2003) the ethical right to share information, the principle of non-exclusion is the leading ethical principle of the information society that is not, I believe no longer, based on a market-driven information economy *alone*.

Charles Ess has analyzed the cultural impact of computer-mediated communication (CMC) and in particular of Western-designed CSCW systems (Computer Supported Cooperative Work) in different countries such as Japan, Indonesia, Malaysia, Israel, and Kuweit (Ess 2002). The social context of use or the "thick" cultural aspect plays an important and distinctive role against the widespread idea of a hard technological determinism. In fact he draws the conclusion that CMC are marked by "soft determinism" (Don Ihde), i.e., their practical implementation is partly conditioned by the local context of use and does not necessarily mean a "computer-mediated colonialization." He writes:

> In contrast with the apparent dichotomy between a global but homogenous computer ethic vs. a local but "disconnected" computer ethic (i.e., one reflecting solely specific cultural values and preferences) [...] Hongladarom's model for a middle ground between homogeneity and diversity suggests rather a "both-and" ethic, i.e., one that serves *both* a global computer ethics *and* local values as expressed in specific traditions, policies, etc. That is: in order to avoid the ethical equivalent of "Jihad vs. McWorld," comparative philosophers need to contribute to a computer ethic for a global communications media such as the Internet and the Web that endorses both global/universal values and decision-making procedures *and* the distinctive practices and values of local cultures [Ess 2002, 337–338].

We need an *intercultural informatics* not only the development of software, say, accessible in different languages but its contextualization according to specific needs and cultural practices as well as a critical reflection on these practices inside and between them.

An outstanding compilation of best-practices in intercultural information has been done, for instance, by *Yois* (Youth for Intergenerational Justice and Sustainability) (2003). It includes examples from an educational system in rural areas of India, learning projects in different regions of Africa, youth empowerment in ICT in Turkey, youth and economic participation in the information society in the Philippines, software development in Bangladesh, alternatives to high-tech computers in Romania as well as contributions from European countries, Canada and the United States.

5. Beyond Cultural Conventions: A Sophistic Argumentation

The sophist Antiphon the Athenian (ca. 480–411 B.C.) questioned legal and cultural conventions (*nomos*) in the name of nature (*physis*). He was a kind of libertarian ethicist and a psychoanalyst *avant la lettre*. He writes:

> We can examine those attributes of nature that are necessary in all humans and are provided to all to the same degree, and in these respects none of us is distinguished as barbarian or Greek. For we all breathe the air through our mouth and our nostrils, and we laugh when our minds are happy (A3) or weep when we are pained, and we receive sounds with our hearing, and we see by the light with our sight, and we work with our hands and walk with our feet [qtd. in Gagarin 2002, 183].

Is this reasoning based on a naturalistic fallacy? The argument seems to me less onto-logical than pragmatic, that is to say that our common nature (*physis*) is based on things that we need as well as on the capacities we have in order to be able to survive than in, say, a universal human reason. In some way we are followers and antipodes of Antiphon. We are followers as far as we are universal pragmatists. We believe in the pragmatic equal-ity of human beings with regard to the struggle for survival. But we are his antipodes as far as we believe that we can better take care of our lives on the basis of the universal *nomos* we call the *Universal Declaration of Human Rights* (UDHR). And even more, we believe that artificial devices such as the Internet are as basic for human survival as the air we breathe and the sounds we hear. From a pragmatic point of view our natural capac-ities are no longer enough for guaranteeing survival. In other words, there are things that belong to artificiality, that is to say to culture or convention (*nomos*) and that are neces-sary to all human beings, although the capacities to use them is not given by nature. We face an ethical dilemma as far as we state *de jure* a kind of universality based on artificial-ity while *de facto* such a common basis is not given. A theoretical path for the solution or *dissolution* of this dilemma in the field of human communication is intercultural infor-mation ethics.

The human right to communicate (in general) is broader than the one to communicate via the Internet, but *de facto* the problem arises today because of the possibilities offered by the Internet as they become more and more necessary for survival. In other words, what seemed to have a relative or cultural character due to its artificiality becomes an object of universal or transcultural interest. At this point a new ethical dilemma arises as far as the usefulness of artificial products is dependent on local needs and on local *nomos* that would give the impression of universality. The sceptic Antiphon would probably say that this is nothing but a domination strategy, which is very often the case, and that we should make a clear distinction between things that are naturally common to everybody and other kinds of cultural things produced by artifice and subject to local laws. He would contest the idea of a universal *nomos*. He writes in the same fragment:

> (A2) The laws of nearby communities we know and respect, but those communities far away we neither know nor respect. We have thereby become barbarian toward each other, when by nature (*physis*) we are all born in all respects equally capable of being both barbarians and Greeks [qtd. in Gagarin 2002, 183].

Antiphon states a *de facto* cultural difference between the Greeks and the barbarians, this difference being not a natural one but a product of culture (*nomos*). Culture is *per definitionem* what makes a difference between human societies and something that, according to Antiphon, we should know and respect, although paradoxically this respect seems something very Greek in Antiphon's view although xenophobia is indeed not something given by nature to barbarians and/or to Greeks. But it seems as if it were the Greeks that were aware of this bias and as far as they were aware they created a cultural difference based on the idea (1) that a natural meta-code makes possible that cultures respect each other. But this code itself is, indeed, a cultural product with meta-cultural ambitions, the alternative being apparently the barbarian code of ignorance and hate that might also affect Greek culture. In other words, Antiphon's solution of the *nomos-physei* dilemma is on the one hand to look for a common natural basis of living together; but, on the other hand, it also requires us to state a kind of transcultural code based on knowledge and respect as opposed to hate and ignorance.

Both codes cannot be conceived as natural properties of any given society. Greeks can behave as barbarians and barbarians can behave as Greeks. The universality of Antiphon's code does not deny cultural diversity but intends to find a *modus vivendi* based on the Greek way of life which is not a property of the Greek people as far as such a way of life can degenerate and become an enemy of human life. But it would be a fallacy to attribute to Antiphon the ideas of, say, French Enlightenment or of the principles of the Constitution of the United States or even of the UDHR. Antiphon was, indeed, a critic of Athenian democratic order. Even his tolerant views on Greeks and barbarians can be interpreted as a kind of cultural imperialism. Natural equality does not mean that we, Greeks and barbarians, are or should be cultural equals. Antiphon's alternative to law and cultural conventions with their arbitrary character is a kind of libertarian ideology based on the individual's harmony with himself (*homonoia*) in opposition to the rights of the *polis*. Antiphon's ethics is eventually not only individualistic but also apolitical. Its kind of pragmatic natural universality is a necessary but not a sufficient condition for dealing with the question of what we call an intercultural and even a transcultural ethics. But we can learn from him the limits of culture, law, and artificial devices when we feel the tendency to overestimate their capacity for creating social bonds.

Conclusion

The ongoing debate on the impact of the Internet is at the core of today's and tomorrow's global and local political decision-making in a world that turns more and more unified — and divided. Manuel Castells puts it this way: "It's not as activists used to say, 'Think globally, act locally.' No, no, think locally — link to your interest environment — and act globally — because if you don't act globally in a system in which the powers are global, you make no difference in the power system" (Castells, 2001, 5).

Questions concerning anonymity, universal accessibility to knowledge, and digital surveillance, are basic to all societies. From an intercultural perspective the leading question is how human cultures can locally flourish within a global digital environment. This question concerns in the first place community building on the basis of cultural diversity. How far does the Internet affect, for better or worse, local and particularly global cultures? How far does it foster democratic processes inside and between them? How do people construct their cultural identities within this medium? How does it affect their customs, languages, and everyday problems?

Intercultural information ethics addresses, secondly, the changes produced by the Internet on traditional media, such as oral and written customs, newspapers, radio and TV, the merger of mass media, the telephone and the Internet, and the impact of the Internet on literary cultures, including the impact of the next generation of information and communication technologies such as ubiquitous computing in the post–Internet era. This concerns new methods of manipulation and control made possible or aggravated by the Internet.

Finally, intercultural information ethics deals with the economic impact of the Internet as far as it can become an instrument of cultural oppression and colonialism. How does it affect cultural memory and cultural sustainability? The question about the so-called digital divide is thus not just an issue of giving everybody access to the global network (a Utopian goal?), but rather an issue on how the digital network helps people to better manage their lives while avoiding the dangers of cultural exploitation and discrimination. The vision of a cultural inclusive information society should be stated in plural not just because there are different visions according to cultural backgrounds but also because there are different possibilities of cultural inclusion from a type of inclusion that excludes the included until different forms of homogenization and cultural colonialism form. Concepts such as hybrid and polyphony are ethical markers that need to be critically analyzed in specific situations.

The key question of intercultural information ethics is thus how far and in which ways are we going to be able to enlarge both freedom and justice within a perspective of sustainable cultural development that protects and encourages cultural diversity as well as the interaction between them. Digital interaction could be used to weaken the hierarchical one-to-many structure of global mass media, giving individuals, groups, and whole societies the capacity to become senders and not only receivers of messages. Cars and highways have lead in the meantime to a rediscovery of car-free localities within our cities as well as to a rediscovery of slowness and the value of natural environment, particularly in Western societies. Shaping our daily lives with mobile communication technologies will indeed transform the ways we construct the social, political and economic world as well as the ways we reshape natural environments. Will they also bring back cultural practices of individual and social self-care such as the art of silence in the face of verbosity, the art of laughing in the face of fear, and the art of choosing paths of liberation (Capurro 1996)? These practices will take place within different cultural horizons and moral traditions that should be critically observed by intercultural information ethics.

Intercultural Ethics Cases

CASE #6.1

A library school faculty member, Professor Rasto, from the United States was invited to visit and lecture in a Chinese university. The visit was well-planned and the lectures were received enthusiastically by students and faculty alike. As a parting gift, a group of students presented the professor with a photocopy of a famous Chinese manuscript. The students had translated parts of it into English, had signed it with a very sincere dedication and note of gratitude, and had bound it themselves. The professor was honored and, when he arrived home, showed it to his colleagues. One of them taught information policy and immediately voiced concerns about the violation of copyright, since the manuscript had indeed been copied in full, and about the "notorious" violations of copyright law that took place in Asian countries. "You should have used this opportunity to discuss the legal issues in copyright law with the students and faculty," the IP professor stated. "By accepting the gift, you are complicit in their disregard of the law." "No," responded Professor Rasto. "This was the most sincere form of appreciation. It would have been amazingly rude if I had not accepted this gift or had raised such issues when they were showing their thanks."

QUESTIONS TO CONSIDER

1. Discuss international differences in copyright laws.

2. Should Professor Rasto have accepted the gift as he claims?
3. Even if it were possible, should western models of intellectual property be used across the globe? Why or why not?

CASE #6.2

Many public libraries across the United States are sponsoring informational sessions on eBay. The sessions typically introduce people to the eBay culture and processes and teach them how to buy and sell across the worldwide auction block. Many flocked to the sessions, in the hopes of making some additional income; it was increasingly popular among elderly patrons. During one session, the instructor asked each participant to list an item for auction. The instructor became concerned when he learned that one of the class members was listing a copy of *Mein Kampf,* a 1934 German language edition. He had photos of the book, which was in pristine condition, and specifically stated that he was selling it for "historical purposes only" and did not agree with the ideological positions represented in the book. He also included a statement that he would only sell to bidders in the United States. The librarian teaching the session was unsure how to respond, as he knew there were laws against such items in Germany and France, for instance.

QUESTIONS TO CONSIDER

1. Does the librarian have an ethical or legal responsibility in this case to suggest the man not sell such an item?
2. How does this case raise intercultural intellectual freedom issues?
3. Discuss the ever-increasing global responsibilities information professionals face.

CASE #6.3

An academic library in a northern European country was promoting the use of a new project and a researcher from the team gave a talk on the project at the ALA annual meeting. The idea was simple: The university population, including students, faculty, and staff, would carry RFID tags with basic identity information and when one approached a smart building, e.g., for an appointment, to do work, to use the library catalog or resources, there would be sensors and a database system in place to be ready to greet the individual (perhaps by way of an avatar on a screen) when he or she walked in any room in any building, to provide with directions to an appointment, or to open up any resources one may need (office, computers, printers, phones), as well as alert the appropriate people that the person had arrived. While the project had been enthusiastically received in a number of EU countries, the American reception, especially among professional librarians, was less than cool. Privacy became a large issue in the ensuing discussion; it became evident to the European researcher that Americans did not have the same level of trust in their government and this trickled down to federally funded libraries. Trust that one's government would protect people and their privacy was very different across cultures, the researcher discovered, encouraging him to consider ethnocentric assumptions related to privacy, technologies, and individual and collective rights in the research.

QUESTIONS TO CONSIDER

1. Discuss the concept of privacy across cultures; review the work of CATaC conferences for references.
2. How do technologies and ethnocentrism coexist?
3. Should libraries as a profession embrace the use of the RFID as described in this case?
4. Would cultural differences in libraries complicate such uses of RFID in insurmountable ways?

CASE #6.4

Hava was a research specialist at a multi-national pharmaceutical company. When he began, he agreed to many clauses in his contract, such as privacy, conflict of interest, and secrecy, as this was no ordinary library position. He was assisting the top researchers in the company as they sought information to assist in the development of important — and profitable — drugs. Hava was particularly qualified for the position, with a degree in life sciences from a prestigious European university, as well as a Master's degree in information sciences. Hava was also well-traveled, having spent a number of years in the Peace Corps, before settling into his profession. He had lived in various African countries, as well as in Thailand and China, to name a few. He felt that his work in the pharmaceutical research center would be a way of helping — his contributions to research could save lives, he truly believed.

A few months into his employment, Hava was asked by a researcher to search STN and DataStar for background information on the Hoodia cactus from the Kalahari desert. The properties of the cactus were of great interest to the company as a potential diet drug, as for years the San people had eaten the cactus to prevent hunger and thirst. He found as much as he could and presented it to the researcher and his team. Not too long after, Hava learned, the company filed for a patent on the cactus. Hava had not quite realized this was what his work would lead to: That cactus, indigenous property for hundreds, thousands of years, now "belonged" to a company and would most likely make millions of dollars for a few people. The San would get nothing from this transaction. Hava felt ill — this was not fitting into his plan to contribute to the global population.

QUESTIONS TO CONSIDER

1. Discuss the ethical implications of bio-piracy.
2. What roles and responsibilities do information professionals have to prevent it?
3. Can western intellectual property models fit indigenous knowledge? Should they?
4. Explore such documents as the UN Convention on Biological Diversity and the UN

Declaration on the Rights of Indigenous Peoples, and their implications for information professionals.

CASE #6.5

Anneh is a South African archivist. She has worked in the field for more than thirty years and has seen dramatic changes in archival practices pre– and post–Apartheid. She was one of a very few white South Africans who kept their positions after the change in government and she was privy to some highly disturbing information. Archival work during Apartheid was a systematic cleansing of certain forms of information, a systematic elimination of representations of the marginalized and oppressed; while conversely, vast sets of data were amassed by the SAS on particular individuals for state surveillance. As Verne Harris has stated, "A key element in [the] exercise of hegemony was the state's control over social memory, a control which involved both remembering and forgetting" (2002, p. 69). Much data was destroyed in the time leading up to the Mandela's presidency and Anneh knew about this; she had never condoned the practices, but she never voiced her professional outrage over them either.

Now, as Anneh prepared to retire, she thought about the historical record — or lack thereof — to which she had contributed. Her entire professional life had been based on a lie. How would she reconcile this? She decided to write a memoir to help herself sort through the life she had led as an archivist. Once the memoir was published, many professionals in the archival community boycotted the work. They felt she should have "come clean" much earlier and that her disservice to the people, the country, and her profession was unconscionable.

QUESTIONS TO CONSIDER

1. Discuss Verne Harris' statement, "Archives is politics." If this is correct, what is the role of social justice in archives?
2. What specific ethical responsibilities do archivists have and how might these be different from other information professionals?
3. Should national archives be digitized, where possible, to allow for a global community of viewers/researchers/users? Is there a cultural identity or ownership issue that would suggest archives should remain "private" for the community from which they came?
4. How, in this Apartheid case, do archives manipulate social memory?
5. How should the global community of archivists and information professionals respond to such state-wide oppression, censorship, and human rights violations?

CASE REFERENCE

Harris, V. (2002). The Archival Sliver: Power, Memory, and Archives in South Africa. *Archival Science*, 2(1–2), 63–86.

CASE #6.6

A Native American student began his LIS program with high hopes. He was interested in children's and young adult librarianship and hoped to gain his degree to then work at the public library near his tribe. After taking his required coursework, he began his electives, taking literature and public librarianship courses. He soon began to question the reading lists of many of the courses. Even the "multicultural literature" course seemed largely to exclude the Native American voice and was heavily dominated by African American and Latino reading. The student voiced his concerns, that there was a paucity of works by or about Native Americans represented in the readings and that the cycle was self-perpetuating—if LIS students weren't exposed to it in their courses, they would not bring it into their libraries, so there would be "no need" for it in the curriculum. The instructor of the course agreed that there was a problem of representation, but that the course was already over-packed with material and thus suggested the student take a course in the Native American Studies Department.

QUESTIONS TO CONSIDER

1. What professional and ethical obligation do librarians building collections and LIS faculty teaching multicultural literature have to reflect all cultures?
2. Explore ALA's diversity initiatives and how they fit into LIS curricula. What is working and what could be improved?
3. Is the instructor's response justified? Is this a reality of such survey courses?

CASE #6.7

Joe and Colleen, two professional librarians sat speaking about the problems their institution faced with spam and, in particular, emails phishing for personal information. Joe remarked, "Have you ever noticed these messages undoubtedly come from some guy from somewhere in Africa?" "Yes," said Colleen. "I read a report on the lack of laws surrounding intellectual property and privacy in Africa. In essence, there is no equivalent of our intellectual property laws. So, it's a free-for-all—information corruption is rampant in Africa—anyone can get away with this sort of thing. If those messages originated in the United States or Europe, we wouldn't get half the spam we do and people wouldn't be losing their money and identities." "So," said Joe, "what can we do about it?"

QUESTIONS TO CONSIDER

1. Discuss the perceptions and realities of information corruption in Africa in particular.
2. Review the Africa Information Ethics web site. What sorts of issues were raised in this congress?
3. Why is it a moral imperative to discuss different value systems embedded in IP laws—or lack of such laws?

4. How can Western information professionals contribute to the global IP and information ethics discourse?

CASE #6.8

The National Library of Afghanistan is in the city of Kabul. The library was nearly destroyed after years of war and civil unrest, but through the outstanding efforts of the national librarian, it is recovering. Western philanthropic efforts, both large and small, along with help from the media, have worked toward the restoration of this library. One grassroots organization in particular has received high praise as noted in a 2002 speech by Donn Marshall, founder of the Shelley A. Marshall Foundation, "When I heard and read about what your organization was doing, I was tremendously impressed both with your effort and the thought behind it. To promote literacy, the freedoms of speech and thought, and the free exchange of ideas will be the key, not just to winning the war on terrorism, but in quite literally making the world a better place. Thoreau once said something along the lines of 'There are a thousand philanthropists hacking at the branches of evil and injustice, but only a few who strike at its roots.' You are striking at the roots." This speech honored Books for Freedom, recipient of the 2002 Shelley A. Marshall Award for The Enrichment of The Human Spirit. According to a press release dated October 31, 2002, "Books for Freedom hopes to aid in rebuilding the country of Afghanistan by donating books in local and foreign languages that will help to create a better way of life for many Afghan men, women, and children. By supplying books on all topics, we hope to increase knowledge and expand minds that were strait-jacketed for so many years under the Taliban," said Melissa Street, president and Founder of Books for Freedom. "Street organized a shipment to Afghanistan that left New Jersey July 11, 2002. Among the 20,000 books in the first shipment are volumes on engineering, agriculture, medical and legal topics, as well as novels and other literature. The books are in both English and local languages."

QUESTIONS TO CONSIDER

1. Do the book topics reflect the current information needs of Afghanistan?
2. Are the choices culturally sensitive?
3. Is book donation the best way to rebuild national libraries that have been decimated by civil war, terrorism, or an occupying force?

CASE REFERENCE

Books For Freedom (2002). *Books for Freedom's First Shipment of 20,000 Books Arrives in Afghanistan.* Retrieved on September 2, 2007, from http://www.booksforfreedom.org/news.html#pr103102.

CASE #6.9

The academic library at Youngstown College required first-year students to take a one-credit course on library and research skills. Much of the class was discussion-oriented; the instructors frequently gave out assignments with inaccuracies and the students were to address and correct these errors as part of the classwork. Students were generally comfortable with this model, but Lyn, the instructor, noticed that non–American students were often very quiet in the course. She understood that there were different models of teaching used and the Socratic method of questioning one's instructors was not readily accepted by all cultures. But, when she had to assign her grades, which included thirty percent for class participation, she was concerned. There were two students who had not spoken in class at all; they had completed their assignments well, but they had not reported back to the class as was expected. Lyn knew their native language was not English and considered this as well in their grading. But, she thought, if she did not raise the issue now, the students might be worse off because of it as they progressed through their studies.

QUESTIONS TO CONSIDER

1. Discuss cultural differences in the teaching environment and how faculty should respond to such differences.
2. Should Lyn grade the non-native students differently?
3. If so, is that unfair to the other students?
4. What ethical obligations do teaching librarians have to address cultural differences in information literacy method and content?

CASE #6.10

Troy, an academic librarian in Toronto, had recently assisted a professor researching human rights issues. Specifically, the researcher was interested in the various UN declarations, such as the Rights of the Child and the Rights of Indigenous Peoples, and why the United States had opposed both of those. Troy never considered the research "questionable" in any way, instead, he considered it important from many perspectives — cultural, legal, ethical, and historical.

As a courtesy, Troy showed the professor how to store and generate citations and reference lists in Refworks, an online research management tool. However, one of his colleagues, Barb, approached him after he had finished with the professor. "Troy, you know under the auspices of the PATRIOT Act, the U.S. government could access that data — it is, after all, stored on servers in the United States. What if they think that is some kind of anti-government work? The PATRIOT Act is quite vague in its definitions of what 'terrorist' activities are. Didn't you hear about the writer who had researched landmines in Cambodia while writing a women's fiction adventure book? She was investigated under the auspices of the Act. I would hate to see our faculty and staff investigated under a law that isn't even ours," Barb continued. "I had no idea," Troy said. "We should inform our patrons about this and suggest to IT that we move the data back to Canadian servers. Let's discuss this immediately with the library and IT directors."

QUESTIONS TO CONSIDER

1. What does this case illustrate about the complexities of trans-border data flow?
2. Is Barb correct that the data could be subject to U.S. law?
3. In the United States, we frequently hear that 9/11 changed everything — and that civil liberties must change in response. How does this mentality threaten potential research and intellectual activities and at what cost?
4. Discuss the implications of such externally housed servers.

CASE #6.11

A Middle Eastern family entered the public library one afternoon. The community had very few Middle Eastern families and even fewer with women who dressed traditionally. The woman was dressed in a burka. A group of teenagers, who had been using the computers, began laughing and making fun of the woman. The reference librarian overheard the kids calling them names, while putting their shirts over their heads to mimic the head covering. The librarian was very uncomfortable with these actions, but was not sure if he should intervene. The family had not heard them, nor seen them, so it might be best to let it go. But, he thought, perhaps he should discuss the actions with the parents when they came to pick up their children.

QUESTIONS TO CONSIDER

1. Should we have policies to prevent such behavior among patrons?
2. Does our professional responsibility demand that we stop patrons in instances such as this?
3. Should the librarian discuss the situation with the children's parents?
4. Consider Robert Hauptman's foreword — "Nothing is more important than the way we treat each other." Discuss this imperative in light of the case.

CASE #6.12

Raj and three of his cousins were attending a prestigious university on the East Coast. Attending this school was a family tradition. Every cousin, brother, uncle in his extended family had attended this school, majoring in either business or law, for the last 20 years. Occasionally, one of the young men broke with tradition and attended the medical school at the same university. Part of this family tradition was to share class notes, lecture notes, papers and exams if the professor returned them to the examinee. Raj and his cousins took full advantage of this extensive archive. One of Raj's cousins was a computer wizard. While he was in India visiting his family over the summer break, he digitized all of the papers and put them into a searchable database that he made available via the website he made for the family.

A professor from the same university stumbled onto the website and discovered 20 years' worth of materials created by his colleagues. He found his own materials as well, including a series of a dozen final exams. He alternated exams from semester to semester in no particular order other than not using the same exam for at least 4 semesters. He thought this a satisfactory way to avoid students having access to the exam in advance. Anyone with access to the database could see all 36 of the essay questions. The professor took his findings to the dean of students and asked her to charge Raj and his cousins with cheating on final exams because they had access to the tests. He also believed that the students were systematically infringing on the copyrights held by all of the professors whose materials were in the archive. This was also a breach of the honor code and, just like the cheating, grounds for suspension. The dean told the professor that she must follow due process and told him she would speak to the cousins within the week. The dean talked to the cousins. The four did not believe that they cheated on any test nor did they believe that they should not share copies of lecture notes. The dean was perplexed and talked to other students from India. They agreed that what the cousins did was acceptable. The Dean decided not to suspend the students and the students agreed to remove the tests and any materials the professors wished to see removed.

QUESTIONS TO CONSIDER

1. Did the professor have a valid argument?
2. Should students who have a different culturally driven perspective on intellectual property be expected to follow rules based on Western rules and norms?
3. How should information professionals best educate students from different cultures about intellectual property models?

CASE #6.13

The academic librarians of a public university in the United States hoped it could help the bombed-out, desecrated libraries of the many war-torn regions around the world, especially in the Middle East, and began a book drive. They would collect materials from the campus community and send them to libraries in need. There were plenty of them — and, of course, many of these libraries needed complete rebuilding before they could consider materials, but the librarians hoped that this deed showed a commitment to civility in general and to the profession in particular, as well as a sense of collegiality with peers who were facing great dangers in their everyday lives. The book drive would, then, raise awareness of the war and its horrible impact on daily life, including such aspects as the right to receive information. Hopefully, the organizers thought, this would encourage people to vocalize their concerns about the perpetual war to their elected officials. The librarians set out collection boxes, with information on the impact of war on people and their libraries. Images of ransacked buildings, among others, were shown with the display. After a few days, the library director received a note from the university president that they should cease this activity as it was "overtly political" and raised questions about the objectivity and professionalism of the library staff. "We would not want to send the message that this library does not support our troops. Your actions, while generally well-intentioned, do raise the question of politics. We have many students in the military and would not want to discourage them or their family members." The library staff was shocked and saw this not only as unprofessional but also as an attack on the very intellectual freedom principles they were extending across the globe. The director, however, instructed the staff to remove the display and disburse the materials they had since collected.

QUESTIONS TO CONSIDER

1. How is this case about the professional foundations of intellectual freedom?
2. What responsibilities do we, in the West, have as professionals to our colleagues in war-ravaged countries? (See also Case #6.8 for further reflection.)
3. Write a position paper from the library director, supporting the book drive.
4. Defend the university president's position.
5. How does this case highlight the global interconnections and responsibilities embodied in LIS work?

CASE #6.14

Academic and research libraries in affluent countries are often heard decrying the cost of medical and scientific journals. These costs have rocketed over the years and yet researchers must have access to remain on the cutting edge of scholarship. If an institution wants esteem, it considers its library collection carefully. However, globally speaking, access to key medical and scientific information is not only important, but life saving. With such global health crises as HIV/AIDS, information and the knowledge developed from it is indeed critical to saving future generations. Information access in many African countries, for instance, is dismal for a number of reasons. First, "brain drain" is taking scholars and researchers from the south, as many researchers have left for northern or developed countries. Indigenous forms of knowledge thus leave with them in many cases. Second, the prohibitive cost of journals keeps many countries from such information. Third, access to online information must be carefully considered. Scholars and researchers within developing nations must have the language skills (usually English) and the requisite interpretive skills to make the best use of western/northern research. Fourth, much of the research that is produced comes from the western/northern perspective, thereby raising questions of cultural relevance or applicability. Finally, with online access slowly availing itself to more people, the quality of information should be considered with critical information literacy skills. As Tan-Torres Edejer rightly suggests, "Even if the woman in the village has access to the internet, she will not necessarily be able to use the information to improve her child's health."

QUESTIONS TO CONSIDER

1. Should medical/research journals be delivered freely to developing countries?
2. What moral imperative should guide information professionals in assisting their colleagues in developing countries?
3. Should LIS programs require a course or component on international/global librarianship or information work?
4. Discuss the five major issues raised in this case regarding information access in developing countries.

CASE #6.15

Web design has quickly become an important skill of librarians and information professionals, regardless of their location. Students emerging from professional programs are typically expected to have this set of skills upon employment. Charles learned quickly that a set of technical skills was not quite enough, however. Charles was multi-lingual and had completed his MLIS in Canada. He was thrilled to land a position in Japan, at an academic library, where he would be responsible for, among other things, the redevelopment of the library's web pages. Charles was very confident with his technical abilities: web 2.0, xml, meta-data, and, of course, his command of Japanese, Chinese, German, and French languages. Charles worked diligently for weeks on the redesign; he hoped to streamline the pages for greater efficiency for the library patrons, who now burrowed through many superfluous pages to get to the real content. He created a logical placement of links on the library's main page, minimized the number of images throughout, creating what he thought to be a nice flow to the site. The pages all had the same template, using a pale color palate. He was certain his colleagues and the patrons would like this improved design. When Charles unveiled the site to his superiors, however, they were not satisfied. They found the site to be impersonal, lacking in imagery and aesthetic appeal. They asked why there was no animation, in particular. Charles left the meeting thinking, "They are less interested in the information itself. We are a library; of course we should think content first and foremost. I would hate to include those silly flash animations; we are a professional setting, not a video game."

QUESTIONS TO CONSIDER

1. Explore the cultural differences in web design through the discussion of Elizabeth Wurtz, University of Copenhagen (http://jcmc.indiana.edu/vol11/issue1/wuertz. html).
2. What mistakes did Charles make in approaching the design from a low-context rather than a high-context perspective?

3. How should such cultural differences be considered as LIS programs increasingly teach technical skills?

CASE #6.16

Many nation-states have voiced concerns about the United States' dominance over the Internet. Most of its super-servers are in the United States. Distribution and management of domain names falls to the U.S.-based Internet Corporation for Assigned Names and Numbers. In the weeks that led up to the World Summit on the Information Society which convened November 2005 in Tunisia, this simmering conflict ignited and the United States' influence on Internet governance came under intense scrutiny. Several nation-states prepared alternative policies, which called for shared governance, for consideration at the Summit. In response to this, the Bush Administration firmly held that the United States would not relinquish its control to others. The administration went so far as to say that the free and democratic nature of Web would be at risk. To date, there has been no significant change in Internet governance.

QUESTIONS TO CONSIDER

1. Would shared global governance provide greater or lesser assurances that the Internet remains free and democratic?
2. The United States government funded the majority of research and infrastructure for the Internet. Is it fair for other countries to demand control without remuneration? Does the United States have a moral obligation to share?
3. Some countries do not respect freedom of speech and are intolerant of dissent — the antithesis of the Internet culture. Do we ignore these values since they conflict with the nature of the Web? Would this be justified?

CASE #6.17

Zimbabwe is a country in deep despair. It is ranked fourth on the 2007 Failed States Index prepared annually by The Fund for Peace and Foreign Policy magazine. Political, economical, military and social indicators of instability are the basis of the rankings. "A state that is failing has several attributes. One of the most common is the loss of physical control of its territory or a monopoly on the legitimate use of force. Other attributes of state failure include the erosion of legitimate authority to make collective decisions, an inability to provide reasonable public services, and the inability to interact with other states as a full member of the international community" (Peace and Foreign Policy, 2007).

There are a million sad stories here and one that is especially disheartening for librarians. For many years, Zimbabwe hosted an independent international book fair attended by publishers from all over the world. In spite of the odds, organizers persevered and held the 2006 event. According to a newspaper article from Comtrex (originally reported in

AllAfrica) dated April 2007, a number of European donors were unwilling to continue their financial support and many publishers left as well. The news report was pessimistic and indicated this was likely to be the last of the book fair. "Zimbabwe was once the publishing capital of southern Africa.... It used to host the best book fair in Africa, complementing the more commercial book fair in Cape Town with a lively forum for debate, discussion and performance which the predominantly white Cape Town fair always lacked. Cape Town hosted its first official international book fair in June, but sub–Saharan Africa must now fit its enormous creativity into a handful of fairs: the Ghana book fair is every other year; Nigeria has an annual fair; Kenya and Uganda both have successful annual book weeks run by the East African Book Development Association. But years of neglect, as with Zimbabwe itself, have rendered it obsolete. As many a wise African has said: 'We cannot eat books.' With few visitors and even fewer sales, neither can the publishers" (Comtrex, 2007).

QUESTIONS TO CONSIDER

1. Was the decision on the part of the European donors and publishers ethical?
2. Is there a role for information professionals in a situation this dire or must we wait until social order is restored?
3. Describe your reaction to the phrase "We cannot eat books."

(Note: The Zimbabwe book fair was held again in August 2007. According to Associated Press reporter Angus Shaw, "The once world-renowned Zimbabwe International Book Fair wound up with a whimper Saturday, with its only foreign exhibitor — the embassy of Iran — packing Islamic tracts and political brochures into cardboard boxes.")

CASE REFERENCES

The Fund for Peace and Foreign Policy (2007). *The failed states index 2007*, July/August, retrieved on September 3, 2007, from http://www.foreignpolicy.com/story/cms.php?story_id=3865& page=0.

Shaw, A. (2007, August 4). Famed Zimbabwe book fair dwindles in a country where 10 children now share a single textbook. *Associated Press Newswires*. Retrieved on September 28, 2007, from http://global.factiva.com.

Symptoms of decline. (2007, April 11). *Comtex*. Retrieved on September 3, 2007, from http://global. factiva.com.

CASE #6.18

Jane was the curator at a well-respected Native American museum that was located in a major city in the United States. She recently received a request from the public relations department at the museum. The request came from a librarian from the main branch of the public library that was just a few blocks from the museum. The request was for a reading list of Native American books for the newly formed Native American Book Club. Jane was not very happy with this request, not because she did not want to help the new book club, but because the librarian did not seem to have any idea of what Native American literature was. This lack of knowledge was significant, given the vast number of indigenous people who lived in the region and the number of well-known Native American authors who lived in the city. Jane emailed the Public Relations Director. In her note, Jane suggested that rather than respond to this generic request by sending a list of "Native American" books, that she send a list of Native American writers arranged by tribe and genre.

QUESTIONS TO CONSIDER

1. Do public libraries have an obligation to develop collections that reflect the diversity of their community?
2. If so, are schools or programs of library and information science adequately preparing librarians for such tasks?
3. Consider the average public library diversity campaigns. Are these campaigns effective? Do they address information issues "globally"?

CASE #6.19

A major, international library cooperative created a list of the books most widely held by their member libraries. The goal was to allow other libraries a look at popular collection items — it was a listing of works judged to be valuable to a library's collection. Such books as the Bible, the U.S. Census, the *Odyssey* and the *Iliad*, and *Huckleberry Finn* were among the top. The majority of the cooperative's member libraries were in North America, with only a small percentage of member libraries coming from Europe, Africa, Asia, and the Pacific Rim. Thus, the listing was heavily dominated by works of western, especially U.S., influence. By creating the list, the cooperative hoped also to show that there was great room for growth by and representation from non–U.S. libraries; such growth, was, of course, a business decision first and foremost. Yet, for many developing countries, there was a catch-22. They could not afford to join the cooperative and thus they could not get their works of non-western perspectives represented. Many began to call on the cooperative to provide free, or at least heavily subsidized, membership for libraries who could not afford the costs — especially given the record profits the cooperative has seen in recent years. The cooperative assured member libraries that the costs associated with membership were necessary and to provide free membership went against the entire model of cooperative sharing. While of course *some* members paid more, it did not balance out to offer *free* membership and, of course, parity was never promised within and across membership.

QUESTIONS TO CONSIDER

1. Why is unequal representation in the cooperative's holdings an ethical issue?
2. Should the cooperative offer free membership to libraries in poor countries?

3. How can business profits and a common good for all the world's libraries co-exist? Can they?
4. Is a worldwide cooperative destined to be biased? Is neutrality a possibility?

CASE #6.20

Tess was a children's librarian and a talented artist. As part of a major library renovation, Tess agreed to paint a mural. The focal point of the mural was a storyteller doll. (Storyteller dolls are clay sculptures that are composed of a large female figure holding dozens of tiny children in her lap.) Tess created a number of detailed sketches to use as a reference point while she painted. The other librarians were excited about the project and they asked Tess to bring the sketches to their next meeting for a "preview." At the meeting, each librarian reviewed the drawings. After everyone had an opportunity, Tess asked the librarians what they thought. Marianne hesitantly commented, "I like the idea of the storyteller, but I am not so sure I like the figure you repeat around the border. I have seen it on the side of a trash collection truck." The other librarians nodded in agreement; they had seen this logo, too. Another librarian, Jeff, spoke up, "I haven't seen the trash trucks, but I do know a little bit about the figure. It is a Gan, a mountain spirit. These are sacred to the Apache. If you have seen a crown dancer, then you have seen a Gan in human form. Although Tess' mural drawings are beautiful, I don't think the figure should be in the mural — it isn't ours to use. For the record, storytellers are part of the Pueblo tradition." The librarians were quiet and Tess wasn't sure what she should do.

QUESTIONS TO CONSIDER

1. Is it acceptable for the trash company to use the Gan figure on their trucks?
2. Is it acceptable for the library to use it?
3. Storytellers are ubiquitous throughout the Southwest. Tourists have abundant opportunities to purchase these figurines and many are inexpensive. Some vary from the traditional look, using cats or dogs in lieu of human forms. Does this information change our answers to questions one and two?
4. Is it possible to get permission to use a cultural symbol? That is, how are western IP models applicable?
5. Do we need to consider Tess' freedom of expression rights?

CASE #6.21

We all have a digital personae; it includes all of our private information, data about our lives from our birth certificates to our medical records to marriage licenses, our address, our credit history and more. The ability for others, individuals or institutions, to gather all of this information has gained momentum. Our digital selves are infinitely more "getable" and various agencies and institutions continue to strive for even greater connectivity. The European Union is no exception and it is calling for proposals for a scheme, which would allow interoperability between the various member states' health care systems. This plan has raised a number of issues relating to privacy, security and other patient rights. Should these millions and millions of records become readily available to other countries? These issues must be weighed against the ability for doctors and other health care professionals to provide optimal care, especially in emergency situations in which the patient could be at extreme risk — severe allergies to medications, diabetes, and so forth. Given earlier data privacy initiatives in the EU, this proposal came as a shock to a number of privacy advocates, scholars, and information professionals, all of whom came out against the new plan.

QUESTIONS TO CONSIDER

1. Is this plan in the best interest of everyone or does it favor the health care industry?
2. What level of privacy and security is necessary in terms of medical information? Is this level of privacy and security possible in trans-border information sharing?
3. Is this scheme riskier or less risky in countries which have authoritarian governments or little private enterprise?
4. Are these concerns coming too late? Is the genie out of the bottle when it comes to our personal digital data?

CASE #6.22

There is a small but rich archive of World War II materials housed at a museum just outside of London. The archivist, Victoria, uncovered a box of recordings. After some searching, she located a machine on which to play the recordings. Much to her delight, Victoria realized what she had — recordings of the Navajo Code Talkers. The tapes were more than 60 years old and showed signs of deterioration. Victoria immediately launched a fundraising campaign to pay for restoration and digitization of the recordings. She was successful and the preservation began. About six months into the year-long process, the archives' board of directors decided to host an event to showcase the recordings. Invitations were sent two weeks ago and Victoria had already received a number of acceptances. Today, she had another stack of replies. She opened one. Instead of a response to the invitation, there was an official notice requesting that the recordings and any copies be returned to the rightful owners, the Talkers, their families and the Navajo Nation.

QUESTIONS TO CONSIDER

1. Who is the rightful owner of the original recordings? Is this party also the legal owner?
2. If the archivist had not made such an extensive effort, the recordings would have been lost. If the recordings belong to the Talkers and the tribe as the letter indicates, should the Talkers, et al., compensate the archives and the donors for restoring and preserving the recordings?

3. Discuss various concepts of "ownership" and "representation" of intellectual property.
4. In this case, is archival work favoring a specific cultural orientation over an indigenous orientation? Is this a moral consideration?

CASE #6.23

The local union, which represented library and information workers in Vancouver, Canada, CUPE 391, went on strike in August 2007. The workers had been without a collective agreement for nearly a year and the negotiations between workers and the administration had not progressed. The library and information workers based their strike on four basic principles: pay equity, improved language for job security, improvements for health benefits, and improvements for part-time and auxiliary workers, of which "almost half of CUPE 391 members are either part-time or auxiliary workers. Of these 380 workers, only 50 members receive any kind of pro-rated health and vacation benefits. The rest of these employees receive only a small percentage in lieu of benefits that comes nowhere near fair compensation" (CUPE 391). According to the CUPE and the striking workers, these issues are basic worker — and human — rights issues and should be considered very carefully by the city, the country — and by the profession. Oddly, little discussion ensued around the strike in the professional LIS community in neighboring communities or countries. The people of Vancouver have been supportive, despite the stoppage in library services and resources.

QUESTIONS TO CONSIDER

1. Is it OK if a library line staff member wants to cross a library strike picket line? Would you?
2. What is acceptable and not acceptable when library employees participate in citizen journalism in the context of a strike and criticize their employer in the blogosphere? Is this workplace freedom of speech?
3. As a library manager, would you go so far as looking into hiring new temporary staff during a strike situation in order to keep the library open? What are the consequences?
4. How should the global community of librarians and information workers respond when their peers are striking in a neighboring community?

CASE REFERENCE
CUPE 391, http://www.cupe391.ca/.

CASE #6.24

Lona was a librarian in university setting, where she was revamping the school's information literacy program to better fit the growing international study population. As part of her background research, Lona started reading blogs from other librarians throughout the world. She saw this as a great way to gain personal insight into the library models used in other countries and hoped to instill a sense of cultural sensitivity into her teaching. Since she was a tenured librarian, she was also responsible for conducting research and publishing. She found such great data within the various blogs she was examining that she decided to write a paper on librarians' perspectives on information literacy across the world. She would use the blogs' entries as data, citing directly from them and attributing the source to the authors, as appropriate. Lona asked a communications researcher if she wanted to be involved in the research, since she was also interested in new media and how professionals used blogs as a communications media. Professor Jeong replied, "Yes, but we will have to seek ethics board permission to use the blogs." Lona had never sought review board permissions and was surprised that blogs would fall under the human subjects review process. But she agreed and began the process of seeking consent from the various authors. Interestingly, many of the respondents didn't quite understand the need for the lengthy and complicated informed consent document, especially given the public nature of blogs. Some did not respond at all, as there was a strong western bias embedded in the language and process of human subjects' research ethics, and the model was truly foreign to many of the authors from whom Lona sought permission. But, as Professor Jeong explained and as Lona knew first hand, many scholarly journals want to ensure that research was in fact reviewed for ethics considerations and they wanted to publish their work in a top-tier journal. By the end of the process, they had many fewer blogs to cite in their research and the perspectives from others Lona so wanted to include were then unrepresented.

QUESTIONS TO CONSIDER

1. Discuss human subjects' protections models from an international perspective. Which ethical principles apply across the globe and which are culturally specific?
2. How do such models affect social science research? Medical research?
3. Explore the research of Maui Hudson, who has explored the differences in Maori approaches and responses to the ethics review process. (See http://repositoryaut.lconz.ac.nz/theses/190/.) What do global researchers have to learn from such explorations?

CASE #6.25

Google claims to be organizing the world's information and making it accessible to everyone. Google's critics raise an important question: Should (or can) Google, or any commercially driven enterprise for that matter, be organizing and thus controlling the world's information? Libraries certainly question Google's ability to do this; they have been trying to do this for thousands of years. But more fundamentally is the question: What *is* the world's information? What is and is not included in this vast enterprise? What of indigenous knowledge that cannot be recorded, packaged, accessed electronically? What of the knowledge and information that exists only as spoken language, where there is no written form — and there are thousands of them? What of the knowledge that exists outside the mainstream of the world's cultures? What of infrastructural issues? What of technological literacy? If we cannot answer these fundamental questions, how would this project succeed in a meaningful way? Unfortunately, despite its intentions, it systematically excludes vast numbers of peoples and cultures from the global discourse of information access and thus power. This case is not about criticizing Google. It is a case about awareness. It is about ethics, rights, responsibilities. It is about thinking critically and acting responsibly.

QUESTIONS TO CONSIDER

1. Discuss the myriad questions presented throughout this case.
2. What ethical responsibility do librarians and information professionals have in questioning such commercial enterprises as Google, OCLC, and so on, who seek to control the "world's information" flow?
3. Review Siva Vaidhyanathan's "Googlization of Everything" (http://www.uwm.edu /Dept/SOIS/cipr/archive.html). Why does the concept of "googlization" raise significant ethical, legal, cultural, and political issues?
4. Discuss the intellectual property challenges raised by such enterprises. Who stands to lose and who stands to gain (monetarily, culturally, politically)?

REFERENCES

Agamben, G. (2002). *Homo sacer. Die souveräne Macht und das nackte Leben*. Frankfurt am Main: Suhrkamp.

Assmann, J. (2000). *Das kulturelle Gedächtnis*. München: Beck.

Assmann, J. (2003). Kollektives Gedächtnis als kulturelle Identität. In J. Golten & C. Erhardt (Eds.), *Interkulturelle Kommunikation*. Sternenfels: Verlag Wissenschaft und Praxis, 61–2.

Barlow, J. P. (1996). A Declaration of the Independence of Cyberspace. Retrieved from http://www. eff.org/~barlow/Declaration-Final.html.

Beck, U. (1997). *Was ist Globalisierung? Irrtümer des Globalismus — Antworten auf Globalisierung*. Frankfurt am Main: Suhrkamp.

Bien, G. (1985). *Die Grundlegung der politischen Philosophie bei Aristoteles*. Freiburg/München: Alber.

Capurro, R. (2004). Eine lateinamerikanische Antwort auf die digitale Spaltung. In R. Scheule, T. Hausmanninger, & R. Capurro (Eds.), *Vernetzt gespalten. Der Digital Divide aus ethischer Sicht. Schriftenreihe des ICIE, Bd. 3*. München: Fink, 225–242. Retrieved from http://www.capurro. de/digspaltung_la.html.

Capurro, R. (2003a). *Ethik im Netz*. Stuttgart: Franz Steiner Verlag.

Capurro, R. (2003b). Angeletics — A Message Theory. In H. H. Diebner & L. Ramsay (Eds.), *Hierarchies of Communication* (pp. 58–71). Karlsruhe: ZKM — Center for Art and Media. Retrieved from http://www.capurro.de/angeletics_zkm.html.

Capurro, R. (2001). Beiträge zu einer digitalen Ontologie. Retrieved from http://www.capurro.de/ digont.htm.

Capurro, R. (1996). Information Technology and Technologies of the Self. *Journal of Information Ethics*, 5(2), 19–28. Retrieved from http://www.capurro.de/self.htm.

Capurro, R. (1995). *Leben im Informationszeitalter.* Berlin: Akademie Verlag.

Cassirer, E. (1994). *Philosophie der symbolischen Formen.* Darmstadt: Wissenschaftliche Buchgesellschaft, 3 Vol.

Cassirer, E. (1985). Form und Technik. In E.W. Orth & J. M. Krois (Eds.), *E. Cassierer: Symbol, Technik, Sprache.* Hamburg: Meiner.

Castells, M. (1996). *The Information Age* 3 vols. Malden, MA: Blackwell.

Castells, M. (2001). Identity and Change in the Network Society: Conversation with Manuel Casells by Harry Kreisler. Retrieved from http://globetrotter.berkeley.edu/people/Castells/castells-con1.html.

Elberfeld, R., & Wohlfart, G. (Eds.). (2002). *Komparative Ethik. Das gute Leben zwischen den Kulturen.* Köln: Edition Ch_ra.

CAtaC. (2004). Conference on Cultural Attitudes Towards Technology and Communication. Retrieved from http://www.it.murdoch.edu.au/catac/.

Charter of Civil Rights for a Sustainable Knowledge Society (2003). Retrieved from http://www.worldsummit2003.de/de/web/52.htm.

Civil Society Declaration to the WSIS. (2003). Shaping Information Societies for Human Needs. Retrieved from http://wsis-cs.org/.

Computer Ethics: Philosophical Enquiry (CEPE 2005). Retrieved from http://cepe2005.utwente.nl/.

Computing and Philosophy (CAP 2004). Retrieved from http://caae.phil.cmu.edu/CAAE/CAP/.

Elberfeld, R. (2002). Vom Nutzen komparativer Ethik für das Leben der Gegenwart. In R. Elberfeld & G. Wohlfart (Eds.), *Komparative Ethik. Das gute Leben zwischen den Kulturen* (pp. 7–21). Köln: Edition Ch_ra.

Ess, C. (2002). Electronic Global Village or McWorld? The Paradoxes of Computer-Mediated Cosmopolitanism and the Quest for Universal Values. In R. Elberfeld & G. Wohlfart (Eds.), *Komparative Ethik. Das gute Leben zwischen den Kulturen* (pp. 319–342). Köln: Edition Ch_ra.

Ess, C. (Ed.) (2001). *Culture, Technology, Communication: Towards an Intercultural Global Village.* Albany: State University of New York Press.

Ethics and Computing. (ETHICOMP 2005). Retrieved from http://www.ccsr.cse.dmu.ac.uk/conferences/ccsrconf/.

Ethics of Electronic Information in the 21st Century. (EEI21 2004). Retrieved from http://exlibris.memphis.edu/ethics21/04eei/.

Floridi, L. (1999). Information Ethics: On the Philosophical Foundation of Computer Ethics. *Ethics and Information Technology*, 1(1), 37–56. Retrieved from http://www.wolfson.ox.ac.uk/floridi/papers.htm.

Floridi, L. (Ed.). (2004). *The Blackwell Guide to the Philosophy of Computing and Information.* Malden, MA: Blackwell Publishing.

Foucault, M. (1984). *L'usage des plaisirs*, 2 Vol. Paris: Gallimard.

Gagarin, M. (2002). *Antiphon the Athenian. Oratory, Law, and Justice in the Age of the Sophists.* Austin, TX: University of Texas Press.

Habermas, J. (1991). *Erläuterungen zur Diskursethik.* Frankfurt am Main: Suhrkamp.

Hadot, P. (1993). *Exercices spirituels et philosophie antique.* Paris: Gallimard.

Hadot, P. (1995). *Qu'est-ce que la philosophie antique?* Paris: Gallimard.

Hausmanninger, T. (2004). Controlling the Net: Pragmatic Actions or Ethics Needed? *International Review of Information Ethics*, 1. Retrieved from http://www.i-r-i-e.net/issue1.htm hausmanninger.

Heidegger, M. (1976). *Was ist das — die Philosophie?* Pfullingen: Neske.

Heidegger, M. (1975). Aus einem Gespräch von der Sprache. Zwischen einem Japaner und einem Fragenden. In M. Heidegger, *Unterwegs zur Sprache* (pp. 83–155). Neske: Pfullingen.

Hoffmann, U. (2003). Reflexionen der kulturellen Globalisierung. Interkulturelle Begegnungen und ihre Folgen. Dokumentation des Kolloquiums "Identität — Alterität — Interkulturalität. Kultur und Globalisierung" am 26./27. Mai 2003 in Darmstadt. Discussion Paper SP III 2003–110. Wissenschaftszentrum Berlin für Sozialforschung (2003). Retrieved from http://skylla.wz-berlin.de/pdf/2003/iii03–110.pdf.

Hongladarom, S. (2001a). *Cultures and Global Justice.* Retrieved from http://www.polylog.org/them/3/fcshs-en.htm.

Hongladarom, S. (2001b). Global Cultures, Local Cultures, and the Internet. In C. Ess (Ed.), *Culture, Technology, Communication: Towards an Intercultural Global Village* (pp. 307–324). Albany: State University of New York Press.

Huntington, S. P. (1997). *The Clash of Civilizations and the Remaking of World Order.* New York: Simon and Schuster.

ICIE (2004). International Center for Information Ethics. Retrieved from http://icie.zkm.de.

IIMO (2004). Centre for Intercultural Theology, Utrecht University. Retrieved from http://www.uu.nl/uupublish/onderzoek/centrumiimo/centreiimoenglis/6725main.html.

Jammal, E. (2004). Krieg oder Dialog der Kulturen? In P. Grimm & R. Capurro (Eds.), *Krieg und Medien* (pp. 17–43). Stuttgart: Franz Steiner Verlag.

Julien, F. (1998). *Un sage est sans idée.* Paris: Seuil.

Kant, I. (1974). *Kritik der reinen Vernunft.* Frankfurt am Main: Suhrkamp.

Kant, I. (1977). *Die Metaphysik der Sitten.* Frankfurt am Main: Suhrkamp.

Krämer, H. (1992). *Integrative Ethik.* Frankfurt am Main: Suhrkamp.

Kuhlen, R. (2003). Kommunikationsrechte — "impart" oder "r2c"? *Information. Wissenschaft & Praxis,* 54, 389–400.

Küng, H. (2001). *Projekt Weltethos.* München: Piper.

Lessig, L. (1999). *Codes and Other Laws of Cyberspace.* New York: Basic Books.

Lipinski, T. A., & Britz, J. J. (2000). Rethinking the Ownership of Information in the 21st Century: Ethical Implications. *Ethics and Information Technology,* 2, 49–71.

Luhmann, N. (1990). *Paradigm lost: Über die ethische Reflexion der Moral.* Frankfurt am Main: Suhrkamp.

Merwe, W. L. van der (2000). "African Philosophy" and the Contextualisation of Philosophy in a Multicultural Society. Retrieved from http://www.polylog.org/them/1/aspmw-en.htm.

MISTICA. (2002). Working the Internet with a Social Vision. Retrieved from http://www.funredes.org/mistica/english/cyberlibrary/thematic/eng_doc_olist2.html.

Moglen, E. (2003). Freeing the Mind: Free Software and the Death of Proprietary Culture. Retrieved from http://emoglen.law.columbia.edu/publications/maine-speech.html.

Nietzsche, F. (1988). Menschliches, Allzumenschliches. In G. Colli & M. Montinari (Eds.), *Kritische Studienausgabe, München: dtv, Vol. 2.*

Paul, G. (2001). Philosophie der Menschenrechte. Ergebnisse eines Projekts. Retrieved from http://agd.polylog.org/3/ppg-de.htm.

Paul, G. (2003). Argumente gegen den Kulturalismus in der Menschenrechtsfrage. (2003, December). *Information Philosophie,* 5, 54–61.

polylog: Forum for Intercultural Philosophy (2004). Ed. Bertold Bernreuter. Retrieved from http://prof.polylog.org/obj-en.htm.

Robertson, R. (1992). *Globalization: Social Theory and Global Culture.* London: Sage.

Rombach, H. (1996). *Drachenkampf.* Freiburg im Breisgau: Rombach-Verlag.

Schauer, T. (2003). *The Sustainable Information Society: Vision and Risks.* Ulm: Universitätsverlag.

Scheule, R. (2004). Digitale Spaltung und Vernetzungsgerechtigkeit. In R. Scheule, T. Hausmanninger, & R. Capurro (Eds.), *Vernetzt gespalten. Der Digital Divide aus ethischer Sicht. Schriftenreihe des ICIE, Bd. 3* (pp. 121–138). München: Fink.

Scheule, R., Hausmanninger, T., Capurro, R. (Eds.). (2004). *Vernetzt gespalten.* Der *Digital Divide as ethischer Sicht. Schriftenreihe des ICIE, Vol. 3.* München: Fink.

Sloterdijk, P. (1998). *Sphären,* 3 vols. Frankfurt am Main: Suhrkamp.

Tavani, H. T. (2002). The Uniqueness Debate in Computer Ethics: What Exactly Is at Issue, and Why Does It Matter? *Ethics and Information Technology*, 4, 37–54.

Taylor, C. (1993). *Multiculturalism and "The Politics of Recognition,"* with commentary by Amy Gutman (Ed.), Steven C. Rockefeller, Michael Walzer, and Susan Wolf. Princeton University Press.

UNESCO. (1987). INFOethics Congresses. Retrieved from http://www.unesco.org/webworld/public_domain/legal.html.

UNESCO. (1980). *Many Voices, One World. Communication and Society Today and Tomorrow.* Paris: MacBride-Report.

UNESCO. Universal Declaration on Cultural Diversity. (2003). Retrieved from http://www.unesco.org/culture/pluralism/diversity/html_eng/decl-en.shtml1.

Universal Declaration of Human Rights (UDRC). Retrieved from http://www.unhchr.ch/udhr/lang/eng.htm.

Walzer, M. (1994). *Thick and Thin: Moral Arguments at Home and Abroad.* Notre Dame: University of Notre Dame Press.

Warschauer, M. (2002). Reconceptualizing the Digital Divide. Retrieved from http://www.firstmonday.org/issues/issue7_7/warschauer/index.html.

Wijsen, F. (2001). Intercultural Theology and the Mission of the Church. Retrieved from http://www.sedos.org/english/wijsen.htm.

Wimmer, F. (2004). *Interkulturelle Philosophie. Eine Einführung.* Vienna: WUV.

World Summit on the Information Society (2004). Retrieved from http://www.itu.org/wsis/.

Yois (Youth for Intergenerational Justice and Sustainability) (Ed.). (2003). Wh@t's next? The Future of the Information Society—A Youth Perspective. Retrieved from http://www.yois.de.

ACKNOWLEDGMENTS

Thanks to Charles Ess (Drury University, U.S.A.) and Thomas J. Froehlich (Kent State University, U.S.A.) for comments and criticisms.   —RC

Epilogue

At the time of this writing, in October 2007, the public librarians and information workers in Vancouver, British Columbia, had been on strike since August 2007. The issue: workplace equity and basic worker—human—rights. Such issues as pay, contingent workers, and workplace speech were paramount concerns. Another chief concern: The strike garnered very little attention in the American library and information community, perhaps because people did not see the implications as personal. It is always easy to ignore that which does not directly affect one's own existence. But information work is always affected by and affecting another. That is why it is so important to become aware of and act responsibly around the ethical responsibilities in our work. And, when we as professionals fail to act, or we respond with silence, to pressing issues of the day, we are sending the wrong message about our profession and its values.

Strikers sent questions to prominent listserves, asking, "A comment on JEESE and the Library Education Community—where are you? As one of the librarians impacted by the current 49-day strike at the Vancouver Public Library in Canada, I continue to be perplexed by the indifference displayed, with only far too few exceptions, by the library education community." A blog post from a Portuguese librarian on *Library Journal* cut to the heart of the debate:

> Our role, as professionals, is imminently a social one, filled with micro-political statements and practices. It doesn't pay to elude this—you only put more distance between you and your users, you dilute your responsibility.... Our social role should be appreciated and cherished and social skills should be a focus in our learning and training along with technological ones. Management decisions concerning library policies—technology included—should be clearly imprinted by this social role rather than by technological warrant [Sequeiros, 2007].

Our social role. We as librarians and information workers often forget about this social role and we overlook the broader implications of our work. We forget that we exist in a globally connected profession. But we can easily become—or accept—status quo. The strikers in Vancouver refused to accept this and instead put fundamental principles of equity, freedom of expression, and rights into a very public forum. Oftentimes, it seems as if we as information professionals work privately, make decisions quietly. And our work *is* very public, with significant social impact. We mustn't take this lightly. We must act autonomously while considering a greater good. We must continually remind ourselves how our work as information professionals actively shapes history.

We encourage more dialogue around ethics, legal issues, social responsibility, and cross-cultural information work. It is through exploration of these deeper issues that we, as a profession, will continue to grow and mature. It is through critical reflection and responsible action that our profession will make a difference — for all.

Action expresses priority.

REFERENCES

Sequeiros, P. (2007). Talkback Blog Posting. *Library Journal* (8/26).

Index

Academic Bills of Rights 25, 69
academic libraries: and intellectual freedom 31, 34, 38, 42; and intellectual property 77–81, 83–86, 88–90, 92–93; and intercultural ethics 137, 142–143, 145–146, 152; and privacy 57, 61, 64–65, 68; and professional ethics 107, 111–112, 114
academic misconduct 79–80, 86, 144
accessibility 1, 23, 92, 83, 85, 115
acquisitions 33, 39, 43
adjunct instructors 103
aging population 38, 115
Aid, Matthew 29
Alfino, Mark 2
alternative lifestyles 43, 107
American Association of Law Libraries 16–17
American Civil Liberties Union (ACLU) 49
American Library Association (ALA) 13, 16, 23–24, 49, 75, 98
American Society for Information Science and Technology 16
American Union of Concerned Scientists 26
applied ethics 10
archives: and intercultural ethics 139, 151; policies of 102; and privacy 52, 64–65; and professional ethics 102, 110; see also special libraries
Aristotle 118
Assmann, Jan 122
Association for Library and Information Science 13

Bailey, Barbara 51
balance of media 38
balanced collections 33, 39, 43
Barlow, John Perry 119
Beck, Ulrich 131
behaviors 9
bio-piracy 138
book banning 36, 39
book fairs 147–148
book sales 106
brain drain 145
Britz, Johannes 131
Burton, Paul F. 2
business records 50, 52

Canadian Library Association (CLA) 13, 26
Capurro, Rafael 11
case studies 12, 18, 19–20
Cassirer, Ernst 122

Castells, Manuel 135
cataloging materials 33, 39, 43
catastrophic events 100
censorship 23, 26, 30, 35, 42
Center for the Study of Ethics in the Professions 96
challenge policies 36, 39
character of use 74
Chase, Peter 51
child abuse 116
Child Online Protection Act (COPA) 28–29
Child Pornography Prevention Act (CPPA) 27
child predators 54
Children's Internet Protection Act (CIPA) 27–28, 98
Children's Online Protection Act (COPA) 27
children's rights 34, 37, 67–68
Christian, George 51
circulation 49, 57, 61
civil liberties 47, 142
classification of materials 33, 39, 43
classification structures 89
classified information 29
Clinton, William Jefferson 29
codes of ethics 13–15, 18, 96
collection development 33, 39, 42, 43
commercial interests 71, 89, 153
commoditization of information 93
common nature 133
communication rights 128, 129
Communication Rights in the Information Society (CRIS) 130
communitarianism 131
comparative ethics 122
compensation for reprints 75, 89, 92
competing stakeholders 71
computer ethics 125
computer-mediated communication (CMC) 132
Computer Supported Cooperative Work (CSCW) 132
computer viruses 56
conduct 9, 95, 96
confidentiality 55, 63, 109
conflicts of interest 102–103, 104
conglomerations 25, 39, 93
consulting services 89
contingent worker models 103
contract renewal 82, 113, 114
contractual agreements 76, 91
contributive justice 131
controversial speakers 32

Convention of the Rights of the Child (United Nations) 26
Copyleft 86
copyrights 71, 72, 98, 136, 144; *see also* fair use
corporate models 81, 101
corporate ownership 89, 151
corporate settings 59
corporate sponsors 35, 71, 106, 153
correct action 3
creationism theories 32, 35
creations 71
critical thinking 6, 9, 19, 26
cultural differences 142
cultural diversity 39, 128, 130, 140
cultural memory 122, 129, 139
cultural reflections 126
cultural relevance 145
cultural sensitivity 140–141, 144, 146, 148–149, 153
cultural symbols 122, 150

data personae 47, 150
data privacy 46
databases 59, 83, 84
Davis, Michael 95
decision-making 1, 6, 9, 18, 20, 96
Declaration of Human Rights (United Nations) 46
declassified records 29
deontological 10
descriptive ethics 10
destruction of materials 58
digital divide 38, 73, 127
digital globalization 126
Digital Millennium Copyright Act (DMCA) 25–26, 71–73, 98
digital ontology 119
digital personae 47, 150
digitization 151
discourse ethics 125
discrimination 81, 107, 108
display arrangements 44, 106
dissemination of information 1
distance learning 48, 63, 76
diversity 39, 128, 130, 140
donations 42, 86, 102–103, 106, 110, 136
Douglas, Justice William O. 23

E-rate monies 27
editing 41
Edson, Gary 12
educationally unsuitable 27, 29, 41, 66, 104
Elberfeld, Rolf 125
electronic intellectual freedom 30–31
electronic mailing lists 31
electronic records 59
electronic trails 55
electronic versions 92
employment contracts 82, 113–114
Ess, Charles 126, 132
ethical principles 17
ethical reflections 132
ethical thinking 121
ethics, codes of 18
ethics training 96
ethnocentrism 137
evolution theories 32, 35

exclusive rights 72
expense reports 112

fair use 72, 74, 81, 83–84, 93; *see also* copyright
Family Education Rights and Privacy Act (FERPA) 69
Family Friendly Libraries Association 16
family friendly materials 27, 41
federal funds 27, 28
Felton, Richard 89
Fifth Amendment 49
file sharing 73, 93, 98
filters 27, 28, 34, 36, 41, 65
fines 61
First Amendment 24, 27, 28, 48
First Sale Doctrine 76
flash drives 60
Floridi, Luciano 119
Foreign Intelligence Surveillance Act (FISA) 50
formats, obsolete 75
Foskett, D.J. 2
Fourth Amendment 48, 49
free expression 24
free inquiry 29
free sequence 120
fuzzy and contingent sets 123

gag orders 50
gaming 36
Ghandi, Mohandas 20
gifting materials 42, 86, 102–103, 106, 110, 136
global cultures 122, 127
global governance 147
global interconnections 145
global librarianship 12
globalization 126, 131
good and evil 9
government repository libraries 38
greater good 97, 102–103
guardian policies 104, 113
guest speakers 32, 35
guidelines, professional 7, 16

Habermas, Jurgen 125
hacking 56
harassment 143
harmful to minors 27–29, 41, 66, 104; *see also* offensive materials
Hauptman, Robert 11, 20, 26
health care industry 151
Heidegger, Martin 120
Heraclitus 118
hoarding materials 87
hold shelves 61, 67
homeless individuals 37
Hongladarom, Soraj 131
Hoschild, Adam 28
human conduct 9
human rights 46, 99, 124, 142
human subjects' protections models 152–153
Huntington, Samuel P. 123
hybridizations 123

in loco parentis 27
inappropriate materials 27, 29, 41, 66, 104
indigenous knowledge 138, 145, 153

individual privacy 46
individual responsibilities 54, 131
information: corruption 140; ethics 11; gathering 59; literacy 152; needs 141
Information Security Oversight Office 30
informed reason 6
infospheres 119, 125
inner-cultural 120, 121
institutional obligations 98
intellectual freedom 19, 53, 144–145
Intellectual Freedom Committee (Canadian Library Association) 26
intellectual property 140, 144, 151
intelligent design theories 35
intercultural informatics 133
intercultural information ethics (IIE) 11
internal disagreements 105, 111–112
International Center for Information Ethics (ICIE) 11–12
International Convention on Cultural Diversity 129
international obligations 71
Internet 36, 54, 72, 78, 119, 147
intranets 82

Jefferson, Thomas 71
Jonas, Hans 125
Julien, Francois 121

Kant, Immanuel 11
keynote speakers 32, 35
Kramer, Hans 119
Kranich, Nancy 50, 98
Krug, Judith 98

labeling, patron 62
legal liability 19
Leonard, J. William 30
Lessig, Lawrence 130
liability, copyright 73, 90
libraries: boards 102; consortia 38; records 53
Library Bill of Rights (American) 24
library schools: and intercultural ethics 136, 140; and professional ethics 103, 109
licensing 76, 80, 81, 83
Lipinski, Thomas 131
login information 59
Luhmann, Niklas 118

Mall, Ram Adhar 120
market harm 75; see also fair use
mass surveillance 25, 47; see also surveillance
McCullers, Carson 2
McMenemy, David 2
McNealy, Scott 48
media conglomerations 25, 39, 93
medical information 151
Medical Libraries Association 16
meeting rooms 32
meta-codes 134
meta-ethics 10
military recruiters 40
monitoring 47
Moor, James 48
morals 9, 12, 31, 118
Motin, Susan 2

movie ratings 43
multicultural ethics 122, 140
music CDs 73, 77, 90

name tags 60
naming rights 71, 106, 153
Napster 73, 77, 90
National Archives and Records Administration 29
national libraries 139, 141
National Security Letters (NSL) 50, 57
nature of work 74; see also fair use
neo-Nazi groups 32
New World Information and Communication Order 127
Nocek, Janet 51
normative ethics 10
notice 49

offensive materials 27–29, 34; see also harmful to minors
Office for Intellectual Freedom 98
official information 65
on-hold materials 61, 67
online classes 48, 63, 76
opt out clauses 31
oral traditions 122, 129
ownership 89, 151

Pape, Helmut 122
paraprofessionals 34
patents 71
paths of thinking 120
patient rights 151
PATRIOT Act 47, 49–51, 98
patron databases 59, 83, 84
patron-librarian privilege 55, 63, 109
patrons, demanding 108, 116
Paul, Gregor 122
peer-reviewed journals 91
personal as the political 31
personal convictions 30–31
personal emails 64
personal information 52
personal interests 113–114
personal morals 12
personal papers 102, 110
personal privacy 110
personnel evaluations 42
phishing emails 140
picket lines 152
Pierce, Linda 2
piracy 73, 77, 90, 138
plagiarism 79–80, 86, 144
plurality opinion 28
policies 34, 97
politics 31, 41, 46, 100, 145
polyphonies 122, 123
poor individuals 37
pornography 27, 34, 37, 60
Poulter, Alan 2
precedents 71
preservation 75, 151
principles 9, 17
print-based intellectual freedom 30–31
priorities 20

163

prison libraries 33, 58; *see also* special libraries
privacy 37, 50, 53, 110, 137, 151
privatized public library services 100
problem patrons 108, 116
professionals 95; codes of ethics 43; conduct 9, 95, 96; guidelines 7, 16; responsibilities 9, 19, 54, 99, 131; values 12–13
proficiencies 20
propriety information 55
protecting minors 104, 113
public domain 72
public education 32
public libraries: and intellectual freedom 32, 36–37, 39–41, 44; and intellectual property 77–78, 81–82, 88; and intercultural ethics 137, 141, 143, 150, 152; and privacy 53–54, 56–57, 60–62, 66–68; and professional ethics 99–101, 104–108, 113–116
public records 113–114
public viewing (movies) 82
publicity principle 48

radio frequency identification device (RFID) 25, 55,137
Ranganathan's second law 41
Rawls, John 11
re-cataloging of materials 33
reclassification of materials 33
Recording Industry Association of America 73, 77, 90
recruiting policies 40
representation 140, 149, 151
reprint policies 89, 92
reproductions 75, 78–79, 151
responsibilities 9, 19, 54, 99, 131
responsible action 6
restoration 151
restroom policies 56
reverse declassification 29–30
right and wrong 9
right to communicate 127–128, 134
right to privacy 48
Robertson, Roland 122
role-playing games 36
roving surveillance 50; *see also* surveillance
rules 9

safe harbor 73, 90; *see also* fair use
safeguarding materials 88, 110, 151
salaries 82, 113, 114
sales of original work 75
Samek, Toni 26
school libraries: and intellectual freedom 34, 36, 38, 39; and privacy 65; and professional ethics 106, 114, 116; *see also* special libraries
scope of responsibility 115
secondary infringement 73, 90; *see also* copyright
security 110, 151
self-censorship 33, 39, 42, 43
Severson, Richard 2
sexual orientation 43, 107
shelving policies 44, 106
signature pedagogy 103
Sklyarov, Dmitry 89
social justice 139
social memory 122, 129, 139
social networking sites 37

social roles, 159
Society of American Archivists 14, 16
Socrates 21
Sonny Bono Copyright Act 25, 71–72
spam 140
special collections 52, 110
special libraries: and intellectual freedom 33; and intellectual property 82, 87, 92; and intercultural ethics 138, 148–149; and privacy 55, 58; and professional ethics 102, 104, 109
Special Libraries Association 16
special populations 37, 38, 115
Spinello, Richard 12
stakeholders 97
standardized testing 35
Statement on Intellectual Freedom (Canadian) 24–25
statistics 114
Statute of Anne 72
student privacy 110
subject headings 38
substantiality of work 75
Sudweeks, Fay 126
surveillance 24, 47, 50, 53, 55, 64
suspicious situations 62, 66
symbolic forms 122, 150
systems, moral 9

Taylor, Charles 124
TEACH Act 76
technical skills 146
technologies 34, 38, 98; obsolete 75; philosophy of 122; and privacy 46
term limits, on copyrights 72
textbooks, copying 78, 79
theoretical contingencies 124
thick and thin moralities 124
third-party privacy 110
Title 17 74, 75
touchstones 121, 132
tracking software 66
trademarks 71
traditional cultures 119
tragic events 100
trans-border data flow 142, 151
transcultural codes 134
transcultural ethics 122
transcultural philosophy 120
transparent society 47

unions 102, 152
United Nations Universal Declaration of Human Rights (UDHR) 24, 27, 128, 133
Uniting and Strengthening America by Providing Appropriate Tools Required to Intercept and Obstruct Terrorism (U.S.A. PATRIOT Act) 47, 49–51, 98
Universal Declaration of Human Rights (UDHC) 124
Universal Declaration on Cultural Diversity (UNESCO) 123, 127
universal pragmatists 133
usage data 55
usage records 49
utilitarianism 10

valuable materials 88, 110, 151
values 9, 12–13

variety of media 129
violence 36
void formula 120

Walzer, Michael 124, 132
web design 146
web pages 115
White, Herbert 12
wi-fi access 78
Wohlfart, Gunter 122
workplace rights 31, 42

World Conferences 123
world ethos 124
World Forum on Communication Rights 129
World Summit on the Information Society (WSIS) 127
worldwide cooperatives 149

Youth for Intergenerational Justice and Sustainability 133

Zipkowitz, Fay 5, 12